COLLEGE OF MARIN LIBRARY
KENTFIELD, CALIFORNIA

D0622921

WITH THE COMPLIMENTS
OF
THE INTERNATIONAL CULTURAL SOCIETY OF KOREA
C.P.O. BOX 2147 SEOUL, KOREA

A GUIDE TO
KOREAN LITERATURE

A GUIDE TO
KOREAN LITERATURE

In-sŏb Zŏng Litt. D.

Former Dean of the Graduate School
The Hankuk University of Foreign Studies
Seoul, Korea

PL
956
Z59
1983

HOLLYM INTERNATIONAL CORP.
Elizabeth, New Jersey   Seoul

Copyright © 1982
by In-sŏb Zŏng

All rights reserved

First published in 1982
First American edition published in 1983
Second printing, 1983
by Hollym International Corp.
18 Donald Place,
Elizabeth, New Jersey   07208   U.S.A.

Published simultaneously in Korea
by Hollym Corporation: Publishers
14-5 Kwanchol-dong, Chongno-ku,
Seoul, Korea   Phone: 725-7554

ISBN: 0-930878-29-9

Library of Congress Catalog Card Number: 82-84416

Printed in Korea

Contents

Preface

Several volumes of Korean Literature have been brought out in English so far, but they were mostly translations of collected poems, short stories, plays, or essays, and no general guidebook has been published yet for foreign readers. It is understood that reading of literary productions piece by piece alone is not enough for the public to taste the ideas, or inner sentiments of the authors, and the literary forms or styles interwoven therein. Particularly when reading a foreign literature, one should be provided with some information on the traditional background of that field or its historical trend as well as a certain amount of descriptive interpretations of models, or comprehensive appreciation of a few targets. Having such a book is all the more necessary for serious study or academic research work in that specific line.

The present book, a genuine guide to Korean Literature, intends to meet such demands on the part of foreign readers or scholars who are interested in Korean Literature. The author also paid much attention in this book to the influences of Western Literature as well as those of other Oriental Literatures on the development of Korean culture, so that foreigners might easily excavate the characteristics of Korean Literature by analogical approach. I hope this book will contribute to a certain extent to the effort of foreigners who are anxious to proceed to the study of Koreanology. As the contents of this publication indicate, it gives necessary comments on all phases of literary harvest of the Korean people, broken down in separate chapters with some unavoidable overlapping lines or paragraphs because of their reciprocal relations.

Proper names are spelt in the Unified System of Romanization drafted and adopted by the Korean Language Society, which is explicitly illustrated, "The Korean Alphabet." It should also be noticed that personal names come first and family names after them as in the case of most Westerners, though the original Korean style goes the other way round.

In concluding it is recommended that those more concerned with the actual examples of literary productions quoted or mentioned here in this book better refer to my other publications of English translation, because majority of them are derived from mine; An Anthology of Modern Poems in Korea, Folk Tales from Korea, Modern Short Stories from Korea, A Pageant of Korean Poetry, and Plays from Korea.

October 9, 1982
Author
Seoul, Korea

Introduction

Korean literature can be segmented into two distinct periods with some overlapping. There is the literature produced before Korea was subject to western influence and the literature subsequent to this influx.

The pre-western literature was influenced by a number of factors. Shamanism taught that inanimate objects were beings and in no way inferior to the human. This suggests close identity to nature, which is the primary aspect of Korean poetry.

The pervading influence of nature is illustrated in many poems. Most of the poetry deals in some way with nature, either nature as esthetic or nature as an object example for human beings to guide themselves by. The fact that most Korean authors constantly use pen names which seem to be culled from nature still indicates that they adhere to oneness between human and nature.

This enabled Koreans to claim themselves to be a peace-loving nation. Differing from the western appreciation of humanism in its love of nature, this Shamanism was further augmented by Buddhist influences which preach reincarnation, the transformation of souls, so that animals can be vehicles for the human soul on its journey to Nirvana.

In addition to such self-satisfied human life of circling quietude, a feeling of fatalism can also be noticed throughout the traditional literature of Korea, because internal disorder and the danger of foreign invasions imposed by topographical conditions were commonplace throughout most of Korea's history. Confucianism with its acceptance of the status quo was responsible in a great part for this fatalism, too.

Korean prose through the Pre-Western Periods deals in the terms of supernatural occurrences, magic, good rewarded and evil punished, etc. Through most of Korean literature, especially prose, various behavior patterns are stressed, such as loyalty to the king, filial piety, respect for seniority, trustworthy friendship and chastity of women. Always the author tries to depict people who have respect for ancient traditions and lead virtuous lives so that the reader might emulate them.

With the introduction of western ideas and culture to Korea the traditional patterns undergo a change. Science with its ways of changing the existing world, Christian humanism which teaches the nobleness and dignity of the individual, and socialism which shows the way to a more equal distribution of wealth—these are the new gods that the authors embrace including the idea of Man-God suggested in the philosophy of a new Korean religion, Czondo-gyo. No longer is it resignation to one's fate but rather the world must and will be changed. Modern literature deals with such things as the breakup of the old tradition, and conflicts arising from them. As a transitory active feature, at the beginning of the 20th century emphasis was on nationalism, on pride in one's country, Korea taking her place among other nations as a free and sovereign state.

Unfortunately these hopes were in actuality short lived as witnessed by the Japanese occupation of 40 years. But this did not dim Korean hopes. Authors and poets were constantly reiterating the ideas of freedom and nationalism with various expression of camouflage under the alien's occupation.

Literature came into its own after the end of World War II in 1945. But Korea was divided into north and south military occupation zones, a cruel partition. The resulting condition could not last long and the Korean War ensued in 1950. After the armistice Korea is still divided.

Thus Korean literature at the present time deals with the uncertainty of modern life, aspirations of nationalism, resistance against communism, a strong desire for reunification and other themes reflecting these troubled anxious times.

Literature plays a great role in human history. The true

greatness of any people at any period of history can be measured by their literature. Great literature also helps to make a
people great. A study of Korean literature shows the sources
of the strength and lasting qualities of Korean life and
civilization.

Literature is important in international relationships.
Ideas have long been exchanged between peoples through their
literature. This is particularly true of the present time. Rapid
methods of communication have made much of the literature
of every land available in both the original language and in
translation. The exchange of literature between countries has
helped to increase international understanding. One of the
most interesting and most rewarding ways to study the psychology of a people is to read the literature of that people.
Korean literature, like that of other civilized countries, offers
a broad area for research in this field.

Literature is the tool through which ideas are freely exchanged and communicated for social education. It is the tool
through which evil aspects of society are depicted and good
ones proposed. In one way, it is the mirror in which the real
self of society is reflected, recorded and transmitted to later
generations. Literature is, of course, important in all countries; however, it has special significance in Korea because it is
one of the most important mediums of the country's social
education movement.

Korean literature as an entity in itself consists mainly of
poetry and prose created by native Koreans. Since Korean
literature began as a creation of the people, it was spoken and
sung long before it was written, but we can gain a knowledge
of it in its origins by examining early folk songs and poetry. In
looking at this early Korean literature, one finds that many of
these writings are also tales and legends sung or spoken about
ancestors of various Korean tribes, often praising them. These
narratives and tales were almost always accompanied by music
and dancing, and they were presented principally at tribal rites
including religious festivals, sacrifices, and political gatherings.

Of the Korean Three Kingdoms, Sinla, Begze, and
Goguryo, Sinla unified them into one and became independent

of continental culture principally due to geographical reasons, being located in the south-east of the Korean peninsula. Since Sinla became an independent culture, she of necessity had to devise one of her own, so a separate Korean culture including language and literature began to develop in this area.

The first individual Korean written language began to appear in Sinla in the last years of the eighth century and was a script-type language partially adapted from Chinese characters by phonetic soundings called *Idu*. Only 25 poems are still extant in this style, and their dates range from the seventh to almost the beginning of the 11th century; they represent the first Korean literature as a separate style. *Idu* as a written language slowly ceased to be used during the first part of the Goryo Dynasty, and nothing was devised by the Korean people to record their native literature until a new alphabet was invented in 1443. This alphabet, now consisting of 24 letters, completely separated the Korean language from the classical Chinese. It is designed on a phonetic basis and therefore makes it truly a language of the people enabling Koreans to further their native literature.

This brief background in Korean literature leads us now to a modern observation of it, some influences in it, themes running through it, some examples of it, and some evaluations. Of course Korean literature of today can be compared to those of other modern nations. The literary taste of Koreans had been influenced by the country's geographical location and its political situation. Korean literature reflected the effects of the surrounding countries of China, Japan, India, Mongolia, Tibet, Manchuria, and Siberia, but now its writers use a new style that is solely Korean.

Of course the principal influence on modern Korean literature has its source in the origins and beginnings of the early literature, but the second principal influence on it is western culture with its new ideas, revolutionary literary forms, its independence and freedom movements, Christianity, and the scientific attitude and method. Subject matters stemming from these ideas are patriotism, social welfare, freedom of love, democratic equality, and subconscious suffering.

These topics penetrate deep into the inner person of each Korean which makes modern Korean literature truly a literature reflecting the values and ideals of the people.

Korea's literature has from ancient times been influenced by the country's turbulent history. This country, whose history goes back in legend more than four thousand years, has been attacked, possessed, liberated, reattacked, and repossessed. It has more often been the center of controversy brought about by neighboring nations whose desire has been to control and develop the country, not for the benefit of the Koreans, but for their own selfish interests.

The literature of ancient Korea reflected the pressures of the times. It was also expressive of the religious beliefs and superstitions associated with the country. After 1900 Korean literature was profoundly influenced by Western ideas and literary forms. It was inevitable that in the vast intellectual and social upheavals of modern times the Korean vernacular should replace Chinese in all written communication. This development had a very stimulating effect on the concern of Koreans with their past; in particular, the literature of native inspiration of all periods was studied as a cultural heritage worthy of recovery and perpetuation. Customs and manners in Korea have changed immensely through the ages. However, they still exert a significant influence on the literature and on the daily lives of Koreans.

A study of Korean literature shows a distinct division of the traditional and the modern. Both have definite causes, subject matter, and style. Each of these main categories is further broken down into various sub-groups. The traditional literature reflects a fatalistic attitude, caused partly by the geographical influences, and partly by religious influences. The mountains form a background setting for many of the writings while the variety of religions that have flourished in Korea contribute important ideals and values. Modern literature shows resistance, both political and moral. This resistance has been influenced by Western civilizations which have invaded the peninsula and subjugated the natural development of the inhabitants. This constant political struggle is gradually seeing the emergence of a modern nation capable of progressive growth in all areas, including the arts.

Since only a very small percentage of the land is fit for agricultural purposes, the Koreans, believing themselves to be moral and worthy people, were pressed to find an answer to this dilemma. They began applying this fatalistic type of rationalization to all their problems. The religions which at that time had pervaded Korea also helped to nurture this fatalistic trend in many of their followers. Buddhism, Confucianism, Shamanism, and Taoism all contained within their philosophies a measure of fatalistic dogma.

There are two primary ways that the Koreans expressed this fatalism in their literature. First we find in the literature of this time a trend toward Love of Nature. Man and nature are one—man is only a small part of nature, and therefore should endeavor to identify himself with his natural surroundings—the oneness or harmony between man and nature. The expression of Love of Peace also was a primary factor in the Korean fatalistic trend in literature. Love of Peace is based on five moral standards. Precisely speaking, these are "loyalty to the king, filial piety, seniority, friendship and chastity." These factors make the traditional literature of Korea a beautiful thing to read.

Modern literature deviates from the restricted subject matter of the traditional era to enlarged and varied subject matter. The style, or call it mood, set by these two different literary concepts is that of an attractive inner beauty, everlasting exhilaration, and a sense of humor. Works are not produced for technique's sake or for the demonstration of a technique.

There has always been a great appeal in the Western Hemisphere for the Oriental methods of reasoning. Their clear-cut, concise logic arrives at a conclusion which should be emulated by philosopher in the West. Its simplicity combined with its universality has gained them a wide area of supporters in the West, and this profound simplicity of expression is possessed also by the Koreans in their poetry and prose. The main feature of Korean literature is their simplicity of expression. They are not writing to demonstrate a style; they are telling a story. One does not play a musical instrument to demonstrate the instrument; he plays it to express a song. Just so, the Koreans tell a story using style, but do not just use a story to demonstrate their skill with words.

Western Literature and Modern Korean Writers

The Reciprocal Influences of the Literature of the East and the West on Contemporary Writers, both in Relation to Aesthetic Values and to their Ways of Life. (Delivered at the 29th Congress of the International P.E.N. Club, held in Tokyo, 1957)

In the remoteness of yesterday, the literature, culture, and philosophy of the East and the West were, like their respective geographies, poles apart. But in the modern age, as we see the mile shortened a little more each day, the hour accelerated, and the vastness of oceans narrowed by the technological advances in transportation and communication, it is apparent that the reciprocal influences in the literature of East and West have likewise become more intensely intertwined.

Long-standing differences in the characteristics of the cultures of East and West are resolved in three major categories: Occidental positive Rationalism is contrasted to Oriental Intuition; European Objectivity finds its antithesis in Asiatic Subjectivity; and the Humanism of the West is pitted against the Love of Nature in the East. These three main differences inspired the three main areas of consciousness among the modern writers of the East. The first—positive rationalism of the West—gives the Eastern writer a feeling of literature as an independent science. The second—objectivity—is the font of consciousness of expression as professional technique. The third—humanism—gives birth to an ideological literature bound to the ways of life.

The West's rationalism produced a modern civilization

through thorough development of natural and mechanical sciences. In this structure of analytical methodology, philosophy was split into various separate fields of religion, politics, economics, ethics, law, literature and others. Literature was required to develop itself as a pure art with separate identity, and with its own criteria for truth, goodness and beauty. In the East, on the other hand, philosophy could not be easily divorced from religion, ethics, politics and economics, nor from literature and art. The ways of life in the Orient in general were hardly rationalized. Literature had hardly been a separate entity, hardly separated from other cultural pursuits. Literature had been more or less a means of discipline for intellectuals in general.

Since the introduction of Western literature into Korea, which began at the end of the 19th century, the earlier pioneers of the modern Korean novel paved the way toward the creation of a real modern literature by modeling their works after European authors. But they never forgot the uncertain situation of the Korean nation when they had been threatened by three powers surrounding her; first by China, next by Russia, and then finally enslaved by Japan.

Upon her compulsory occupation of Korea by force in 1910, the then imperial Japan employed every possible means of ruthlessness to oppress not only Korean political leaders but also Korean intellectuals. Particularly, the Korean writers were considered as the so-called undesirable and dangerous elements and deprived of their basic rights as human beings including the freedom of speech and expression. Under such a difficult circumstances, however, the Korean writers stood firmly against the Japanese oppression with their pen. So they used modern literature, thus emerged as the tools of resistance against the alien rulers over them. They began cooperative efforts for national enlightenment and at the same time furthered the development of literary merits for that purpose.

The contrast between Western objectivity and Eastern subjectivity is pointed up lucidly in the technique of expression in modern Korean Literature.

The history of Korea dates back 4,290 years to the first

King, Dan-gun, the mythical founder of Korea. Her people are an ancient and homogeneous race, distinct from both the Chinese and the Japanese. In the cultural field Korea was the channel through which the civilization of China and the religion of India were transmitted to Japan. Also by the ingenuity of her people, she made a great contribution to the world through many inventions.

Traditionally, however, Koreans along with others in the Orient, were more interested in their spiritual home behind reality and were not so concerned with conquering the concrete challenges in the forefront of reality. Their harmony was with the nothingness or timelessness that led to an inner ecstatic feeling. They tried to appreciate the seeming stillness that was at the centre of the spinning top that was reality.

And so it was that symbolism became a dominant factor in oriental art and literature. Simplicity and mystery were preferred. A graceful gloom, an elegant humility pervaded the literature. These traits are exemplified in the poems of Omar Khayyam of Persia, Tagore of India, Tupao of China, Classical poems of Korea called *Sizo,* and others.

Since the advent of modern Western civilization in the East and its accompanying scientific methods, there was a steady development of free verse, modern prose, modern drama, modern essays and other forms of expression,

But not only all works of writing of the Korean writers were strictly and ruthlessly censored by the Japanese authorities concerned but also many of them were prohibited from the publication thereof for one reason or another which was hardly reasonable and convincing. Furthermore many of the Korean intellectuals including writers were ruthlessly arrested and punished by the Japanese authorities concerned under the pretext of violating the so-called public security maintenance law of Japan.

During World War II the Japanese prohibited Koreans from using their own mother tongue even in their daily life with an obvious intention to deprive Korean citizens of their own national language and letters and to erase the Korean chapter of the cultural history of the world. The Japanese also

prohibited Koreans from learning western languages. It is true
that such a measure taken by the then imperial Japanese government hindered Korea's literary development to a great
extent, but the Korean writers made their every effort to
prevent their culture and literature from being wiped out by
the Japanese.

So Korean writers developed underground their own techniques deeply rooted in Oriental aesthetics, plus the sentiments
of an oppressed nation. For example a modern poem, *Heartache* by a contemporary poet, Gwang-sob Gim, illustrates
these points:

> By a lamp-light twinkling in the heart of the sea
> The sea at night is endlessly dark.
>
> The waves
> Are leaping under foot, broken by the rocks!
> Freedom, too,
> Is spreading eternal sadness in this land.
>
> Gull's cries from far through the darkness
> Come to my ears and die, tearing a wound in my heart.
>
> Ah! bird of poetry, flying afar, crying over the deep,
> So full of darkness is your flight uncharted.
>
> I, a poet of sorrow, filled with heartache,
> Will be a lifeless form with you on the sea tonight.

And also trying to satisfy their national pride as well as to
identify the written language with their own speech, they
tended to abolish the use of Chinese characters in their belles-
lettres, because it differed from Korean in morphology and
syntax. The Korean alphabet of 24 letters, one of the world's
most highly-regarded phonetic alphabets, has been used exten-
sively as the best medium of expression in modern Korean
literature.

The Koreans are entitled to enjoy their cultural heritage

from their ancestors. However, due to the fact that many of literature and objects of artistic, historical and archaeological value belonging to the cultural heritage of Korea were also taken away by the Japanese during their compulsory occupation of Korea for 40 years, the Korean scholars as well as writers had great difficulties in their study of literary works on things Korean with the historical background of ancient Korea. It is firmly believed that such literature and objects as referred to above shall be returned to Korea.

Next, speaking of the ideological influences, we see that Humanism has had some impact on the literature of the East. Hellenistic Greece, the cradle of Western civilization, was based on Humanism. Eastern culture, on the other hand, is deeply rooted in the subjugation of human to God and Nature. Christianity, which geographically and basically is an eastern philosophy, shows considerable humanistic characteristics when compared to Chinese philosophy or to Buddhism or even Mohammedanism. The personality of Christ is more self-conscious of human values and more adaptable to the philosophy of the West. Thus it flourished more in the West. But it must be understood that, without the strong influence of this Oriental spiritualism in Christianity, the human materialism of the West might have faced bankruptcy. This contrast or combination of materialism and spiritualism produced contrasting or synthesizing ideologies throughout the historical development of western literature.

Turning to the East, modern Korean literature developed under the influence of western literature but in a fashion that might be called retroactive to that of the western world. Our periods of modern literature were Neo-idealism, Naturalism, Decadence, Romanticism and finally Classicism. The process thereafter coincided with that of western literature.

Forerunners of contemporary Korean literature began publishing in the 20th century their poems and novels, which embodied the neo-idealistic sentiment of the West. They were idealists but nationalists. In their works they always appealed for the solution of the problems of their unfortunate nation which was under the yoke of the Japanese. Christianity now became highly appreciated by the people through their own identification with its humanitarian aspects.

When the first world war ended, spirit of self-determination of people, as proclaimed by western leaders, prevailed in the minds of Korean intellectuals. On the first of March, 1919, thirty-three Korean patriots launched the independence movement with the publication of the proclamation of independence and other patriotic documents. This spirit of independence still prevails in the minds of many contemporary writers in Korea.

Soon after, a literary magazine called "The Creation" began to produce works from more artistic motivations. They insisted on Naturalism as the best ingredient for descriptiveness in writing novels. But they tried to visualize under the guise of realism the distressed life of the nation and twisted character of the suffering people.

In 1920 a magazine called "The Ruin" and in 1921 a periodical called "The Rose Village" were published by the so-called "decadent group" who were influenced by Western literature's fin-de-siecle. This leaning towards decadency was spurred by the economic and political situation of the time, when Korea was under Japanese control.

In 1926 in the magazine "The White Tide," a brighter interpretation of these pessimistic elements of the Korean situation began to appear. They showed a sort of twilight nostalgia. This feeling evolved into the Romantic movement of Korea, which is exemplified in a work of a contemporary poetess, Yun-sug Mo, whose poem *A Rose* begins:

> In a corner of my heart,
> In the secluded shade,
> A lone rose blooms.
>
> At night, it is not dark,
> The stars are not far away.
> Even at night, the rose sleeps not.

The most significant activities in the import of western

literature into Korea were initiated by the Society for Research in Foreign Literature, which in 1926 began the movement of translating world literature into Korean. Its brother-in-arms, the Society for Research in Dramatic Art, was established in 1931. These societies contributed much to the appreciation of foreign literature and dramatic art of the world. They were soon merged into the Overseas Literature Circle.

In addition, all the familiar ideological currents were active in Korea in varying degrees. But all of them in Korea centered around one purpose—it was their heart-felt desire for the attainment of freedom and independence of their Fatherland from the Japanese yoke.

Touching for a moment, finally, on Korean literature after the liberation of August 15, 1945, all the literary intellectuals seemed united as one as they began a strong national movement with their pens, celebrating the independence of Korea. Soon they found the unexpected barrier of the 38th parallel dividing Korea. The Korean Writers' Association was organized on the 13th of March, 1946. Most of the nation's fine arts organizations were allied with the Federation of Korean Cultural Associations which was begun in February of 1947.

On June 25, 1950, the communist forces invaded us from the north in one of the most inhumane aggressions in the history of mankind. We stood up and fought the aggressors with a determination to win over freedom at all cost, because we know then, as we know now, that the freedom is the most precious possession of mankind, and that no freedom can be won without sacrifices. We paid heavy sacrifices to preserve our freedom and independence and suffered the worst destruction and devastation of our economy in the course of fighting against the communist invaders. Many writers were killed in the war or are still missing.

Despite the heavy sacrifices and sufferings on our side, the United Nations failed to win the war in Korea which they could have won militarily and instead concluded the so-called armistice agreement with the communists. Thus the armistice left our country divided. Under the circumstances, more and more emphasis in all of the literary groups is on a national plane, stemming from the strong desire for the unification of the fatherland by expelling communist aggressors out of their territory in the north. Thus, in 1955 the Korean Free Writers' Association was newly established. It is the strong view of the Association that literature under a communist regime can only exist to be a means of assisting the aggressive scheme of the communist, for there exists no freedom of speech or publication under the communist rule. Many of Korea's eminent authors of today are now members of the Korean Center of the International P.E.N. Club which started in 1954.

Thus modern Korean writers have been suffering for a long time from the political and economic difficulties which have been imposed on them from outside. Their pleasure was to seek something in literature. This is why we have been more interested in liberal arts than in science.

We have a hidden power and hope for the future, with which we will overcome our difficulties. We have shown in our modern literature as well as during the recent Korean War an ability to integrate the western science with our spiritual home life, and thus we are equipped to fight against any aggressions whether political or cultural. As a whole, modern Korean literature can be called "*The Literature of Resistance against Imperialism and Communism.*"

The character of Korean literature for the future hangs unmistakably on the settlement of the problem of unification. For Korean literature, as well as for every Korean, the future is unquestionably dependent on the erasure of the artificial line that divides our nation at the 38th parallel.

Every Korean's life is tied to his country—and its future is his future: as the poem, *I Am a Son of This Land* by a contemporary poet, Zu-dong Yang, suggests:

> The people of this land—
> Their minds whiter than their clothes,
> Loving wine and song as their wives,—
> I am a son of this land!

Appreciation of Korean Poetry

LOVE OF NATURE AND PEACE

Traditional Poems

The Koreans were long known for their contributions to the cultural development of the east. To appreciate the beauty of Korean poetry to its highest degree one should be familiar with the country. One should know something of its mountains, lakes, rivers and physical features. It is further necessary to understand the philosophy of its people, their dreams, their hopes, their ambitions, etc.

Poetry in any society is a personalized expression of the literature and culture of that society. Its meaning and interpretation can vary from person to person; and its symbolic and subtle meanings reflect many of the social influences of that society. An analysis of a country's poetry can often produce the key which opens up the door to its philosophical thinking. However, even with a mind's eye view of the Korean landscape and an understanding of its people and their mystery, Korean poetry may be enjoyed to its ultimate only if read in the vernacular. The loss in meaning must necessarily be great when translated into another language.

Korean poetry has evolved from traditional simplicity to modern complex meaning. Traditional Korean poetry was closely related to nature and the Korean geographic situation. It was symbolic of the beauty of nature, and also of the love of peace that evolved from this true life state. Modern Korean poetry has also centered around nature, but the modern poets have seemed to try to draw out a deep or hidden meaning.

They try to relate objects of nature to reality. It seems that traditional poetry shows peace and tranquility, whereas, modern poetry drifts toward a distant mental thought slowly cracking out of its encompassing shell.

The earliest records of the ancient tribes of Korea relate to us that they had many Shamanistic festivals along with the worshipping of many different events of nature. And also the reader must bear in mind the practices of Animism—belief in "spirit beings" to cover animals, plants and even inanimate objects, and Fetishism—the attributing of spirit qualities to the sun, moon, stars and other objects of nature. Through justifiable means it has been evidenced that the Korean people had produced poetical literature from their very earliest days. Through the early stages of the Korean culture, most of the poetical creations were connected with some sort of myth or legend, revolving around or influenced by such religious sentiment.

First of all the "Love of Nature" in Korean poetry can best be considered by dividing it into two distinct parts, the traditional and the modern. One does not have to go very far into Korean culture to discover that the Korean's affinity to nature is an indigenous of his culture. Rugged mountains seem endless in number on the Korean peninsula. Within the rugged terrain a hardy Asian stock has been able to develop a culture distinct from its two neighbors, China and Japan. The Korean's ability to adapt himself to the soil and to the harsh climatic conditions which prevail in the higher elevations of the peninsula has, in the process, made him associate very closely with the terrain. In passing, it should be noted that traditionalist poets identify themselves with the physical aspects of nature. Korea is a land of mountains, hills, valleys, and other physical feature that make it a most beautiful and legendary country. These physical characteristics, as well as others, have played a major role in the development of Korean culture through the ages. One can find a number of excellent examples of traditionalist poetry.

For instance, in a poem by In-hu Gim *The Blue Mountains Are as They Are* we have an excellent example of a

Korean's close identification with nature:

> The blue mountains are as they are,
> So are the green waters!
> Mountains and rivers are as they are,
> So am I as I am.
> I that grew up among them
> Will grow old as they do.

Here, one can readily see the effect that the geographical terrain of the peninsula of Korea has had on this particular poet. This poem expresses the traditional belief of accepting nature for its beauty and not trying to find out how nature is utilized for human life. The author tells us that the mountains and rivers are as they are simply because they were so created. Man is as he is because he was so created. He will die and reproduce the earth by returning to dust. Koreans living close to nature understand its messages.

The person possibly sees the mountains as they appear to him. They may be enveloped in a mist of some type and appear to be a blue color. And the waters that he talks about are probably green in color. The mountains and rivers, then, appear as one sees them. He then says, 'I am also what you see before you.' He also states that as the mountains and rivers grow old with age, so will he also grow old just as everything else does. It is something that cannot be stopped.

Here the poet accepts life as it comes to him. He is part of nature which is always present around him. He is a very tiny part of this large world, being surrounded by the blue mountains and green waters. They are present everywhere. However, after many centuries, even the mountains sometimes lose their majesty. Some of the rivers become streams. They grow old. Our period in the present world is but for a short duration and they will be here for others who will follow.

In the first line, "blue mountains" and "green waters" are paired together. They would seem to suggest two aspects of nature, one the stable and the unmovable, and the other undergoing constant change, thus being different attributes of the one substance nature. In the second sentence nature (mountains and waters) is paired with "I am as I am," which indicates that the person is one with nature. Or, as the Taoists whose concepts are reflected in much of Korean literature would say, 'He makes his spiritual home in the Tao (nature), in which all things lose their distinctions and merge into one,' the third sentence, "I grew up among them," and "will grow old as they do," reflects the fatalistic approach of the traditional poet for he even gives up his identity to become one with nature, completely accepting its course.

Thus in this poem, oneness or harmony with nature is emphasized, and the poet presents an abstract philosophy that man is nothing but a mountain among mountains. He is trying to equate man with nature by saying that nature's phenomena and man grow old in the same way. The poem illustrates Oriental fatalism with its inherent parallels between man and nature. He implies that mountains are destined to crumble and rivers are destined to run their course with time. He also implies that man similarly follows nature's fatalistic path and grows old as do nature's phenomena.

This poem is written in the most typical form of Korean lyrics, known as *Sizo,* or "melody of time," a standard genre comparable to the English sonnet. This poetic form is one of the most rigid and demanding of those in any language, as it requires strict adherence to the established phrase, syllable, and line structure. Originally limited to only three lines though I arranged them in six lines each, the *Sizo* poems are intricate, compact and condensed so that not a single word is wasted. Their concise message is at once profound and universal, and so stated that it has always appealed to the learned men as well as to the common people. This message in this lyric concerns man's harmony with nature, and his fatalistic willingness to let it direct him.

The repetition of stating that things "are as they are," in these lines conveys the consistency with which the partial forms and conditions of matter unite in the "one."

Thus the author submits his own life process to the vast cosmic continuum. This passive unification with the all-encompassing harmony of the cosmos is the honest expression of traditional fatalistic "oneness." The poem is so condensed and complete in itself, that it is a symbol of the unity it expresses.

The author of the next *Sizo, Butterfly! Let's go to the blue mountain,* is unknown. The poem is as follows:

> Butterfly, Let's go to the blue mountain.
> Spotted butterfly! Come with me.
> When it grows dark on our way,
> Let's stay the night in a flower.
> If the flower refuses us both,
> We will sleep content on a leaf.

The mountain to me again signifies the love that the author feels toward nature. This harmony with nature is evident in the way he says "Butterfly! Let's go to the blue mountain." He wants to be united with nature and with, perhaps, one of nature's creatures—the butterfly. In asking the butterfly to accompany him to the mountain, he again shows his desire to be with nature.

He indicates his love for the mountain by letting nothing —not—even darkness—stop his journey. The butterfly is stressed as his intimate and companion because of its fleeting but essential contact with the natural world, and because it represents the poet's capricious aspirations. In calling it a "spotted butterfly," he indicates the insect's natural camouflage which allows it to merge with the rest of nature, or stand conspicuous in the sky above it. It further portrays the whimsical mental activity that taunts man into activism.

He expects it to "grow dark," as he shows foreknowledge of his predestined retirement in nature. It would then be comforting to "stay the night in a flower," or to be consumed within nature and consoled from his fear of mental loneliness. In the last line he states symbolically that he will be content with his companion to rest atop nature if he is predestined to be alienated from within it. Like the first poem we see his desire to be included in the "oneness" of nature, and the same passive acceptance of fatalism, even if that should mean exclusion from the harmony of the whole.

The butterfly symbolizes a vagabond searching for lodging during the night. (He is looking for protection in nature from the night.) Both the flower and the leaf are symbolic of lodging in nature. The parallel is drawn to conclude that man belongs in nature and at night nature will protect him. The author depicts man living in harmony with nature through his man-nature equivalents. The vagabond poet is a simple man close to nature without many needs, who is content to be left under the protection of nature. This goes along with the traditional aspects of Korean poetry in that the author is of the view that man can live harmoniously within nature and nature will protect him from its complexities.

> "When it grows dark on our way,
> Let's stay the night in a flower."

This I interpret as, when the pressures which are imposed on man in society become too great, man looks toward nature (in its various forms) to console and protect him. With this in mind, the love of nature is exemplified beautifully, the butterfly symbolizing the female and the male bidding her to come and live with him. The last two lines,

> "If the flowers refuses us both,
> We will sleep content on a leaf."

seems to indicate that even though in the road that they will transverse together they should encounter rejection, the element of togetherness will exist for them, giving them contentment. Evidently, as the author became more aware of himself, there appeared some noticeable examples of animism in Korean poetry. Animism refers to the ascription of human traits to inanimate objects and souls to animals. Animism usually indicates that man is confused as to his role in nature.

"Let's stay the night in a flower" means that they will find some shelter to sleep under. If this is not possible, they will sleep under the stars. He indicates this by saying "We will sleep content on a leaf." Leaves are carried by the wind in all directions. To me, this means that they will just make a bed wherever there is space. The most ideal spot would be under the stars—with nature again.

The above two poems show in the traditional sense the love of nature for what it is. Nature—just for the simple feeling of nature. The central theme is carried out in the above poems by the feeling of oneness that the person creates with nature. I think that the physical setting of the land—what nature has made—causes this harmonious feeling between people in the poem and nature itself.

The butterfly is a sign of not being tied down or without a house. Its spotted wings indicate its adaptation to nature. Going to the mountain is symbolic of the trip through life. The darkness stands for some interruption in the achievement of our goal, the mountain. In achieving our goal we are forced by some things to decide, and if we are rejected on that decision we can be content with less as long as it is but a step towards our goal and we are not permanently bound by it. The poet goes on a journey to the blue mountain. He beckons one of nature's most beautiful creatures to accompany him and they begin their adventure. When does it end? One cannot say. The poet sets no time of return. When it becomes dark he and his winged companion will sleep in the fields and continue their journey the next day.

Planning for Ten Years by Sun Song also expresses closeness to nature.

> Planning for ten years,
>   A house I built,
> Fresh air occupies the half,
>   The moon the rest.

In the above lines the author brings out the fact of the closeness of nature to the people. The author feels that nature surrounds the life of the people and they long for its beauty.

No room for mountain and river
They're to be around.

In these lines the author further brings out the traditional idea of the vastness of nature.

For ten years a man planned to build a home, yet he thought of only two things to occupy it. Air and the moon will occupy the house, but is this enough? Must he not think of the mountains too, and the rivers as an essential of life? Though man plans for ten years his job is not perfect. He has forgotten the many substances of life. The beauty of the earth is always around but men fail to see it. The Divine Planner had the only perfect plan and man cannot duplicate it.

In this poem he writes of a house that he has built which allows itself to become engulfed by the crisp air and the nightly moon. The air and the moon have taken over his house so that there is no room for the mountains and the streams, but he does not despair since the mountains and the rivers are all around him and his house. To enjoy the true beauty of nature one cannot be a casual observer who goes to a particular place and stays for a short while. One must spend a great deal of time around nature.

Traditional Korean poetry is sometimes a meditation, but it can be a crying out against social injustice. It can be peaceful, but it also can be turbulent. It almost seems to be likened to a river. It has its swift, turbulent sections, but then it flattens out into a broad, placid section where it will do nothing but lull the boatman into a restful state so he will be unprepared for the next drop into turbulence. And yet, hasn't the history of the country itself accounted for this crashing white water and then the leveling out into the broad placid section where there is hope for the populace to regain once again that which they have lost?

The correlation between the Korean and his early, serene surroundings is no more evident than in the lines of the traditional poet's consideration of his environment. He is awed by the natural wonders which have been thrown up around him by his creator. Because of this awe, he has gradually come to feel that he is but a minute atom in the cosmos that has been created by the one supreme being. Nonetheless he is able to feel a kinship with the nature elements in his environment. This is no more easily illustrated than by the short lines of verse written by the poet Son-do Yun.

> How many friends have I?
>   Waters and rocks, pines and bamboos!
> Now the moon rises on the east mountain
>   And how glad am I to see him!
> Then whom else do I need
>   Than these five friends of mine?

This is the friendship that has evolved from time immemorial between man and his natural surroundings. But in these days how easy it is for men to disregard that heritage of beauty that is our one true inheritance of the past! It takes ages to mold and rot away the papers and paintings, the sculpture and other art forms that are tenderly cared for. It takes but a few hours or days to blast the mountains down or burn the forest to the ground.

He conveys friendship between an incurable idealist and five facets of nature. This person has found stable friendship among the waters and rocks, pines and bamboo, and the phases of the moon rising over the mountains. He also feels that these are all the friends he needs. With friends like these, he is close to a nature he must love. This poem in *Sizo* form shows how friendship can be found in nature. The lap of the water against the rocky shoreline lulls one to sleep at nightfall. This will be repeated nightly until the end of time. What could be more consistent? In the beauty of nature true friendship may be found that death will never mar.

The Modern Concept

There is a constant motivation in the natural setting of things for both humans and animals to have a burning desire for the Love of Nature and particularly the mountains. In effect this means that the mountains are a sanctuary for the

Lovers of Nature. Hence the mountains assume that which is true nature. Poetry in this classical tradition has made the mountain the practical reality of the Love of Nature. In verse the mountain is the objective of attaining the true appreciation of the Love of Nature.

Korean modern poetry has taken the concept of the mountain in the expression of its poetry and has given it a different role in its relationship with man and then combined relations with nature. The mountain in its justification for satisfying the human desires is still very powerful in its drawing men to it. In the poem *The Mountain Road* the characteristic reflection of its role is quite in the Love of Nature. This modern concept has a feeling of ideas stemming from the new or modern civilizations of the west. It originates from such concepts as science, a feeling for independence, and the political conflicts that are quite common in the modern world of today.

THE MOUNTAIN ROAD

by Zu-dong Yang

I am going on the mountain road silently.
I am going on the mountain road alone.

The sun sinks and the bird's song stops.
Footfalls of the beasts are heard.

I am going on the mountain road silently.
I am going on the mountain road alone.

Tranquil is the night,
Dark the forest.

However dark the forest I go on.
Forest so dark that no star may be seen.

The mountain road is steep;

The mountain road is endless.

On the dreamy mountain road
A single torch is seen.

When will this uncertain mountain road be ended?
When will this dark night be lightened?

On the rocks
A single torch is seen.

The central theme of this poem indicates a specific goal that a person is trying to achieve. He is trying very hard to accomplish the feat which he has before him. It is not an easy thing to do, for the mountain road is the path he must follow. And he is alone and silent on his journey. It is a hard thing to do but no matter hard it is he must go on. His journey seems endless. The torch gives reference to the goal he has set before him. He asks, when will his goal be reached? This is shown by the statement "When will this dark night be lightened?" He then sees his torch or goal in life.

In looking at this poem, we see a rather free construction, one that is not so rigidly bound and shaped. In this poem man is less tied to fatalism, but instead gives resistance. The mountains refer to knowledge, the attainment of which is desirable and is our goal. The road to this knowledge must be transversed "alone" and "silently" as symbolically stated in the first sentence and then restated again in the third. Things which people consider as the truth, the way, etc., soon prove not to be; thus, "The sun sinks and the bird's song stops." Thus, in the fifth sentence, "However dark the forest I go on," shows perseverance in acquiring this knowledge, the path to which is difficult and never-ending.

> "The mountain road is steep.
> The mountain road is endless."

But on this path to seek knowledge, "A single torch is seen."

So, then he asks,

> "When will this uncertain mountain road be ended?
> When will this dark night be lightened?"

He is asking, when will "I" find the truth? When he accepts
that there is no ultimate truth, he accepts life and his movement within it. In this poem he is resisting and fighting to
achieve a goal; there is not the complete fatalistic acceptance
shown in earlier works.

This new attitude in Korean poetry involves less identification with the topographical setting and more inward contemplation. It becomes, I believe, a much more stimulating
philosophical association and, at the same time, one feels a
greater sense of helplessness and loneliness and bold struggles
against it in the various modern poets. While the traditionalists
enjoyed nature for nature's sake, the more modern poet seeks
to discover an answer, or a new truth in nature. One feels that
the modern poet is rather alienated from nature and is seeking
to rediscover its true beauty.

The Mountain Road was written during the Japanese occupation of Korea. It is a patriotic poem which depicts hard-
ship and a severe political situation countered by the indirect
resistance of the poet. He describes a man journeying on a
mountain road alone, symbolic of the road of life. The inherent
meaning of this is a direct contradiction of the fatalistic philosophy of earlier poets. The poet is saying that no matter how
difficult the road of life may be, man must not give up, but
rather go on in search of freedom. No matter how bad the
situation may be—in this case a supressed nation occupied by
foreigners—man must persist in his search for the light of freedom, "The sun sinks and the bird's song stops," expresses
symbolically the downcast state of the author's land at the
time of occupation. "Footfalls of the beast are heard," indicates the alien soldiers marching through the streets of his
supressed nation. In the third stanza, he sees the light symbolized
by the torch from the mountain road, a torch which is also
symbolic of freedom. He then asks the proverbial question,

"When will this dark night be lightened?" meaning when will the supression be lifted and give way to freedom. From the rocks, he can see the torch—the light of freedom—but he leaves us with the feeling that he has a long way to go before he reaches his ultimate goal.

Thus in the modern school of Korean poetry, we see a change in attitudes towards many things. The new poets challenge man's predestined limitations. They see man as a free agent setting out to explore the possibilities of new knowledge. The style of the earlier modern poems immediately reveals the new western influences. The highly disciplined form of the traditional poet is no longer allowed to restrict the artist. They experiment with new styles, asserting their freedom and individuality. *The Mountain Road* exhibits a more conversational style. Free-will is exposed in the opening line. The poet has left nature's valleys, and aspires individually to conquer the "mountain." He is now active rather than passive, but isolated and not able to communicate with unified nature. Thus, he goes "silently" and "alone," a mixture of reluctant fatalism.

As he leaves the well-illuminated valley of natural harmony the "bird's song stops," and he falls in the shadow of doubt symbolized by the sinking sun. He now hears "footfalls of the beasts," or the insatiable appetites of the will. The worldly knowledge that he has plunged into is dark, misleading, and passive. He must find his own way through the true and false knowledge, as it will not come to him of itself. And yet, in spite of the obstacles, and the absence of a standard to guide him, his will drives him on.

Again we have the stylistic portrayal of laborious repetition, as "The mountain road" is repeated in lines 11 and 12. It is here described as "steep" and "endless," indicating that the climb into intellectual involvement is indeed a difficult one and will never be completely accomplished. He admits that he will never reach the summit where all the world would be illuminated at his command.

The "dreamy mountain road" of the 13th line suggests that the repetition has been so exhausting and frustrating that his quest seems to become blurry and he may doubt the reality of existence. At this his conviction may be vacillating. Then, "a single torch is seen," an inspiration that will guide him onward, the first thing that he has actually seen. At this point he is sure of the objective uncertainty that he is committed to, and expresses questions instead of pronouncements. They are weary questions about the extent of worldly knowledge and the possibility of shedding light on this knowledge. Yet, they are fundamental to constructive thought. These questions reflect western philosophy.

Finally in the last stanza, his inspiring "torch" reveals in its light the composition of the mountain. The "rocks" of which the mountain is built are the cold, hard, bare, irregular facts of existence. He is free to see and examine each fact separately and in its relation to the mountain, and to pursue his never-ending quest towards a body of enlightened knowledge and its structure. This places the Korean poet directly amidst the world of western thought. His style has likewise assumed the already indicated western characteristics, although fortunately he retains his native composure of lyrical beauty, simplicity, and profundity. In expanding the scope of his subject, the modern Korean poet has not allowed his universality to diminish. The early modern Korean poets indeed exhibited a great shift in both style and theme. Their most outstanding original qualities, however, suffered no change. These qualities are the truth and honesty of expression, and the pervasive inner beauty of form.

The next poem is *Mountains* written by Dog-zin Yi.

As if always waiting for someone
Even on the day of death sentence,
You hold solemnly in yourself,
The legend never to be solved.

The beautiful feature
Occupies itself in gentle dreams,
And far and near
Listens to sounds, and sounds...

answers to its hidden secrets. Man's inquisitive nature leads him to the physical and metaphysical laboratory in which he examines the nature of things to discover the true meaning of existence. Nature offers the poet a great deal to contemplate upon mountains, or rivers, the sun, rain, etc. How are they related to man? Are they a part of man or are they apart from him remote, brooding, silent? That is the question which Korean poets present and attempt to answer in their poetry.

The poem was written during the Korean War. The mountains' sentiments have been personified and a contrast between the beautiful mountain and human sentiment has been established. The mountains, regardless of time, remain standing aloft. "Even on the day of death sentence you hold solemnly in yourself" illustrates that no matter what the day or what the time the mountains continue to stand, overlooking the human element. The mountain, symbol of high ideals, is clearly represented by "the beautiful feature occupies itself in gentle dreams." During the Korean War, as always the high ideals were still symbolized by the mountains, and even though the times were different (tragic), the mountain remained a transition (link), between the sky and humanity. For "thousands and millions of years" the mountains have remained the same, even though the world around them changes. They symbolically embrace the changing features of the face of the earth and more specifically of Korea. "As if waiting for someone," indicates the longevity of their presence and seems to say that they will always be there giving man a goal in which high ideals are the primary aim. "Brooding silently the smile from time immemorial," seems to say that the mountains have seen history go by and have the wisdom of an old philosopher, still remaining silent but ever present. The poem contrasts men who are at war and changing constantly with the mountains which remain stationary with high ideals and are peaceful.

The modern aspects of the love of nature have an overtone of political and moral resistance. Before 1907 the needs of the Korean people were reflected by traditional poetry. After the Japanese occupied the country, these needs changed from those of satisfying a free people to those of satisfying a surpressed people. Modern poets took up a resistance cause which became the new mode of expression. In this resistance movement, the people were given new hope which was to keep the fires of traditional poetry lit. Since the true feelings of the Korean people are rooted in traditional poetry, it will surely be only a matter of time and freedom that such poetry will again reflect the thoughts and emotions of its people.

Mountain Climbing written by In-sob Zong (the author) is in contrast to the above-mentioned poem. A child thinks he can achieve any ambition. But after much experience, he finds that reaching his goal is a long and arduous path. After one obstacle is overcome there are additional tiers of mountains or obstacles to overcome. Life is not clear but still goes on. There are colors other than black and white; there are controversies in life. Will there be happiness in the valley on the other side of the mountain? Would it be better to strive to attain our happiness within ourselves? People feel that the grass is always greener on the other side and when they reach the valley on the other side of the mountain they find the grass to be no different from that they left. Foreign ideologies have placed another obstacle in the pathway blazed by Korean patriots.

The poem is an allegory in which the poet compares learning and becoming educated with the hard and tedious task of mountain climbing. For example,

"How many return of those who up the mountain swarm?
From the wisdom of ages some drops of water form,
And dark-gathering clouds above forecast a storm.
Illusion is but vain, create your own sun,
Although the sun in the sky be undone,
The sun in your heart can be dimmed by no one.
The sun of all the ages is your very own.
Having passed the peak of thirty years what words have
I then?
After much thought and reading these words alone I
pen."

Again one can see the deep symbolism which Koreans see

in the various elements of nature. Korean poets attempt to discover their relationship to these massive earthly symbols. Man, as he grows older, reaches the peak of manhood and then begins to decline—in this manner he is not unlike the mountains which, when they are young, reach a high peak and, as they grow older, begin a steady decline. There are, though, certain elements that never seem to change; the sun and the rain never seem to grow older and, in the same respect, what one feels—that inward glow—never seems to change even though one grows older.

Mountain Climbing is a comparison between the reality and fantasy of mountain climbing. The mountain is a target where they could climb up and find hopes. The poet has ascended and was disillusioned by reality, and so to establish another truth in life has to climb on to another peak and find reality elsewhere. *Mountain Climbing* is a poem about the poet's search for truth. The mountain symbolizes the heights of truth to which he sets his goals. In a dream he begins to climb this mountain of truth and imagines the beauties he will find at the end of his climb. As he goes further up the mountain, the phenomena of reality clouds his child-like image of the truth. The poet climbs and climbs but never reaches the top and finally becomes weary and begins to regret his journey. In the fourth stanza he offers a prophesy to the children of the coming ages who would search for truth. He tells them not to waste their time dreaming and goes on to tell of the graves of the men who came before in the search for truth. The poet is plagued by coming face to face with the reality of the situation. In the seventh stanza he comes to the realization that the search for truth was not as he had dreamed it to be. As a final word he tells the coming generations to learn from those who have gone before them in search of truth. This is well illustrated by the lines "From the wisdom of ages some drops of water form... Illusion is but vain. Create your own sun, Although the sun in the sky be undone, The sun in your heart can be dimmed by no one." The point of the poem is simply that man should not indulge in supernatural dreams but should establish step by step his own struggle for existence. The poet counsels those who would follow his path to beware of fantasies in their search. Above all, man should be national in his search for truth and avoid fanciful dreams. No rung of the "ladder" on the way up should be overlooked.

In the poet's fanciful state, he says that he is disillusioned in the face of reality. He finds that people who have gone before him have not succeeded in finding the truth. He counsels others who would attempt the feat to use more rationality rather than fantasy and with this thought he leaves them with hope. "Credulous travellers, over this pass go not!" means literally, people who are inclined to believe anything on slight exigence should not attempt the symbolic mountain. "Look down, and on the earth your footsteps keep" says that one is better off staying with realism and staying away from fantasy. The end of the poem leaves us with the feeling that he has been disappointed and disillusioned in his search, but yet he leaves us with the hope of using rationality, and keep our feet on the ground and plan our search instead of just dreaming about it. If one does this, he might be able to reach the heights. Men should look to their own resources rather than grasp at dreams and illusions; thus the poet rejects the fatalistic viewpoint and advises man to turn inward to himself. Taking all this into account we can see how this poem turns away from the fatalistic theme of traditional poetry and offers some moral resistance of the newer school of thought.

POETRY OF LOVE

In the traditional poem, *The Long, Long Night of the Eleventh Month* by a poetess, Zin-i Hwang, the love hoped for is peace of mind, tranquility of soul. She was a talented girl. A son of the next house died of his unrequited love, and when his coffin was carried by her house, she removed her underwear and threw it on the coffin. When news of this action became known, she could not find a husband. Thereupon, she determined to become a dancing girl. She became famous and associated with prominent people, though in the course of her associations she lost her virginity, and this of course made unacceptable for marriage. Her poem, *The Long, Long Night of the Eleventh Month,* is her admonishment to good girls not to wander astray. She symbolically explains that if she had to live her life over, she would do much differently than she had done in the past. She has deeply missed the real affection of married life and the tranquility of soul pursuant to such a relationship.

While the traditional expressions are expounded through the *Sizo* form of three lines of regularized syllable and phrase structure, the modern approach, both structurally and emotionally, is a more sophisticated and more flexible approach. Also the modern approach has taken on a conversational style, which adds to its readaptability and general attractiveness. Since about 1907, Korean poetry has also added to its repertoire of topics many western ideas and approaches.

Included within the category of modern poetry of love is the freedom of love. In the modern poem, *The Azalea,* by Sowol Gim, the poet talks of the sadness he will experience when his mistress departs. "When you take your leave, tired of seeing me, Though I should die, I shall not weep." He realizes she will leave him sooner or later, but he knows that this must be the end of the emotional parabola of all love-mistress relations. On the first level of meaning, the sentimental treatment of free love is dissected. In looking for the second level of meaning, nothing is more striking than the use of the imperative, which always indicates urgency. "Go now, I pray, with short steps. Let each foot-step gently tread the flowers which I have spread for you." This act of patience, then, as opposed to the patience of the traditional view, separates this poem from those of the earlier period.

Modern poems as will be seen digress from this fatalistic standard, and show much more optimism. Here the new experience of freedom is expressed. One should be free to do what one wants to and should not have to be tied down against his or her will. This poem is similar to the traditional in the respect that it uses nature, but the idea that is expressed is truly a modern concept.

It portrays the independence and freedom of love not on the fatalistic level but on the social. The author is saying when it is time for his love to depart from him, he will silently say "go," and he will regret this but will not show his grief. He wishes the parting to be as sweet as possible. Also the author is telling the person to go onward onto a path of beautiful wonder but not to tread too fast. The new experience of freedom is expressed in the poem; an individual should be free in what he wants to do. The individual should have his own choice and freedom to leave, although he may feel sadness in his heart.

The underlying message of this form of literature was to accept what comes and make the best of it. The modern seems to represent beauty to be sure, but one gets the feeling the author is trying to express something more than this. He is trying to express a feeling of something new and different. This new feeling is the freedom of his mind.

THE CANNA FLOWER

by In-sob Zong

The lips of canna erupt flames of fire
As the crater of passions from the axis of the earth.
Hoping to swallow the warm summer sun,
It blooms like a fire-god in the garden.

The lips, kissed still to be enjoyed,
Holding the bright red dreams in the mouth,
Now riding on a green horse carriage,
Merge way bearing my melancholy.

The canna, longing for the sound of waves,
Pricks up its ears over the fence.
My mud-stained fingers
Draws silver bells on the horizontal line of the sea.

This poem compares the warmth and emotion of a loved one to the beauty and passion of the canna flower, a flower of the banana family, with thick roots, large leaves, and brilliant flowers. The canna is given human qualities when the poet says "The lips of canna erupt flames of fire...The lips, kissed still to be enjoyed, Holding the bright-red dreams in the mouth, Now riding on a green horse carriage, Merge away bearing my melancholy." Here also, then, is a break from the traditional, sheltered expressions of emotion, and they are presented here as being natural (the flower) and warmly passionate (flames of fire), dealing with love set in a modern mood. It advocates a freedom of love.

A SECRET

by In-sob Zong

My rumpled hair
   Combing neatly,
I put on the little comb
   You sent to me.

My mud-stained fingers
   Washing neatly,
I put on the little ring
   You sent to me.

While the little comb
   And ring I wear,
In the glass I gaze at myself
   Reflected there.

Oh, in my hand
   And in my hair,
Is hidden a secret
   That none can share.

It seems that this poem deals with the story of a secret love. The girl who owns the comb and ring seems to be the only one who knows where she got them. They are the gifts of her lover who remains a secret to every one but her. It is a very pretty little love poem. Looking quickly, then, at *A Secret* with these principles in mind, we again perform the analysis.

Universal appeal here is based on the universal practice of giving gifts. This theme strikes the hearts of readers everywhere because of the international spirit of achieving satisfaction. For individuality, the poet has struck the basis of this practice by hitting on simplicity as the theme. Perhaps the old proverb of "It's not the gift that counts, but rather the thought behind it," should be kept in mind while reading the poem. Associational value is provided for the reader by the mention of common, everyday articles. The comb and the ring, which are naturally associated with marriage and love, provide a point of reference for the reader. Even more striking for its associational value is the phrase "mud-stained fingers." We naturally associate this phrase with nature and this leads one to recall the close association between man and nature.

As the first of the intrinsic factors, unity is maintained by the consistent use of the personal pronouns, "I" and "me." The repetition of these pronouns, especially in such a short poem, keeps the thought of the individual in the mind of the reader. Variety, on the other hand, is attained through the omission of the pronoun "you" from the last two stanzas after it is mentioned in the first two. Balance and proportion are achieved by this same method of the use of "you" and "I."

FRIENDSHIP

How Many Friends Have I? by Son-do Yun, already quoted as an example for traditional Love of Nature, also attempts to symbolize true friendship. The poet asks how many friends he has and then looks at the world around him. This poem was obviously written in solitude, that is, the solitude of the mind of the poet. He looks around and sees the things that are common in his life; water, rocks, pines, bamboo, and the moon. Each of these inanimate things welcomes him in its own way and he silently returns the greeting. It is my belief that the author realizes that these things, although inanimate, symbolize sincere and true friendship in that they are dependable in both times of happiness and strife. In this poem, the author uses non-human things to symbolize the way human friendship should be.

The poet gives the utmost respect and importance to the elements by referring to them as his five close friends of nature. This friendship must be quite important to the poet as a value of life, because he has capitalized each of the words referring to nature. This technique of capitalizing certain words emphasizes the importance the poet gives these terms in relation to the poem itself too. The reader of this poem could almost say that the poet is in love with nature and that he wants everyone to understand his deep feelings of friendship.

This poem illustrates the basic concepts of the traditional period of literature. Here man is seen as only one fragment of nature, and the other parts are represented by the water, rocks, pines, bamboo and the moon. By seeing these as man's friends one might find peace within oneself and with nature. This is the only way peace can be found because man and nature are one. The friendship between these other elements of nature and man also expresses the Love of Friendship which is part of the traditional outlook. The fatalistic precept is evident in this poem, and it can be seen that it is an elementary factor behind the expressed ideas.

WHEN WINE AT YOUR HOUSE IS RIPE

by Yug Gim

When wine at your house is ripe,
　Please ask me to visit you.
When flowers at my cottage bloom,
　I will invite you to come.
And then let's talk of the things,
　Forgetting worries, over a hundred years.

In this poem the author shows that everyone has something to contribute to the world. Each race, each nation, each individual can help the others in the world even if it is only in some small way. The author is trying to convince us to forget past prejudices and hatreds and come together for a better life for all concerned. Again this poem is from the traditional feeling of friendship. The author is trying to convey the thoughts that when things at your house are perfect, please invite me to visit you. I will do the same when things are perfect and beautiful at my home, because it is only then that we can speak as true friends without worries of the past or future. This poem shows the feelings of fatalism and goodness and piety.

The new literary movements from early twenties were characterized by two points: A new conversational style which was freed from the old traditional form written in the Chinese classic style, and new ideas influenced by Western civilizations. An example of this poetry is *My Dear Friends!* written by Gwang-su Yi.

MY DEAR FRIENDS!

Oh, brothers and sisters!
Do you hear, do you hear
The sound of the song I sing,
As I sit beneath the ruined wall
Bowed down and kneeling low?

Oh, brothers and sisters!
Do you breathe, do you breathe
The fragrance of the sandalwood oil
Which I burn with a trembling hand
In the broken censer bowl?

Oh, brothers and sisters!
Do you see, do you see
I stand and wait weeping
Outside the city wall and yearn

For you, for a place in your heart?

As quoted above, there seems to be a new conversational tone in this poem. The poet seems to be pleading with his reader to take notice of the world around them and to have greater respect for the people around them. Notice that in this earlier modern poetry there are not as many references to nature, and that each line of poetry begins together, as written. There is definitely a freed delivery in this poem as compared to the *Sizo* type of poem. The themes of the earlier modern poems also involve elements which are blunter than those involved in the *Sizo* poems, or in other words, more serious in nature.

This poem was written during the Japanese occupation, and the subject's life seems to have been shattered by the horrors of oppression. His brothers and sisters have suffered. He is trying to comprehend the situation and take hold of a new life but the shattered world around him and the thoughts of his family are not to be suppressed. The occupation of Korea by Japan was the start of this mood of rebelliousness, for there was one to find a friend in those times which were fraught with peril for anyone who said one simple word that sounded as if it were against the reigning power controllers. It is the problem of all surpressed people to communicate with each other. And so the poet tried to produce a product that was filled with double meanings to attract those peoples who were more interested in liberty than in their personal safety.

The poet uses the terms, "brothers and sisters" with much emphasis to express the newer ideas of Christian brotherhood and Democratic equality. When he asks if they see him and if they hear his song we know that he is referring to something they are unaccustomed to, an aspiration yet unfelt. He is pleading with the use of some traditional and familiar items, that they might see the "new light." "Outside the city wall," he yearns for them to join him. Finally, he has the freedom to love his country and this world with a hope of not living in vain.

These examples of traditional and modern Korean poems have given us an insight into the feelings and beliefs of the

Korean people through history. The fatalistic precept seems to show a people that feel hopeless; they do not feel that they can help themselves because everything is determined by fate. Yet, we can sense in the modern literature that their minds were searching for something, some belief or new concept that would give them a purpose in life and a feeling that they themselves had some control over their destiny and the world in which they lived. As we look at the trends in modern litera- ture we see the result of new ideas, ideas which previously had been beyond them. These ideas of struggle for existence bring the whole aspect of life into a new light for these people. This light, which is still prevailing, gives them a spirit, a new self.

IN THE NIGHT WITHOUT A LIGHT

by Zi-hyang Gim

1

Solitude does not weep.
Solitude does not lie.
We, forlorn and lost,
Better meet together
To live with no one else.

The night without a light!

2

The breathing life
Is a ball of flames
Rolling hither and thither.

All surrounded
Being locked up,
Life takes the lead
In the front alone.

Is there a rescue
On the surface
Of a flat ground

In the night without a light?

3

The poet alone
Silently goes
To the pure extreme.

We, forlorn and lost,
Better meet together
To live with none but us

In the night without a light.

The poem seems to describe a group of survivors of some conflict who have been thrown together by some grace other than their own. The difference between this poem and the previous one is that the people in this poem have realized that they cannot afford to give up because they must stay together and rebuild their friendship, their country and their culture. These lines express the feeling of confusion and harshness which exists in the country. It clearly expresses the feeling that the people have of being locked in and surrounded by darkness. Then she asks, "Is there a rescue?" The author is wondering if there is some way that we can overcome this confusion. Can we, who are so forlorn and lost, meet together and solve this problem? Can we ever overcome this darkness and find the guiding light which will enable us to live peacefully as one undivided country?

In comparing the traditional and modern sentiments in Korean poetry there has been a great effect on the minds of the Korean people because of the many years of strife and conflict in which they have been involved. In the traditional sentiment the emphasis was on genuine friendship. This modern sentiment seems to be one of friendship or brotherhood lost and the acquiring of new friends. The tone of the modern poems gives the feeling that Korea is not a stagnant nation but that it is progressing not only in the field of literature but in other political and cultural facets as well.

Darkness is a strange thing. Everyone responds to it differently. Men are in the dark, scrambling, grasping for unity. Continuity is nowhere to be found. All seems hopeless.

We all search for a shoulder to lean on, and a light for seeing. Some of us, unfortunately, remain in the dark. This might be expressed thus:

> All surrounded
> In the midst of a vast wall
> Being locked up,
> Life takes the lead
> In the front alone.

Our past is forgotten. We only rationalize in terms of our present dilemma. We wait for the rope to pull us out. It's a fruitless type of patience. A light begins to shine. A realization becomes all too obvious. A situation is conquered through self-perseverance. We can expect from a relationship only what we ourselves add to it.

This poem is a complex one of modern sentiment. It does not have one simple theme, but several related ones. There seems to be a struggle between choosing solitude and society. Even if a person is an intricate part of society, he experiences alienation and loneliness. He is at odds with society and feels this alienation, but he is still compelled to seek out the companionship of other human beings. This plaintive pleading is but a small example of a people who are torn asunder from one another and weep at the gates, for they know there is no chance to be so free again to decide their own fate. Friend has been torn from friend and they have become bitter enemies.

They are condemned. Is there any better example of this than the words?

> Is there a rescue
> On the surface
> Of a flat ground
>
> In the night without a light?

Darkness has prevailed and without the light of reason stupidity will remain in the fore and no more can there be a beautiful life. This poem dealing with friendship is sad but beautiful. The subject is loneliness and to conquer loneliness people must unite no matter what has brought them in search of one another. When desperation prevails in the lives of men, is there hope of finding an escape? No man should live alone and face the darkness by himself. Human beings need to feel wanted, need to feel secure, and need to feel cherished. People united can be the answer in order to survive. To remove the mask of ugly fright, fear, and hatred is the answer for a modern new world. If man believes in himself, then only can people believe in him. To trust, to work harmoniously and to love is the answer for long, happy friendship.

This is an example, to a certain extent, of the traditional influence on modern poetry. The fatalistic precept is expressed here, too, and the other elements are inevitable results of this. Line three, "We, forlorn and lost," the title, and stanza three are all good examples of this fatalistic belief. We are lost in the sense that we are unable to help or hinder ourselves. Our lives and our minds are locked in an unescapable cell and the key is in the hands of fate. Man finds that the only solution to this dilemma is to accept it rather than to try and change anything. Only the poet is capable of coming to the link which leads to peace because he is the only being that can grasp such a peace in this vain effort of life. The rest must unite "solitude" into a friendship which has some peace of its own, that they might continue to live with the sole friend "solitude" in this "Night without a Light." Thus, we can see why a people with a fatalistic precept would have to centralize their new ideas on such things as a Love of Friendship in modern sense.

To sum up, then, the following must be said. The traditional form of poetry contains a simple elegance and grace of a time when there was the simple factor of environment to be dealt with. It shows a people who were content with the life that was offered them and did not ask for more than was given them by their creator. The modern style shows the repressed resentment that has slowly built up because of the constant marauding of the strong against the weak. The materially strong have had the physical domination but not the mental domination so long as to force an insidious hatred into the hearts of a peaceful people. Let us hope that they will not be consumed by this hate.

The literature of Korea is very expressive in that it appeals to the senses. It seems they appreciate the small, simple things of life that are so commonly taken for granted. It is among the most moving and symbolic poetry ever to be written that represents an amazing and mysterious culture. The ways of the East Asian countries are beautiful and strange, but through the communication of poetry all people in all lands can understand and appreciate their world. Through literature, perhaps, some day, man will cease to be ignorant of the culture of others, and learn to love his fellowman.

LOYALTY AND PATRIOTISM

Traditional Features

Korea, a nation steeped in the traditions of a history that transcends centuries, gives an insight into her basic composition, her people. The consideration of patriotic poems enables us to more fully explore an important facet of Korea. This can give us a much clearer understanding of the people and their attitudes. Patriotism most clearly brings a more lucid concept of a country's people. Patriotism may be manifested in all classes of people and the poetry of a nation may be said to express their attitudes most beautifully.

Korean poetry about the Second World War and concerning the Korean War seems an interesting and worthy segment in the study of poetry, if only for the situations which Koreans were involved in during these war periods. Serving under Japanese rule no doubt greatly influenced Korean thought, and this was expressed through her poetry as well as other mediums. Because of contradictions in national situations as well as racial prejudices, much of the most heart-felt Korean poetry was suppressed and went unpublished. However, many of the war poems that were published since the independence can be considered indicative of true Korean thought.

Heart-felt solemnity was carried over to the Korean War, as the poets of this time wrote of humility and justice for mankind, as well as about the fears and emptiness of embittered war times. These situations brought about the awakening of new poetic talent, as do many important events in world history. Through these talents come a rich and beautiful portrayal of a nation's thought and heritage.

Among many characteristics expressed in Korean literature are the traits of loyalty and patriotism. Nations sometimes need, as do people, a great crisis or terrifying event to bring forth some quality previously hidden or held in check. So it was with nationalism in Korea. With the oppressive rule by the Japanese beginning in 1910, there gradually grew a movement of resistance and a return to independence. This movement of nationalism, or feelings of loyalty and patriotism, are easily seen in the wave of literature which resulted, particularly after the Japanese were defeated in 1945 and fear of punishment no longer existed. Loyalty to country obviously did begin in 1910, and has always been a characteristic of Koreans. It only emerged greatly strengthened and changed in nature at that time. Traditional loyalty was paid to the king. The following poem expresses this clearly. It could easily refer to a medieval knight of the roundtable in Europe.

FATTENING A SPLENDID HORSE

by Hyong Czoe

Fattening a splendid horse,
    And washing it in the river,
I will ride on it with a sword
    Well polished and very sharp.
Thus will I serve the King
    In my country's need!

This poem is a traditional *Sizo*, and in it the author expresses his love for his king as well as his devotion to his country. The traditional patriotism of Korea is shown in this warrior's actions. The soldier will only ride with a "splendid horse" and a "well polished sabre." This portrays that the author wants only the best for his king and his country.

In *This Mortal Dying and Dying* by Mong-zu Zong, as in "Fattening a Splendid Horse" the author expresses his true patriotism and nationalism in the traditional sense. Whether his country is dying or is ravaged by foes, he will not lose faith in it. His heart is with his country. He ends by asking a question, "Will my heart ever change?," but it seems evident due to the traditional strong patriotism of the Korean people that his heart will never change.

Just as the good historian must not neglect the social, economic, and religious counterparts of a political-historical movement, so particularly must one be cognizant of the background and general climate of opinion of the period when a poet produced his work. To read a poem out of context without the reality of the situation in which the poet wrote is both a loss to the reader and a disservice to the author. Sacrifice and patience are the keynote moods to the traditional view of peace held by the Korean people. Sacrifice actually may refer to self-sacrifice on the part of the poet; this self-sacrifice is, however, not the exclusive passion of the older poets, but also can be claimed by modern poets. Patience also seems to be possessed by all poets, though the modern poets are somewhat more demanding in their claims for peace and freedom from restraint than the traditional.

In *Candlelight in the Room* by Ge Yi, the poet speaks of the sadness of an extinguishing candle, slowly burning away. The poet's remorse and sadness came from his failure to establish the dethroned King, Danzong. Although Ge Yi was finally executed for his part in the restoration plot, he was nevertheless able to express succinctly his feelings toward his failure and the injustice extended to the rightful king. In this poem the author is expressing his loyalty by comparing himself to a candle.

The candle light in the room!

> Whom have you sent away?
> Outwardly you shed tears
> Not knowing your heart is burning.
> Like me the candle light
> Does not know its core is burning.

This poem is very symbolic. The wax of the candle melting is the shedding of outward tears. The heart of the candle burning is the wick aflame. The very last two lines of the poem show that man himself sheds without knowing exactly what it is that pains his heart so. The author expresses his love for the king as he compares himself to the candle. The outward appearance of the candle is comparable to the author himself. The melting wax is his tears. His lonely heart, although he does not feel anything deep inside, is the burning wax. His grief is caused in seeking whom the candle has sent away. It is probable that something sad gave him this feeling of remorse, but like the candle, he does not know the core is burning.

In *The Stream that Wept Last Night* by Ho Won, the circumstances which surrounded and brought birth to the poem are much the same as those of the above poem. When Sezong came to power, Won was already a prominent person in the government. Faithful to the deposed young ruler Danzong, he resigned his post and followed the deposed king into exile. He remained near his king and devoted himself to writing in seclusion. When Danzong finally died, he mourned for three years and then returned to his own birthplace. In the poem here reviewed, he speaks of the fact that his king will never be restored and he remains loyal. Here, the peace itself is a sacrifice, for the king cannot be restored by anything less than violence, yet the idea of violence is also repulsive.

> The stream that wept last night
> Still flows with a sad voice.
> Now I realize and realize indeed
> That the weeping sound was sent by you.
> I wish it could flow upstream,
> So that my weeping might reach you!

Then main idea of this poem is that of two people mourning and one person realizing the weeping of the other while the other mourns alone. The person weeping alone wishes that he could give the other person the comfort and knowledge that he too is weeping. This idea can be seen in the last two lines of the poem. The interpretation can be analogous with that of a child weeping for its mother or even that of someone who has been lost to this world and sees the weeping of this world. This may show how the stream even feels one is sad because the lover or the king misunderstood him. But, if only the stream could reverse itself, it too would return the same sad sounds. It would tell the lover or the king to come back and join his loved one so that the stream, too, would be united and not sad. The saddest words of tongue or pen are, "It might have been." The poem also expresses similar feelings as the poem *The Candle Light in the Room* above mentioned. Again using comparisons of nature to express his feelings, Won is comparing the sad sound of the flowing river to a messenger sent by a loved one. The weeping sound he hears is that of the king who has ignored him. He wants to try and change the cause of events by turning the river and making it flow the other way, taking him to his loved one.

Recent Poetry

Korea has been a country under foreign domination several times in its history. In order to escape from this unhappy life the Korean people have turned to poetry to express their hopes and desires. At times the Koreans were so oppressed that their only outlet was through literature. Following World War II the poets turned to themes of patriotism and sorrow because of the unexpected division of the country. Right after the war poets wrote freely but later they returned to more constricted writing. North Korea became a communistic country and South Korea remained free. There were two distinct groups of poets in Korea after the war. One group wrote of hate and repugnance, while the other group wrote ideas for rehabilitation of the country. After the Korean War the poets once again began to write on the subjects of justice and hope for a united Korea.

I Am a Son of This Land, by Zu-dong Yang, is an excellent poem written under the Japanese control, from which one may gather a lasting impression of the patriotism of a people as viewed through the eyes of one Korean. The first few lines express the psychological make-up of the people. He pictures them as a fun-loving people, happy with their lives and their enjoyment of life. He also expresses their mental frame of mind in the following lines:

> The people of this land —
> Their minds whiter than their clothes,

The reference to white clothing, white being the traditional color of Korean dress, also imparts the feeling to the reader that the Korean people harbor no desire to conquer, revolt or impose their will on others. Although it is not stated, one might gather by inference that the Korean people want only the peace and tranquility they have been denied so long by other neighboring nations.

The poem goes on to point out that Korea is a land of humble and good people. They always have a dream and a smile. Indeed, their countenances must shine in the face of all adversities. Though a poor nation, still the people are not filled with expansionist desires, but rather, are guided by an everlasting quest for peace. Yang writes of Korea's struggles under the yoke of conquerors. Though depressed and downtrodden, they still prevail. How many nations could survive Japanese conquest and still emerge a vibrant nation at the end? This spirit of patriotism and the will to survive must surely exemplify a strong people. The writer expresses his personal patriotic feeling in stating that he is proud to be "a son of this land."

The selection *Open the Door* by Yun-sug Mo gives a view of patriotism after World War II through the eyes of a woman who is about to leave this earth. Her only desire is to become a useful part of her country. She wants the door opened so that she may give of herself to Korea.

Open Thy door and grasp the pale hands of me,
Before the lantern light expires.

Even this woman with death at hand does not think of herself but rather of her country. I think most Westerners lose all concept of patriotism at the time of approaching death and attempt to salvage their souls in last minute repentance. Perhaps this is an appropriate contrast in the desires of two cultures. I do not, however, believe that this would provide us with a sound reason for concluding that Koreans are more patriotic, but rather, they seem to be less concerned with the darkness of death itself. In the poem the narrator wishes that the enemy were dead, so she could return to her home again before she dies. This poem depicts the feelings of many people who have been separated from their land. One last look upon the free Korean soil is very important to all the people of Korea.

In *My Fatherland* by Ze-zun Son, the poet describes the beauty of the land. The foreigner or alien has invaded his land, and the roar of bullets may be heard, yet people must go on about their daily tasks during this disheartening period. Even though he gives his life for his country the beauty created by nature will live on. He draws a vivid picture of Korea's vast fields and mountains and lakes all abundant with the fruits of life. The most significant point voiced is that the land is not only beautiful, but it is also enduring. Poet Son states that aliens trampled on the land and iron bullets pierced into the sky. He is referring to the Communist invasion and the Republic of Korea's defense against the invaders. He says that Korea may have to continue to fight for freedom, but nothing can destroy the beauty, the existence of the land. Truly the fatherland shall not perish.

The author expresses his great love and admiration for his country. Although it is not exceptionally large and it possesses much the same as other nations, his heart is always there because it is his homeland. The beauty of nature and the white purity of the people work with this abundance of mind. No matter how war-ravaged, the people will remain as they were before. The people will not give up the love of their country. This is exemplified by the fact that the country may be war-torn, but the people continue to produce peace and work for their families. When all hostilities have ended nature will still maintain its beauty and the people will begin to rebuild their wonderful homeland. It too raises the possibility of future suffering, but it offers some hope, and prays for a rebuilding of Korea to its former grandeur.

In its first stanza,

> "Not so large nor so small
> Is the land where the sun rises, surrounded by the sea.
> This is my everlasting fatherland where I was born and
> grew up."

The author shows his nationalism (This is my everlasting fatherland) and some degree of ethnocentrism (the land where the sun rises).

The next stanza shows a considerable amount of local color:

> "The high sky and the blue land—mountains and fields
> I love.
> Every season bloom the flowers and they ripen.
> Abundant are the lakes with fishes.
> The thirsty history in the endless noisy waves
> Indicates the long-suffering soul of white clothes shed
> blood.
> However aliens tramped on the land,
> And iron bullets pierced into the sky,
> This wonderful nation would never fling off their white
> clothes.
> Mother and brothers produce rice and barley
> To maintain our families in peace.
> And azalea will bloom even after my death."

This shows the author's desire not to forget the war and its evils but at the same time he wants to look to the future and to the prospects it offers in peacetime.

In the final stanza he states that here may be more problems before there is a final solution, but he offers the hope that Korea will again become a world leader. Thus the poem ends with,

"We may have more troubles as in the past.
Yet the pretty colour of the azalea will shed blood
To build a pattern of history again
In the midst of folk-songs that lament."

It can be seen, then, that modern Korean poems generally dwell on the evils of war and the problems that it has brought to Korea. Most poems are pessimistic in attitude and almost all offer the possibility of future wars, but they also hold a faint ray of hope that Korea can be unified so that it may once again ascend to its rightful place among the leaders of the world in the arts, politics, and learning.

Patriotism manifests itself through adversity. Waves come to the shore endlessly, and so, one might deduce that suffering has been endless to the Korean people. They have shed blood in their quest for independence and freedom from foreign conquerors. Even though they are beneath the heel of a conqueror, still the Korean people will not capitulate entirely. The author uses the azalea flower, everpresent in Korea, as a parallel to the heart of the people.

Sang-og Han's poem, *The Day Cried for Joy,* gives a view of the Korean people and their reaction on the anniversary of their liberation from 36 years of Japanese domination. Liberation and a republican government are hard won and the Korean people express their joy at such an auspicious occasion. The background of the poem gives us a relevant view from a historical standpoint. It was written 13 years after liberation from the Japanese and 10 years following independence. The writer recalls how his father and he participated in the celebration. Korea at the writing is still partitioned and not yet unified.

In the poem the son recalls the jubilation of the Korean

people on the day of independence. The father and son celebrated it together. So clear is the young man's memory that he
writes:

> "This is the day you closed your eyes, embracing me
>   abruptly
> And said there will be no more enemy."

He also remembers taking a cup of wine with his father.
He marched in the parade on that clear day and was as much
a part of the celebration as he was a part of Korea. He also
recalls his father's joy as he holds his grandson up and fortells
that he will be president some day. Although his father has
been dead nine years, the son remembers how hopefully they
viewed reunification. The reader of this poem cannot help but
feel the growing frustration of a people liberated from the
conqueror who now must live with partitioning of their homeland by arbitrary decisions of outsiders. Still the Korean
patience prevails, a testimony to the Korean will to preserve.

This is a plea for unification with a touch of filial piety. A
son is talking with his father and is remembering how his
father had assured him in his youth that the independence and
the unification of Korea would take place. The son believed
his father's words, but now years later, unification has not
been realized. This affected the son emotionally, because he
believed that his father had betrayed him, and because of his
intense desire for a unified independence that had not yet been
brought about in Korea.

POEMS OF WAR AND THE 38TH PARALLEL

During World War II, the Koreans were promised their
freedom by the Cairo Declaration. At the end of the war,
Korea was divided roughly in two parts. Soviet forces occupied the northern part of Korea, and American forces took
over the southern part of the country. A United States-Soviet
Joint Commission was formed in 1946 to create a provisional

government for Korea. Soviet representatives objected to a democratic form of government. The question was referred to the United Nations and, in 1948, a commission was sent to Korea to supervise elections. It was refused admittance to the Soviet Zone, where a "People's Republic of Korea" was soon proclaimed. But the commission sponsored an election in the American Zone and in August the Republic of Korea was proclaimed.

The country remained divided, but the People's Republic of North Korea claimed jurisdiction over all of Korea. Communists raided South Korea from time to time. On June 25, 1950, North Korean armies poured into South Korea. The communists ignored the United Nations Security Council ceasefire order. Then, for the first time in its history, the Council invoked military action against an aggressor. The United States, Great Britain, Australia and other non-communist countries sent forces in to assist the South Koreans. A successful United Nations, offensive pushed across the 38th parallel and up through North Korea toward the Manchurian border. But early in November, 1950, the armies of communist China entered the war against the United Nations' forces. In the summer of 1951 a series of truce talks were held in the city of Gesong. But the North Korean and Chinese delegates continued to block the armistice discussions. The fighting continued in Korea with no decisive gains for either sides. Finally peace talks were resumed in October, 1951, at a new site, the village of Panmunjom. On July 19, 1953 both sides announced that they were ready to conclude discussions on the armistice. The signing ceremony was held on July 27, 1953. The principal agency to supervise the implementation of the Armistice terms over the 155 mile frontier was the Military Armistice Commission. Established under the Armistice Agreement, the Commission consisted of 10 members, five appointed by each side.

The Thirty-eighth Parallel by Sang-yon Czoe is the dividing line between free and communistic land in Korea. Many poems and stories have been written about this line that separates the free people from the oppressed one. It is hard for the Korean to understand the reason for this line. "Where is the thirty-eighth parallel? I could not realize it, though I crossed over." This statement tells of the confused feeling of the people of Korea. They do not understand why their country should be divided. This poem was written in May 1946 soon after the country was divided. The division seemed to come so quickly and no one was prepared for the horrors that would soon come. The poem reflects a strong desire for unity among all Koreans. Patriotism and nationalism are definitely important in the poetry after World War II.

The 38th parallel emphasizes, more than some other works, the uncertainty of why Korea is divided. It contains a humanist element, in that the author is uncertain as to just why the 38th parallel exists. He states that the geography of North and South Korea is similar and that the appearance of the North and South Korean people are similar, so why does this division exist? Underlying this, the author seems to question why ideological differences must exist.

Actually, nature was rebelling. How could the grass, the fields, the mountains, the rivers be divided? What had they done? Were they not innocent? They all looked alike and yet they were divided by aliens. How could one tell where nature was divided? The views voiced here state that the 38th parallel as a division of Korea is an artificial one. The poet states that the land on either side is one and the same. The poet can not understand the reasoning for such and arbitrary division. The poet either does not understand the reason for division or is unwilling to accept such a decision. It is a bitter pill that he must swallow.

"With restraint and patience in my restless bosom
I reached stealthily near the 38th parallel,
And shrunken, cast my eyes carefully around.

The sad heart turned my steps into secluded lanes.
My hairs stood up at the ordinary sound of grass-leaf.
And every step of mine was full of hatred.

Children of a village whispered about the uncertain
border.
They should have been more cautious in their answer
to me.
Whatever action the enemy may take, the children and
I could be confident.

Where is the 38th parallel? I couldn't realize it, though
crossed over.
Forests and fields, South and North, were the same
colour.
Who could have thrust the arrow in the innocent land?

This poem can easily be classified as modern because
"resistance" is the main idea of the poem. This can be seen by
the manner in which the man in the poem emits a desire to
have his country united into one glorious state. This man is
like this despised line to be forgotten forever.

One of the main subject matters of modern Korean poetry
is its strong feeling for patriotism. In this poem, the reader can
feel the love of country that the poet has. The patriotism becomes very evident in the poem when the poet expresses his
love for his beautiful but divided country. This poem
obviously shows the influences of the modern world. This can
be seen by the subject matter, political division of a country
because of political problems. It is evident in this poem and
many other poems of this period that South Koreans have a
strong drive to unite their country.

In the first line of the poem, "With restraint and patience
in my restless bosom," the poet demonstrates the feeling of
the Koreans towards partition. This line shows how the
Koreans dream of uniting their country but realize that unification will take a long time. The poet emits a smoldering
hatred for the 38th parallel in the line, "My hairs stood up at
the ordinary sound of grass-leaf." Why in the middle of his
own homeland should he have to be afraid of everyday noises?
Yet, even with this fear the poet still is drawing towards the
hated parallel. In reading this line one cannot but be reminded

of the Berlin Wall and how it stands as the 38th parallel, dividing its people. The poet writes how the children seem to have little concern of the 38th parallel; he is putting the hope of a united Korea in the hands of future generations. This idea relates back to the idea that South Koreans realize that unification will require a lot of patience before it is realized.

In the last stanza, the poet gives the impression that the 38th parallel is something that is unreal; yet, it does exists somehow. The 38th parallel seems to present a frustration to the people of South Korea and maybe even North Korea. One of the most significant line in the poem is the last one, "Who could have thrust the arrow in the innocent land?" Korea has been surrounded by aggressive powers, Russia, Japan, and China for centuries. The Koreans are an industrious and peaceful people who have never caused problems to their neighbors. Yet, Korea stands today as an innocent victim of international power politics, ripped into two parts. The poet seems to be dismayed at the problem his troubled land faces; considering the fact that Korea cannot be held responsible for their dilemma; they just want to solve their problem and forget the 38th parallel which became a hated word to the Koreans. This poem shows how they hope for its destruction because it divides their homeland. The author is questioning the division of his country by outsiders and asking why they had to fight their war in Korea. His nationalism for a united Korea is evidenced by his repeated questioning of the creation of an artificial border within the country.

The poem *Panmunjom* by Zong-mun Gim is a very sad, bewildered, and nostalgic poem. It describes the place where the communists and their representatives of the free world met in order to attempt to draw up an armistice. The total bewilderment of the author is shown as he says the following:

"A baby donkey could not escape and was left utterly perplexed." The author cannot understand how aliens can be left in a land not theirs. They should have no right to negotiate for a stolen land. This seems to be the sentiment of all free South Koreans. Communism and its aggression should be stopped at its beginning.

It reflects a fatalism apparently wrought by the ravages of war. The first stanza:

"As if I had visited a place in China
Somewhere very far,
I was sad and lonesome."

This seems to show that the author feels lonesome, as though not in his own country, but rather in some unknown, depressing setting.

The next stanza alters the depression with:

"The blue sky of autumn is already deepened,
As if the grey air had been roughly dyed.
Blue, yellow, red, white, and crimson—
Balloons of five colours
Are floating in the air."

This is not as much as saying he is joyous though, since he comments on the grey sky. It seems as though he is speaking of the false joys of celebrating a war's end when the fighting is still going on.

The stanza returns to the pessimistic attitude:

"It seemed now as if from somewhere
Far over the mountain or across the river
The sounds of bugles
And of striking drums
Had noisily been heard."

Here the author is frustrated by the attitude of the negotiators who act as though the war were over and there were little chance of it reoccurring.

The author's final stanza gives in completely with:

"Hair-braided witches
Fluttering five-coloured dancing costumes."

This gives an estimation of the people conducting the armistice
and shows a low opinion of both sides.

A poem filled with much emotion is *The Demilitarized
Zone* by Ho-gang Zang. This poem best voices a Korean's
indignation for a barrier of 155 miles from east to west and
four kilometers north to south which divides Korea at the 38th
parallel. He gives a vivid description of this once beautiful
land now scarred by war. The demilitarized land is a no-man's
land where the trees in which birds once dwelt are destroyed
by war. The poet wants to know who to appeal to in this ultra-
atomic age. Finally the poet asks the question of how long he
must live in such a situation where war once raged and divided
his land.

In the first part of the poem Zang points out the destruction that war has brought to this area of Korea. "In the
valleys of hill-pass where the mist is now cleared, There is no
single pine tree where birds may dwell, Nor a wild chrysanthemum where bees or butterflies may stop. Is it because
the heat of the earth is already cooled off, or the bullet-scars
are too deep in the naked surface of the earth?" "What nightmare are you going to plot again, You, Demilitarized Zone,
entangled with barbed wire...? Pondering all through the
long, long autumn night, I admit the map is our own. Only
the hostile aliens whose speech quite unknown to us." In the
last paragraph of the poem Zang points out the hope for unification—"How long must I keep standing here, face to face,
Vacantly with you, the fallen leaves as my friend, As if I were
a fading pine tree of drooping branches?"

The next poem is *Near the Armistice Line* by Yong-te
Gwon. This is a poem concerning the demarcation line at the
38th parallel. The author views the line where enemies face
each other and where a country, destined to be free, is divided
artificially, one part free in the south and the other part enslaved in the north under communist rule. Even though this
division exists, it is not a just and natural division. Fighters for
a free Korea are disgusted over this unexpected division,
instead of the real just division, a unified free Korea, both
north and south.

In the second paragraph Gwon asks the question why alien soldiers are in the Korean homeland. In the third paragraph the stupidity of the armistice line is shown. "Only there were inevitable compromises between lines and lines, Yet they were not obstacles set up in reality. In front of passionate eyeballs and decorated joy, Sun-flowers stretched along the luxurious rails of the sun, Even in this area where controversial warnings brooded." Every paragraph and line shows the Korean asking the question: Why is my homeland separated along an artificial line and why are alien soldiers desecrating my homeland?

Buried in This Earth by Zong-on Bag is a poem about the destruction in Korea telling of buildings, crops, lands, etc. destroyed. The poem implies much more than that, however. It implies that many intangible things have been destroyed, too. There are, however, glimpses of hope in the poem. The author implies that the Koreans feel that they still have their land, and thus their name, traditions, and ideas. It predicts that a rich future still awaits the free Korean people after they return to their land. He says that people's homes and belongings may be destroyed because of the once ravaging war. But he adds very sincerely that the land holds the key to a new Korea. The future of Korea is buried in the earth where homes can be rebuilt and food grown again. The land could not be destroyed by war. It has not perished. Korea will gain a smell of new life, buried in the earth.

Optimism is expressed in this poem. In the poem people are looking for something that could be left after the horrible "bullets showered pelting rains." This thing might be a hope or a dream. These Koreans were not so destroyed that they could dream or hope for a better life. If they did not have hope how could life flourish again and how could man live?

In the communist zone of Korea the people became strangers in their own land. In the poem *In a Strange Village* by Myong-mun Yang this idea is shown. A man was in a village and he had asked a pretty young girl for a drink of clear water. The girl gave him the water but stared at him as if he had been a foreigner. This is a very disheartening fact. Who would like to be considered a foreigner in his own land?

The poet expressed his sentiment in his *Moonlit Night*. A man was enjoying the beauty of the mountains and the fields. A crow flew over him; he remembered from childhood days this was an omen of trouble. Soon the crows were so numerous that they blackened the sky. He began to shoot and the dead crows covered the earth in disorder. He likened this to what happening in his country. The crows were replaced by the enemy and its flock, but the Korean soldiers were watching and guarding as he did to protect and save his country. The average South Korean was peacefully enjoying life when like a bolt out of the sky thousands of invaders from the north stormed across the 38th parallel. Man's structures of wood, concrete and steel may be destroyed by the havoc of war but nature's glories will survive.

The central message in this poem seems to be what maddening, terrifying war can do to even a peaceful, loving countryman when he is thrust into its perils and destruction. This war madness claws senses in firing and killing the crows, which themselves depict at and grips the guard of his homeland causing him to lose his evil, dark, and foreboding enemy, with their stealthful movements and searing cries. There are other examples of the terrors of war. For example, the war concept of "man taught and drilled to kill the dangerous and evil enemy" is shown in the guard's recollection of his grandmother's somber warning about crows and what they bring and can do.

Yang sets a somber, mysterious mood in the beginning of his poem. One senses and understands the loneliness that the guard feels, even in his own fatherland. The concepts of endless quiet and pale moonlight lend to the sinister, almost deadly mood. The coming of the crows typifies the sudden terror of an attack as they seemingly come in droves, blackening the sky in gloomy, deadly fashion. The guard recalls the words indoctrined into his mind and loses control of himself as he fires endlessly at the enemy.

But as suddenly as the thousands of crows appeared, just as suddenly they are gone, leaving their dead scattered around their killer, the guard. Again the serene loneliness returns, and one again becomes aware of the pale moonlight and quietness. But one also becomes aware that the guard is really a lost identity, "transparent staff," among his countless other fellow countrymen, who, like himself, are just one of a number who are firmly guarding what they hold dear to them, their homeland.

A man is enjoying the night and moonlight of a peaceful Korea. This is the peace after a war. Suddenly he sees a crow which is a bad omen as his grandmother told him in years past. This crow calls other crows and they attack him (Korea) by the tens and hundreds. The Korean shoots crows using all his bullets and in reality all the resources of the land. Peace comes again as many crows are dead and the rest are driven away. The Koreans are now aroused to reality and vow not to let this same thing happen again.

"A hundred I's and five hundred I's
Are guarding in the moonlit night.
Guarding my fellowmen and my land,
Thus firmly are they standing."

And so from just a few select poems a person may grasp the significance and desire of a stubborn people, using every means they can to live in peace. They desire neither power nor subservience from other men, just peace. Their patriotism gives one an insight into the character of the people. Korea is a product and direct result of her people.

Hyo-sang Gim in his *The Mind of War* has as his objective the loneliness and lament that is indicative of the minds in war. Spring, normally a gay time with life beginning to bloom again, is now sad with stealthful rain, a good indication of this as used by Gim. War is eating away at the gaiety of spring and the soldiers, only wet, sad "names" in the empty fight are alone really unknown.

Not even crows should be seen in the sky on such a day as is depicted in this poem, but a new day awaits, says Gim. And on this day the broken promises and sadness will be forgotten, and the birds will again come out and fill the sky, and the dew will glisten and cheer the heart. Only then will men's lives mean something, awakened from the nothingness of war, after lying dormant in the heavy, snow-like sadness that winter as well as war brings. Gim says that the mind of war is lonely and meaningless, really waiting only for the time when it can be a non-existent entity, replaced by the waiting "mind of season," with its hurrahs and brightness, and therefore, meaning in life.

Yong-sang Yi's *An Ode to White Flowers* seems to praise the beauty of the white flowers, the fresh green, the bright sun, and the floating clouds, and asks the question, "How can the flowers remain so white and beautiful when they are blooming on the bloodstained battlefield?" This question seems to come to a battalion commander as he pauses for a cigarette before having to return to the battle front. He stands near a war-battered temple, which seems to depict the decline of things man-made during war times, while nature goes on unaffected. As he stands there while all is quiet for at least a moment, he asks himself the question, "Why are the flowers so white?"

In his opening lines, poet Yi shows that a weather onslaught even as forceful as hail does not necessarily ruin the beauty of nature, as the onslaught of bullets and bombs ruin the temple almost beyond recognition. During these war times, Yi, through the eyes of the battalion commander, finds his peace and beauty in the color and apparent durability of nature. So it seems that the trials and ugliness of war times can be told in many interesting ways by poets who receive their inspirations at these unfortunate times in history. The moods of this poem are set in excellent fashion, and it would seem that this poet had something to say and did so successfully.

Ho-gang Zang's *If I Fall Down* tries to point out the hope of a dead Korean soldier that someday the unification of North and South Korea will be brought about by both of the governments. The style of this poem is decidedly sad and melancholy. "Do not let my fellow-soldiers prick wild flowers! Do not let them cover my bloody breast with our national flag! I would not expect the list of my properties to be inherited.

Nor do I wish any grave post to be erected near my grave."

The poem *Nineteen-Fifty* by Bong-gon Zon is a work which tries to identify how a war which lasted three years and one month was to interrupt the progression of nature and life in Korea. The people lost that time in which they could be tilling the soil and living in peace. Instead the free Korean people had to fend off an unwelcome and ruthless foe. This poem paints a beautiful picture of the land which existed before the war and which will exist after the conflict.

Many poems have been written about the division of the country. Korean poets express the desire to free their oppressed countrymen in the north. They cannot understand, and rightfully so, why a truce was drawn before complete victory was obtained. They are not willing, therefore, to live in coexistence with the "red bear in the north." *March on to the North* by Yong-te Zong signifies this loyalty to those countrymen in the north.

> "Do not forget those numberless eyeballs
> That were frozen gazing at the Southern sky
> Somewhere under the sky of the North.
> Unification only is the true peace;
> Mixing blood with the waves of River Amnog,
> We must raise up the cup of victory!"

The poem is related to the Korean War and the post-Korean War period. This poem is filled with the great emotion of the Korean people who strive for unification. It is in this poem that we see the indignation of the Korean people who were invaded by the communist hordes from the north in 1950. This poem voices just this indignation of a people who have been wronged by their neighbor. This poem is a plea by the poet to urge his free breathren to march to the north and take back their stolen land. With this, the poet wants the kidnaped breathren be freed from their evil red yoke of communism. He states that these Korean liberators should not stop till victory is reached, for those who died should have not died futilely.

The tragedy of the Korean War magnified not only by the loss of life and property during the conflict, but also by the settlement which was to follow at Panmunjom. The armistice did not achieve the objectives of repelling and punishing the communist aggressors from the north. The ultimate goal of national unification is still an unfulfilled goal. A divided Korea is a situation which is neither natural nor just. The Korean people are one people, ethnically, culturally, and politically. Every Korean understands these basic facts of an unjustly divided Korea. This poem notes the intense emotion and passion of a young Korean poet who in various manners questions the division of Korea, the communist aggression, and the need to revenge fallen comrades.,

As we know the Korean culture has been spread by peaceful means for over 4300 years and has never made an attempt to conquer her neighbors. The poet I have noted either deplores this aggression toward Korea or wants to gain revenge for his fallen comrades. But the desire for peace and the opportunity to develop themselves according to their ability has been and remains the fundamental desire of the Korean people. Whatever differences the Korean people have on this point of Korean action toward the communist aggressors, all Koreans of whatever class or creed are unified, and all speak with one voice saying, Korea must be unified.

Pearl Harbor by Dong-myong Gim relates what glorious, noble illusions of grandeur the Japanese had as they prepared for their attack on Pearl Harbor, an event which led the United States to declare war on Japan and which subsequently led to the defeat of the imperial powers. But Gim relates, when the real wager of war was carried out, he felt the majestic illusion of grandeur no more, there is left the bare confusion and havoc of the typhoon, depicting the attack.

Gim calls Hawaii "a lotus flower floating on the vast blue waves," thus setting at first a beloved and beautiful scene. Then Japan holds these illusions of wonderful glory through war, and the "waves of yearning" cause the Far East country to be blind to the emptiness and ugliness of the realities of war. The poet continually refers to this glory as only an illusion, dream, wish, or yearning, never a real glory, which he feels is never really attained. "Time does not cast smiles forever on... illusion," says Gim.

Reference to December 8, 1941 as a doomed day relates Gim's true feeling of the attack. Perhaps it is not only doom for those Americans killed on Pearl Harbor, but also to any glorious hopes of conquest for Japan; the grandeur becomes confused, the attack an "outrage." In his last lines Gim sees both the glory and the horror, but the horror is the real part, with its "firy pillars and black smoke." Then he remembers what majestic thoughts had been entertained the previous night in planning, but now the typhoon has broken loose, laying horrifying havoc in its path.

Although *Pearl Harbor* is written on the American disaster of December 8, 1941, I would like to show the similarity between this day and the day of the North Korean invasion of the Republic of Korea. Just as Pearl Harbor shook America out of an idyllic sleep, so did the onrush of North Korea wake South Korea to the realities of communism.

> "Even on every hair of your head
> The typhoon does dwell."

And so they saw an impending danger but paid little heed to the warning before the storm. Had South Korea heeded the danger signals, the first month of the war might not have gone as badly as Japan did at Pearl Harbor. Peace and tranquility cannot go on endlessly. Here we see a resolution or sort of fatalistic attitude. Whatever must happen will happen. The Korean invasion gave the world its first look at communist imperialism in Asia by outright aggression and not the customary "people's uprising."

> "Oh tempestuous eve of history!
> The typhoon at last broke out."

Peace has left Korea and the world. The communist horde or typhoon has unleashed its fury. Korea's Pearl

Harbor Day should be June 25, 1950.

The poem *A Sad Parallel* by Sog-zong Sin also takes a pessimistic attitude toward the problem of a divided Korea. The person speaking is an old man. He wants to see his native land again because he is old and he is afraid that he will die without seeing his country once more. His attitude is pessimistic because he feels that the problem of unification is not going to be solved. This train of thought is shown in the lines "I wish I could walk to my native place riding on a donkey in the late afternoon. Spring comes, I become old...." This poem was written in 1952 and at the time it did not seem a solution was present.

The poem *The Gate* by Gum-czan Hwang expresses the idea of hopelessness. A man is standing in the zone while trying in vain to get to the free zone. "Now in the imminent zone which is beyond my power, I knock at the gate impatiently." He wants to escape but fate has closed every way of escape. He also does not see any solution in the future, "and ten thousand years more in vain." He finally realizes that there is nothing more he can do but wail and cry.

Another poem, *The Gate Is a Stone Fence* by Zong-sam Gim, is about a people's lack of freedom. In the poem the author describes a stone fence which is blocking people's freedom. This fence is a personification of the thirty-eighth parallel. The fence can be broken when people escape but soon the people are caught and killed and the means of escape is cut off. The author takes the view that, no matter how many people try to find freedom, they will be caught. He says that the fence was built to keep the people enslaved and infers exactly it will continue to do for many years to come.

The poem the *Half-Bloods* by Zang-hyon An is another pessimistic poem. It describes the children who were born after World War II in an "alien area which is not alien." These people were born in North Korea yet their land was not ruled by Koreans. He describes how sad the children are with the fear of death hanging over their heads. The author indicates that these children will never be happy because they have no hope for the future.

"Rise; the students Toward the just, Die; the youth For the perennial light." These are lines from the poem entitled *Rise; the Students* by Sung-mog Yang. This is a very patriotic poem which tells of students standing and fighting for truth and justice. This poem contains an everlasting idea that it is the job of the youth of Korea to fight the enemy with knowledge of justice and right.

In all the poems that I have described very strong feelings were expressed. I believe that if these poets of the post-World War II period are representatives of the Korean people, then Korea will be unified once more. All these poets had deep feelings toward freedom and the rights of people. These writers have enhanced the understanding of the Korean from post-World War II up to the present. Many of the modern poems have patriotic ideas, or ideas of reunification. One common idea expressed in these post-World War II poems is their extreme nationalism. The Koreans are a proud people who love their land, want to see their people reunited. The poets of Korea have tried to show this love of their country through their poems.

SUBCONSCIOUSNESS

In *Toward the Light* by He-mun Yi, the poet is trying to describe to his readers not only his goal but the goal of all mankind. "The light" he mentions makes a reference to the goal we seek, which is truth, understanding and a reason for life.

The author starts the poem by describing the earth as a "street where falls the thick darkness," and he (or all mankind) is running toward the light. This is merely Yi's way of saying that the earth is confused and is still searching. He also implies here that not all people are trying to light this darkness, but that some people are bent on smothering the light for their own selfish motives. But he saps that he is eager to reach this goal and is therefore "Running toward the light."

The second stanza is a short three lines. In these lines he

again describes the earth, but this time as a "dusty street." He
tells of himself as "seeking the land of dreams." Next, and for
the first time Yi tells us that the search is not without its hardships and that one must endure great suffering to even think
of obtaining the goal.

In the third and final stanza, Yi tries to show us that this
dream he is trying to find, even though it be imperfect and
confusing in itself; he still holds to be a better existence than
that which he now lives. He tells us that this land of dreams is
"struck by a dark lash" and that is broken and shattered but
still he is "Running toward the light." Yi seems to imply that,
although this dream far surpasses the life we live now, it still is
not a perfect or complete answer to all men's needs. This
poem falls into the category of the suffering subconsciousness.
It is a poem about an unknown destination, which the author
is seeking. It is only logical that the poem be placed in this
grouping, for it is something which we all are trying to obtain
in one way or another.

DARKNESS

by Si-yong O

In the dark night
Alone and still,
When I light a match in the thick gloom,
It burns sputtering.

Burning the darkness by so small a flame
Through that small hole,
I wish to look beyond the gloom.

Even when seen, it cannot be grasped
And though possessed, it does not appear.
Sorrow-like darkness,
Darksome sorrow.

As one colours white thread jet black,

The darkness may not dye;
As one tears at his gloomy heart,
He cannot attack this gloom.
Sorrow-like darkness,
Darksome sorrow.

Life is most difficult at certain periods of our development. At times we feel that we are faced with something where there is no answer for us. We are tempted to give up hope. Yet we have to face these situations by ourselves. However, even in the darkest moments of despair and unhappiness there is this small ray of hope—how slim or tiny it does not count. It is there and we must grasp it. Here the poet speaks about the light from the match and how it only flickers. We must "hold on" too! We can work out our problems with maturity although many times it is unpleasant! This poem reminds me of the expressions—"things look black."

FIRE

by Ze-hyong Czoe

A fire broke out.
A fire broke out in the house of fate.

My wife and my kids,
Sins and tears,
All my numerous husks,
All fates that made me suffer,
—All these are burning!

When the dreams of bygone days
Flare up their red-tongues in the night sky,
I wish to live on with my best.

Nothing is regrettable.
The fire is burning all through the night.
I dared not positively burn my body

And waited till the day broke out.

Smell,
Smell,
Smell,
The smell of the burning of evils.
The smell of the burning of nihility.

This poem is an example of contemporary Korean poetry. The abstract symbolism employed in it is evidence of the Western influence on the poet.

Fire in this poem symbolizes death. The author is dying, and as he is dying, his life passes in front of him. He feels that as he dies his vices and his virtues go with him; but he tries only to recall his virtues. Nevertheless, he regrets nothing. As the end of his life rapidly approaches, he realizes that his life was a negative factor. His past actions were nothing in comparison with the universe. He doesn't feel that his life has been wasted, but rather that it is important to no one but himself. Although the author doesn't state it, we are left to draw the conclusion that he is now entering another state of being, far more important than his life on earth has been. This poem definitely reflects the Korean view of life, as seen through the eyes of Buddhism. The poet is contemplating the small value of life, and the material aspects of it. He expresses his belief in the unimportance of what occurs here on earth.

In the modern age, Korean poetry has reached the point at which nature is used only for imagery. In *The Poet and the Goat* by Hwa-mog Bag uses the goat as a symbol of the vision which had possessed him for years until experience and knowledge destroyed the desirability of the image for the poet. This poem also represents another new tendency in Korean literature acquired from the West, that is, concentration upon the more somber problems of man instead of the appreciation of nature.

I Am Not a Leper by Ha-un Han is a poem that shows the equality of man. The father and mother of a child might both be lepers; the child need not be a leper because leprosy is not inherited. The child could have been born out of wedlock but yet he was born of love. He is not registered as to legitimacy and he cannot understand this. In fact, in his own mind he has built up the idea that he is miserable. However, this is all in his mind and he is debating as to whether or not he is a leper. Can a man inherit inequality because of the sins of his parents?

In considering this poetry it appears that basically human nature is the same the world over. The problems of all peoples follow a similar pattern. A mother's love for her child differs not in the East nor the West. The symbolism may vary, the setting might fluctuate, the color of the skin might differentiate but the true feelings of the heart are the same.

A BLUISH CHINA PITCHER

by Za-un Gu

Serenely expanded down
Curved jade is moulded.

As if worms crawled
Among the grasses silently,
The colour of a mother's breast
Reached at last
This pitcher dyed and fair.
Even pears
Or the floating clouds in the sky
Cannot close down this quiet place.

The whitish feature
Mingled with naive delicacy,
The tight mouth,
The surged pose quietly rolled,
Resembles the round smiling moon
Over the rolling sea.
Thin and frail is the crane in the clouds
Softly designed

And mysteriously made up!
The existence!
Oh, neighbouring death,
A sad worry is to be grasped
With its prettiness!

Today
Whose love is so as this?
I am here
To pick up with my hands the moon beams through
    the night
Because of the petals fluttering.
Oh, pitcher!
You are a burlesque

Controlling my wrist;
When the wind blows breezes
As if softly wet in rain and dew,
My longingness,
Creates jade unconsciously.

I wonder if the author was inspired by Keat's beautiful
Ode on a Grecian Urn. It has the same haunting melody as
does the Keat's masterpiece. Like its Western counterpart it is
a description of an object, not a person. Simply but beautifully it describes not just what one sees on first glance, but
what one feels after careful and deep meditation. I enjoyed it
the most of any that I read. I think that its remarkable re-
semblance to *Ode on a Grecian Urn* (my favorite Western
poem) may account for my feelings.

In *The Face* by Nam-zo Gim, the poetess depicts a man
who sees himself dying from a broken heart. The authoress
begins the work by showing a person who has practically given
up his struggle for love. Here is a man faced with a fate he
may not be able to change. He is fighting for his very existence
as a man, but is weakening very fast.

In the second stanza he is almost on the brink of giving
in, as described in the line, "The wink of a white flag for the

defeated." Next comes the great moment of truth. Is he able to find the will to go on or is he going to give in and be buried with the rest of the self-pitying people of the world? I also believe the authoress is saying that all people are subjected to such decisions sometime in their walk of life, and everyone must solve these innermost conflicts in his own way or suffer the inevitable results.

In the next short stanza she describes love as the goal of all human who are lost within themselves. This point is amply stated by the line, "Love is the star for a human in a dark night." The line which follows, "it weeps by the window of a lonely soul," means that only through the heart can a lonely man find goal. The next to the last stanza tells of a person who has lost all. A man who is alive, but is dying in his heart and soul. At the end, he is finally broken as a man and accepts his fate. "The black seeds ripe with sorrow continuously fall and pile in the deep caves." This poem follows the modern trend in Korean poetry.

All of the poems which I have mentioned are clearly works of literature. First, the extrinsic factors are all good and clearly distinguishable. Both types of poems appeal to the individual's feelings, as well as the feelings of the nation. They are universal because the feelings of love of peace and of nature in the traditional types, and the feelings of resistance, patriotism, independence, sorrow, in the modern type, are all the feelings of the masses of the people and not just a few. Secondly, the intrinsic factors of the poems themselves are all well-balanced. The poems all have unity, because in each separate poem the author takes a central idea and by different wordings is able to transpose the thoughts from the paper into the minds of the readers. The harmony, rhythm, and balance of each of the poems is also of very fine arrangement. All of these factors combined together into each poem and to the superiority of the work which the authors have produced.

Dawn Poems in Korea

There is explicit evidence in ancient Chinese records (as was only to be expected) that the Korean people had their own style of music and song. Of the oldest recorded poems in the Korean language, known as *Hyangga,* twenty-five which survive, scarcely one can be called a love-song. *Hyangga* belong to the Sinla Dynasty (57 B.C.-935 A.D.) and were written in *Idu,* a system whereby Chinese characters were adapted to the very different genius of the Korean language. Under the Goryo Dynasty (935-1392) a popular type of verse now called 'Longer Verses' came into fashion. Such verses often of love, but of clear example of a dawn parting or meeting has come down to us. Towards the end of this dynasty, it appears, the standards form of a new kind of lyric was fixed, that of the *Sizo* or Extempore Song. Its syllabic pattern was:

(Line 1) 3 4 3 (or 4) 4
(Line 2) 3 4 3 (or 4) 4
(Line 3) 3 5 4   3

This pattern seems to be the one best suited to the genius of the Korean language and is capable of expressing the most refined poetic sentiments. *Sizo* have been appreciated by high and low alike and have flourished through many generations, markedly so after the invention by King Sezong in 1443 of a new Korean syllabary which has been used as the national script. *Sizo* take their whole range of human existence. Various kinds of love-poetry have been attempted.

Of the three dawn songs quoted in this section two are *Sizo* (Nos. 1 and 2). They call for no comment. But several others, not all dawn songs, or even love-songs, contain points of interest.

It is typical for sad partings between lovers to take place not at sunrise but at sunset:

> The horse neighs to be gone—
>   yet she does not let me go.
> The sun sets behind the hill
>   and the way is a thousand li.
> Dear love, rather try to stop the sun
>   than cling to me and weep.[1]

On the other hand, lovers are discovered at dawn in a mood of lonely longing.

> The dawn is frosty—the moon at dawn!
>   A lone wild goose cries in passage.
> I fondly hoped the bird would bring
>   Happy news of my dear love.
> But through the clouds, vast and unending.
>   That lone bird's cries echo in vain.[2]

or again:

> He promised to come, but he is late—
>   the peach-blossom will fall.
> The magpie crying in the dawn
>   is still in doubt—
> Yet I will paint my brows,
>   looking in the glass.[3]

(The lady prefers to think that her belated lover will come at last, and applies herself to her mirror encouraged by the morning cry of the magpie, a sign of good omen.)

The following *Sizo* illustrates the well-known inventiveness of the Korean race. Surely there is no other song that gives such practical advice on how to secure a long night.

> This long, long night of the eleventh month,
>   I will sever it at the waist!
> I will stuff one half
>   under the quilt of the spring wind:
> Then on the night of my lover's return,
>   I will unfold it for him[4]

Korean love-poems in fact are much more concerned with the night, above all midnight, than with the dawn.

The Yi Dynasty (1392-1910) saw the development of two new forms, *Gasa* "Song Words" and *Zabga* "Popular Songs." *Gasa* consisted of 8-syllable lines subdivided into groups of four syllables, through variations were permitted. They were more elevated in tone than *Zabga*. As if in harmony with the more popular sentiments expressed in *Zabga,* the rhythms are quite irregular, permitting all combinations of 2 3, 3 4, 4 3, 4 5, 5 4, and 5 5 syllables. The "Song of Parting" (our No. 3) from the area of Seoul is an example of *Zabga* and will be recognized by European readers at once as folk song. The following twelve lines are taken from a *Zabga* of 455 lines collected in the Pyongyang area: They show more marked traces of learned influence than in the ordinary sort of European folk song:

> When the cuckoo cries with choking voice
> And the moon hangs low—
> At the sobbing of that bird
> How I long for my love!
>
> When dusk returns
> And the moon shines and blossoms fall—
> By the light of that bright moon
> How I long for my love!
>
> Come, boy, come.
> Look at the eastern sky!

The dawn moon hangs low:
Where has my dear love gone?

All because of my love
I am as if mad and drunk:
I cannot forget for one moment—
I must go in search of my beloved.[5]

The boy in the third strophe is the house-boy, who is in attendance on his master. Once again we find the dawn in association with a lonely and unhappy love.

The impression, conveyed by our examples that there is some stability in the use of imagery, is borne out by Korean poetry in general. The loneliness of a girl at dawn, whether she has spent the night alone or with her lover is reflected in the flight of the wild goose overhead (No. 3 and the *Sizo* "The dawn is frosty ..." above). The croaking of the magpie at dawn is a good omen (see the *Sizo* "He promised to come ..."). The sobbing of the cuckoo (see the *Zabga* just quoted), like the chirping of the cricket in other poems, has echoed the sad mood of lonely lovers for generations. But the crowing of the cock as a sign that lovers must part is unusual, since his normal function is to awaken sad dreams in lonely lovers during the night. Nevertheless, as Song No. 2 shows, this motif is not entirely unknown. It also occurs in a developed form in the fourth strophe of the following modern folk song:

1. Plain-bean and red-bean
   Do not grow well:
   Camellia and castor bean
   Flourish in their stead!

2. Let us meet, let us meet,
   Both you and I,
   Beneath the shade
   Of the castor bean.

3. When I climb the fence

The dog may bark—
If only a tiger
Would kill that dog!

4. When I stay with my love
   The cock may crow—
   If only a weasel
   Would kill that cock!

5. She promised to come out
   When I knocked on the fence:
   But she does not come,
   Though I've broken the gate!

6. A northern room
   Nay yet prove sunny:
   Your coming to me
   Is far less likely.

7. Where the mountain is high
   The valley is deep;
   A small woman's heart
   Is like to be shallow.[6]

Note: Names and other Korean words have been spelled in the
the Unified System of Romanization. In names, personal
names come first, surnames follow.

All the poems quoted have melodies to which they were
sung to the accompaniment of instruments.[7]

Anonymous   No. 1   18th century(?)

dungzan bul
  gumuro galze
czang zon nomo
  dudon nimgwa

sebe dal

zogal zogui
dasi ana
nuun nimun

i momi
bbyoga gallidoendul
i zulzuri
isirya

The light of my candle/Was growing dim/When through
the window/He stole to my room.//The dawn moon/Was
setting fast/When on my couch/He embraced me again.//
Could I forget him—/So dear to me?/Though my bones
moulder/I'll have no regret.[8]

Anonymous   No. 2   post 1400 A.D.

guridun nim
mannan bamun
zo darga
bude uzimara

ne sore
obdosoni
nal selzul
nwi moruri

bam zungman
ne urum sori
gasum
dabdabhayora

In the night/When I meet my love—/Oh, the cock!/
Please do not crow!//The day would know/Without your
warning/When it should break,/And the dawn come.//Hear-
ing your voice/I should be sad:/For day will dawn/Before its
time.[9]

Anonymous   No. 3   20 century

CHORUS: Farewell, farewell!
           You and I are parting now.
GIRL: If you are going, when will you return?
           Tell me, please, when will you return?
MAN: Sail a ship, sail a ship!
           On the blue waves of the boundless sea.
GIRL: Please don't go, don't go away,
           Don't leave me alone!
           I'm coming with you, I'm coming with you,
           I'll follow my love, I'm coming, too!
MAN: Farewell, my love, and live at peace.
           Have a care for yourself and live at peace.
GIRL: Come back, please come back again.
           Please come back in peace.
           The cold wind is blowing through the dawn
              frost,
           A wild goose is crying.
           If you fly past Seoul Fort,
           Please give my greetings to my love.[10]

1 *New Comments on Old Sizo,* edited by Yong-czol Sin (1948), Anonymous (late Yi Dynasty?).
2 *Ibid.* Anonymous (18th century?).
3 *Ibid.* Anonymous (Yi Dynasty?).
4 By Zin-i Hwang, a poetess of the early 16th century. She was a daughter of a noble family. A young man of her village died of unrequited love for her and his coffin would not move past her house during the funeral procession until she covered it with her jacket. The gossip thus gave rise to prevent offers of marriage being made to her so that she became a dancing-girl, with the name Myong-wol (Bright Moon). When she died she asked her family not to bury her in a grave but to throw her body outside the East Gate as a warning for having loved too many. But her family buried her by the roadside and so eased her spirit. The Governor Beg-ho Yim, who was also a poet, held a memorial service for her at the grave-side, but was severely criticized by the scholars of the time and obliged to resign. Hwang's grave is still to be seen in Zangdan, near Gesong (better known to the west as Kaesong).
5 From *Folk Songs of Korea,* edited by Gyong-rin Song and Sa-hun Zang (1949).
6 Each strophe is followed by a refrain.
7 Those who wish to improve their acquaintance with modern Korean poetry are referred to my *Anthology of Modern Poems in Korea* (1948), in which the original texts are accompanied by my own translations, and also my publication, *A Pageant of Korean Poetry* (1963).
8 *A Sizo from an anthology of songs, Gogum Gagog* (Songs Old and New), edited by Yonwol-ong Songgye (1765).
9 Yong-czol Sin, *New Comments on Old Sizo* (1948).
10 Gyong-rin Song and Sa-hun Zang, *Folk Songs of Korea* (1949). This *Zabga* or popular song was collected from the area of Seoul. It is available also as a gramophone record Polydor No. 19039-B, as sung by Yong-san-hong Yi and Zin-bong Yi to an accompaniment on the fig-flute by Gye-son Gim.

Background of Korean Poetry

The Korean peninsula and the vast plain of Manchuria were once occupied by the nine tribes of the Korean people since the new stone age. The earliest records of the Korean tribes tell us that they had Shamanistic festivals for worshipping the God of Heaven, *Hanunim,* and the Deities on earth; Yong-go (the Welcoming of the Drum) in Buyo (-494 A.D.) in the kingdom of Goguryo (first century-668) in the tenth month, Muczon (Dancing to Heaven) among the Ye people, also in the tenth month, and among the Mahan people in the south, there were two in each year, one in the fifth month, when the sowing of the seeds was finished, and the other in the tenth month, after the harvest. There were also several sorts of festivals among the people of Zinhan and Byonhan. In these annual services of worship or festivals, the Korean people, young and old, recited songs, and danced to tunes day and night, eating and drinking in joyous gatherings.

This means that the Korean people had produced poetical literature from the very earliest days. The earliest poem among these records, the Song of Welcoming God, which is presumed to have been sung in the third month of 42 A.D., in the kingdom of Gaya (?-532 or 562); there is also the Words of the Sea Song, which was recited in the time of King Songdog (702-737) of the Sinla Dynasty (third century-935), a prayer of worship, whose purpose was just to discover the mysterious turtle hidden in the mountain, or to save a lady from the dragon in the sea.

Most of the poetical creations of the early stages were also connected with some sort of myth, or legend, colored by religious sentiment. Religion in these days was directly controlled by the kings or political leaders. So that obedience to royalty and piety were usually combined into one in many of the myths and legends which had been the background to the earlier poetry.

For these reasons, the two oldest extant schools of Korean stories, Samgug Sagi (Historical Records of the Three Kingdoms), written by Bu-sig Gim (1075-1151), and Samgug Yusa (Remaining Records of the Three Kingdoms), written by a Buddhist monk, Il-yon (1206-1289), are worth noticing, The former has for its sources early Korean records and Chinese history, and the latter deals with historical materials about the first king of Korea, Dan-gun, and other historical, mythical, or legendary heroes and heroines.

The latter is more important, especially for those who wish to trace the ancient Korean literature. Poems are inserted in the stories, an integral parts of them, and the stories may also be appreciated individually. But unfortunately, this book was written in Chinese, because, until the Korean alphabet was invented in 1443 by King Sezong in cooperation with linguists of the time, the Koreans had used Chinese as the medium for expressing themselves in writing.

But Chinese was not the language the Koreans spoke. It differed in grammatical and phonetic structure. So some Koreans used a variety of Chinese character, called *Idu* or Official Reading, which was commonly assumed to have been invented by the scholar Czong Sol of the Sinla Dynasty, but might have been gradually developed by people after the Chinese characters had been introduced. This system was a mixture of various uses of the Chinese characters. Some were used in their Chinese meanings, and given pronunciations analogous to the Chinese; some were used merely to represent the phonetic value of the Korean words, and some were to be translated into the Korean sounds which gave their meaning.

This system was introduced in the book, "the Remaining Records of the Three Kingdoms," already mentioned, for describing the native poems at the time, being inserted in the stories which were written in Chinese classical style. And one

more book, "the Life of Gyun-nyo," edited by Hyog-ryon
Zong, in 1075, adopted this system. And these poems were
called *Hyangga* (Native Songs) and are regarded as the first
Korean literature recorded in the vernacular sounds, though
there were many poems earlier than these which were written
by Koreans in Chinese classical style.

Besides the above-mentioned system, Koreans adopted
some parts of the Chinese characters to denote the particles of
the Korean words, but this was not used for describing the
Native Songs.

Hyangga, or the Native Song now found is only 25 in
number, and it can be noticed that some are written in 4 lines,
or 8, while others in 10 lines divided into 2 stanzas (8 and 2),
and that each line consisted of 2 or 3 phrases, whose syllables
vary in number (2, or 3, or 4, or 5, each). 17 poems among the
total number of 25 were written by Buddhist priests and the
themes were usually for religious motives or appreciation of
nature.

Next in the dynasty of Goryo (918-1392) "Longer Verses"
were composed in continuous series of many stanzas, usually
more than 10 lines, often with the repetition of same lines, or
refrains at the end of each stanza. This was the developed
form of the above-mentioned *Hyangga* and became a popular
form of folk song among the people. Many of them were
written on love sung in the Korean vernacular words, such as
The Song of Gwa-zong Zong and Spring Fills the Mansion.

There was also a peculiar type of poetry called "Gyong-gi
style poems," because every one of its two stanzas had the
fixed refrain of "Gyong-gi yoha" or "the scene, how is it?" at
the end. Each line consisted of the preceding 2 or 3 phrases,
each of which was usually in the combinations of syllables of
3, 3, 4, though slight varieties were allowed. Generally speaking the form resembles the Chinese poetical productions called
Tzu and *Ssu Liu,* applying many classical phrases to the lines.
The social background of this poetry was in the time of King
Gozong (1214-1260), when the military men assumed authority
in the Government and the literary men were excluded from
the high ranks, so they were obliged to organize social clubs

among themselves and eased their distressed feelings by composing these poems which usually appreciated natural sceneries or antic curio, and they recited their compositions in turn at the gatherings. This type of poem was solely confined to the scholars of classics, so that it was not exercised by the people in general. And romantic themes or love songs are not easily found in this form of verse.

Then comes the most typical form of Korean lyics, named *Sizo* or Melody of the Time (Korean sonnets in a sense), regular form of which was fixed at the later period of the Goryo Dynasty. It consists of 3 lines, the first and the second to be 4 phrases each (the number of syllables in these phrases being 3, 4, 3, or 4, and 4), and the third line is also the composition of 4 phrases, but the number of syllables is different (3, 5, 4, and 3). The arrangement of syllables in these 3 lines and their rhythmical effects have been traditionally approved as the most suitable to the Korean poetry like sonnets in English poetry or *Waka* in Japanese poetry. This form of poetry has been appreciated by both of the learned men and the people and flourished through the ages. It contained the themes in human life, and some of modern poets tried to apply this form to their poetical creations by repeating stanzas to mould the more complicated idea of modern life.

Then other types of poems called *Gasa* or Words of Songs, and *Zabga* or Miscellaneous Songs appeared. The former developed in the Yi Dynasty (1392-1910) and was popularized among the people. The basic rhythm of this poetry consisted of 8 syllables in a line, which was to be further divided into 2 phrases of usually 4 syllables each, though some varieties were admissible. The latter has been composed a little later, but the number of syllables in a phrase was quite irregular, and there were various combinations of 2 and 3, 3 and 4, 4 and 3, 4 and 5, 5 and 4, and 5 and 5. *Gasa* was a more formal poetry with noble idea, which could be compared to epic in western poetry. It usually described geographical beauty of scenery, or diary of traveling or general themes of human life, so that it consisted of tens of lines or hundreds.

For instance In-gyom Gim, who visited Japan as a clerk
accompanying the Korean envoy, wrote a long description of
his travels, the Song of Travelling to Japan; Sung-hag Hong, a
clerk who followed the Korean envoy to Peking wrote a long
epic on his travel to China, the Song of Yonheng; a certain
Hansan-gosa wrote the Song of Seoul, an epic of the capital;
In-ro Bag wrote on the self-satisfied Life in Poverty, and
Naval Maneuver; Czolzong (1536-1593) wrote the Melody of
Fair Beauty and others. Women at home also wrote of their
domestic lives in epics, especially those living in the south-east
of Korea.

While on the other hand the above-mentioned *Zabga* was
a free delivery with more vulgar element and became the folk
songs among the people. Many of them are still surviving at
present being sung to their fixed tunes often accompanied by
musical instruments.

One more traditional style of poetry is so-called *Czang-
gog* or Singing Melody, or *Czang-gug* or Singing Play, which
has been the Korean opera. This is a dramatic poetry, and the
most famous one is *Czunhyang-zon* or the story of Spring
Perfume. The hero of the story, Mong-yong (Dreaming Dragon), who was well-born, loved a beautiful young dancing-girl,
Czunhyang (Spring Perfume), at Namwon in Zonla province,
(there is still the historical garden Gwanghan-lu now), and
gave his pledge to set up a home for the two of them, on the
completion of his studies. Suddenly, however, his father was
promoted to a higher official position in the capital, Seoul,
and he, being still a dependent, had to go there with his
father, leaving Czunhyang behind. Now a newly appointed
magistrate, who was evil-minded and amorous, tried to make
love to her. But she was chaste, and did not yield to his
wishes. So she was whipped and tortured, and finally cast into
prison. After three years, Mong-yong became a Secret Royal
Commissioner and started on a tour through the country in
the disguise of a beggar, to see the real condition of the
people. He met secretly Czunhyang in prison, who was then
awaiting the carrying out of the death sentence on the following day by the cruel magistrate. He drove away the magistrate

from the banquet of the latter's birthday, and finally saved her life.

There are many other operas of this type composed on the different basis of moral, royalty, filiality, chastity, brotherhood, and others.

The movement for the new poetry in Korea began from 1907, when Nam-son Czoe (pen name, Yugdang, Six Houses) first published his poems in the magazine, Sonyon (Childhood). And next comes Gwang-su Yi (pen name, Czunwon, or Spring Garden), who tested free verses in the magazine Czongczun or Youth. These two pioneers embarked on the new literary movements, which were characterized by two points: The new conversational style free from the old traditional form written in the style of Chinese classic and the new ideas influenced by the Western civilization.

Thus, since 1918, many new magazines were published, such as Hagzi-gwang or the Light of Knowledge and Yoza-ge or the Woman World. Samgwang or Three Lights and Gebyog or the Beginning of the Universe, and three pure literary magazines, Teso Munye-sinbo or the Journals of the Western Literature, Czangzo or the Creation, and Pyeho or the Ruins.

In these years, an idealist, Yo-han Zu (pen name, Song-A or the Singing Child), and a pure lyrist, Og Gim (pen name, Anso or the Dawn on the Bank), wrote many lyrical poems, and Yong-no Byon (pen name, Suzu or the Land of Trees), Byog Namgung, and Il Yi (pen name, Dong-won or the East Garden) also published their favourite poems. Besides these there were other poets, Yong-un Han, a Buddhist poet who wrote meditative verses, Sog-u Hwang (pen name, Sang-a Tab or the Ivory Tower), who was known as a symbolist, and Zong-sig Gim (pen name, Sowol or the Pure Moon) who was a genius in writing subtle lyrical folk songs.

The movements of new poetry developed to a considerable extent, and its foundation became wider and stronger. And after these beginnings, several monthly periodicals were newly published. Sogwang or the Light of Dawn, Gongze or the Mutual Aid, Sinczonzi or the New Heaven and Earth, and Sin-czongnyon or the New Young Men were some of them.

Up to this time our Korean poets worked as a whole, but now they were gradually divided into groups, each insisting on its own philosophy and technique. In 1921 a poetry magazine Zangmiczon or the Rose Village was published, where Zonghwa Bag (pen name, Woltan or Moon and Shallow) and Yong-hui Bag (pen name, Hoewol or Thinking of the Moon) wrote decadent poetry. In the following year a literary magazine Begzo or the White Tide produced three poets, Sa-yong Hong (pen name, Nozag or the Dew Sparrow), Sang-hwa Yi (pen name, Sanghwa or Thinking of Fire), and Gi-zin Gim (pen name, Palbong or the Eight Peaks), and they were rather humanistic. In the same year a poetry magazine Gumsong or the Venus was published by a group of nationalistic lyrists, Zu-dong Yang (pen name, Mue or the Endless), Zang-hui Yi (pen name, Gowol or the Old Moon), and others.

Then the poetical literature of Korea began to develop under the atmosphere of criticism, and there were arguments among these poets. Hyong-won Gim (pen name, Sogsong or the Stone and Pine), the editor of a magazine Songzang or the Growth, wanted to be a democrat, Dong-hwan Gim (pen name, Pain or the Banana Man), Byong-gi Yi (pen name Garam or the Lake), Un-sang Yi (pen name, Nosan or the Heron Mountain), and Un Zo intended to be nationalistic poets. Pal-yang Bag and Do-sun Yu were rather humanistic. Poetess Il-yob Gim and Za-yong No (pen name, Czunsong or the Spring Castle) were romantic poets. Those magazines where their poems appeared were the Renaissance, Sin-Munye or New Literature, Yongde or the Stage of Inspiration, Donggwang or the Light of the East, Zosonzi-gwang or the Light of Korea, Munye-Undong or the Literary Movement, and Zoson Mundan or the Literary Circle of Korea.

In 1926 came the group of foreign literature poets. They were democratic nationalists and introduced Western literature and poetry in academic atmosphere through their magazine Literae Exoticae. Among them were Son-gun Yi (pen name, Susog or Water and Stone), Ha-yun Yi (pen name, Yonpo or the Lotus Garden), U-song Son (pen name, Nozebi or Donkey's Two Noses or Lococo), Myong-yob Gim (pen name,

Soghyang or the Perfume of Stone), and In-sob Zong (pen name, Nunsol or Snow-Pine). And later more poets joined this group and enlarged their literary movements through theatrical performances. They were Hon-gu Yi (pen name, Soczon or Night Spring), Hang-sog So, Czi-zin Yu, De-hun Ham (pen name, Ilbo or One Step), Gwang-sob Gim, Hui-sun Zo, Yong-czol Bag, and others.

From 1923 the socialists challenged against the above-mentioned poets of various groups, and produced many radical songs for class-warfare. There were very serious disputes among them from 1927 to 1932, some between nationalists and socialists, and others between artistic poets and humanists, or democratic liberalists and communistic leftists.

During those years three Korean newspapers, Dong-a Ilbo or the East-Asia Daily News, Zoson Ilbo or the Korea Daily News, and Zung-ang Ilbo or the Central Daily News contributed a lot to the development of these arguments. The first edited two monthly magazines, Sin Dong-a or the New East-Asia and Sin Gazong or the New Home, the second edited monthly Zogwang or the Morning Light and Sin Yosong or the New Women, and Sin Sonyon or the New Childhood, and the third issued a magazine Zung-ang or the Centre. There was one more Daily News called Meil Sinbo, sponsored by the Japanese Government General at that time. And then more magazines were published, such as Samczonli or the Three Thousand Miles, Dezo or the Big Tide, and Dezung Gongnon or the Opinion of the Public.

Meanwhile a pastoral poet Dong-myong Gim, a romantic poetess Yun-sug Mo (pen name, Yong-un or Clouds on the Hill-Pass), a Christian poetess Zong-sim Zang, a poet of local colour Sog Beg, a translator of Korean poems into Japanese So-un Gim, a poetess of *Sizo* O-nam Gim, a modest poetess Su-won Zu were to be remembered.

In 1930 the above-mentioned poet Yong-czol Bag published a poetry quarterly Simunhag or the Poetical Literature and a literary magazine Munye Wolgan or the Literature Monthly, where the poems by Yun-sig Gim (pen name, Yong-nang or the Eternal Man), Ha-yun Yi, and others were introduced and it also contributed pages to the translation of Western poetry.

In 1935 Hui-byong O (pen name, Ildo or an Island) published a quarterly for poetry named Siwon or the Poetry Garden, and introduced his own poems and those of other poets such as Sang-yong Gim (pen name, Wolpa or the Moon and Waves), the above-mentioned poet Gwang-sob Gim, the present author, a poetess Czon-myong No, Sog-zong Sin, Hui-sung Yi (pen name, Ilsog or a Stone), Czi-hwan Yu, and Dal-zin Gim.

Besides these poets Te-o Gim (pen name, Solgang or Snow-Hill), Gon-gang Yun, Zi-hun Zo, Zong-zu So, Mog-wol Bag, Zong-hwan Gim, and others contributed much to the poetical harvest with their valuable verses. During the 2nd World War poets could not produce genuine poetry, because of the contradictions which existed between the external situations of the nation which forced them to serve under the Japanese control and their own racial prejudices which made them refrain from the heart-felt contribution to the warfare. Consequently some artistic or imagery poems appeared but they soon went underground. Some war-poems were exercised, but they were not to be considered as the literary compositions of the Korean people in their true sense.

After the war, poets composed many new patriotic poems and poems about the sorrows caused by the unexpected division of the country. During the first year right after the war authors could express their ideas freely and worked as a whole, but from the second year when they realized the difficult situation of the country caused by the 38th parallel, they returned more or less to their shelters of mystic romanticism, symbolical pessimism, or sometimes abnormal radicalism. And when the literary circles were divided also into two, the nationalistic right wing and the communistic left wing, there occurred the most fatal arguments and maneuvers of the former against the latter.

Then since the Republic of Korea was inaugurated in the south these leftists ran away to the north, and after the Korean War broke out, poets sang of justice and humanity or described the deserted country with their sorrows and tears. Now many young poets sprang out of these ordeal and they sing their sentiments with the whole nation.

Korean Folk Tales and Modern Stories

LOVE STORIES

Traditional Features in Folk Tales

Folklore of Korea is the basis dealing with the many strange customs and practices of the Korean people and especially those concerning the Korean women. "Feminine Shyness" and the "Marriage Customs" deal with the former customs of the Korean love.

To many, the women of Korea may seem unfriendly. But they have a long heritage of being more or less left alone. For many years, the Korean women have remained very shy. This treatment is still found even today. The extreme separation that existed between the men and women of Korea lasted up until the beginning of the twentieth century. Today, tradition still keeps the women from doing many things and going to many places.

During the past centuries, the Korean marriage has been arranged. The marriages are arranged for many reasons, from political gains and alliances to a large dowry for the parents involved. In Korea, there were people who arranged marriages. It was not uncommon for the "makers" to add many qualities that did not actually exist. To guard against such a fictitious outcome or to induce good results, the people of Korea usually tried to find someone else to work with them in making a match for their son or daughter. If and when the families did get together and agree on a wedding, the local fortuneteller would be called upon and a suitable date for the wedding would be arranged. In old days the two people getting married did not actually meet until the wedding ceremony took place. The home town of the bride was the scene of the wedding. During the entire ceremony, the bride could not smile or speak. Everyone tried to coax her into smiling and enjoying herself.

Today, this custom of having one's mate picked has often virtually disappeared. Many have a free choice in who their life time partner will be. This, they have gotten from the western world. The relationship between husband and wife has also changed. This too can be attributed to the western world. The traditions of the Korean people are slowly but surely changing, not only in marriage but also in the many other traditions and customs of the country.

The early love stories depicted social conditions that prevented contact between men and women. This relates back to the days when Korean women were strictly segregated from the men, and even within a household extreme formality was the general rule. It was noted that many of the fables described the delicate sensibility of Korean domestic life. Gradually a change was sensed. The arrangement of marriage with little or no regard for the immediate wishes of the two people is still done in rural areas today, but the urban trend is toward greater freedom of choice in selection of mate.

The Koreans take a much more serious view of love than westerners. People are willing to die for love and a failure in love may often end in suicide. The Koreans place much more emphasis on chastity than do Western civilizations. The western way is more fun, but Koreans still prefer a virgin for marriage. The strictness of the Korean code of chastity is a little too strong for western taste, but so is the western code too weak.

In *The Legend of the Virgin Arang* the virgin's father was a magistrate and of all the suitors that came to woo his daughter he could find none suitable for her. There was a young official of low rank who fell in love with Arang. He set a date to meet her through the girl's nurse without her knowledge. The nurse tricked the girl into going out one night to see the moon, the river and the reeds from a tower where the nurse knew the young official was waiting. The nurse left her there and the young official showed himself and proclaimed his love for her. Arang was frightened and tried to flee but the young man stabbed her to death and threw her body into the bamboo bushes. The next day the magistrate learned his daughter was missing and no trace of her could be found, so he resigned. And then a new magistrate showed who her slayer was. He confessed and was executed and the ghost of Arang appeared no more.

The legend has several very important morals within it. The first is the power of the father to select his daughter's husband and her complete faith in her father's wishes. The second shows the importance of virginity for this young girl, for she gave her life to protect her virginity.

The traditional characteristics of shyness and chastity with respect to relationships between men and women are the most important elements in the Korean character. The story of *The Three Foolish Brides* who lost their husbands because of embarrassing moments on their respective wedding nights is indicative of the old Korean customs which have separated the sexes and placed women in an actual state of seclusion. In the present century, however, these restrictions have been relaxed so that today there is much more contact between the two sexes. Nevertheless, Korean women still maintain a certain bashfulness in their relations with men.

The hero, Mong-yong, a wellborn young man who falls in love secretly with a dancing girl, Chun-hyang. The girl is beautiful and talented. The courtship flourishes and they are to be married when his studies are completed. The romance is interrupted when his father is promoted to a higer official position in the capital. The hero, in deference to his father, must accompany him to the new residence.

The newly appointed magistrate is evil-minded and attempts to woo Czun-hyang. Being chaste and an ideal of Korean womanhood, she refuses his attentions. This enrages the magistrate. He orders the dancing girl whipped, tortured, and cast into prison. Here she leads a miserable, wretched life.

After three years our hero has completed his studies. He

becomes a Secret Royal Commissioner. Disguised as a beggar, on special order of the king, he tours the country to observe lesser officers of the law. He arrives at his former town one day before his lover is to be killed. Czun-hyang is to be tortured in front of guests as part of a birthday entertainment for the magistrate before her execution. Happily, she is saved by the hero. This is a tale of love and ultimate devotion. It shows local government practices of the era.

One of the marriage customs of Korea in olden times is of the parents making a match for wedding. Not only did they bring the boy and girl together, but also many times other factors besides the happiness of the children enter in the picture.

In the folk tale *The Wedding Day,* Meng-zinsa was a wealthy man but he wanted more. So he figured that he could find a wealthy boy for his daughter. Meng-zinsa was able to get an agreement with Gim-panso. Gim-panso was very influential and had a brilliant son named Mion. The deal was made for Gabbun, the daughter of Meng-zinsa, to marry Mion. In his haste to make the engagement Meng-zinsa had failed to meet Mion.

The gifts were exchanged. Gim-panso gave many expensive gifts and this of course pleased Meng-zinsa very much. A poor traveler came to the home of Meng-zinsa for food and shelter. The maid met him and the stranger was given dinner. During the course of conversation he mentioned that Mion was completely helpless and an invalid. This shocked Meng-zinsa. Gabbun flatly refused to go through with the wedding. By not going through with the plans much disgrace would fall upon the family name. It was decided that the maid Ibbun should take Gabbun's place in the wedding. Since the maid must follow the orders of Meng-zinsa, she had no choice but to marry Mion.

On the wedding day Gabbun was taken to a relative's house to stay in hiding. Ibbun was dressed in a jeweled dress. She was beautiful but she was unhappy. There was nothing she could do for she did not want to hurt the crippled Mion anymore. When the procession appeared and the groom was seen,

Meng-zinsa was shocked. Mion was truly a strong handsome youth. His uncle walking with him turned out to be the stranger who had visited them earlier. Meng-zinsa quickly sent for his daughter but she arrived too late. Mion and Ibbun were married.

That night in the bridal chamber Ibbun thought that Mion would send her away. But Mion explained that he and his uncle set up the whole plan to test the intentions of Meng-zinsa. He said that he was sure Ibbun would make a fine wife because she was willing to marry an invalid and help him. He said that this was the kind of woman wanted for a wife.

Importance is placed upon chastity for married women as shown in the story *The Mud-Snail Fairy*. A fairy from heaven appeared to a poor farmer and they were married. One day the farmer became ill so his beautiful wife went into the field to work. The magistrate ordered her brought to him but she did not want to do it. She offered everything she had to let her remain with her poor husband. She finally had to submit to his demands and came to him with only her panties as apparel for she had given him all else. The farmer killed himself and became a sad blue bird and sang in mournful tone in a tree by the magistrate's house; the fairy refused to eat and she became a bamboo comb but she preserved her chastity.

This sad story points out the extremes which are placed upon chastity. The fairy could have happily gone to the magistrate and lived well instead of wishing to stay with the poor farmer. She knew her destiny, yet she refused to give up her chastity for material gain.

The story of *The Young Man from Andong* takes place during the Goryo Dynasty. A young man was about to be married to a young woman from a neighboring village. The marriage was arranged by a marriage broker. She was supposed to be wealthy, beautiful, healthy, and of a good family. At the wedding the man discovered that his fiancee was not beautiful, and was extremely poor. Moreover she was totally blind. The young man was about to break off the wedding, when he was overcome with sympathy for the unfortunate girl, who, after all, was not to be blamed for misrepresentations of the unscrupulous marriage broker. They married and lived happily until the husband's death. His widow was reduced to a poorer existence, and she took her son to Seoul where she established a restaurant that became very successful and she became very rich.

Upon deciding to retire, the widow displayed grief that there was a hill on her home estate that blocked her view. How could she remove it and continue her charity toward her neighbors and the poor of the city? She hid money on the hill and told the neighbors that they had to dig for it. Yes, they dug, got some money, and removed the obstruction. This is a perfect illustration of the virtues of honesty, piety, and charity. It is an example of how great difficulties can be overcome by energy, determination and integrity.

There is another story which underscores the traditional virtue of chastity. This is *The Story of the Three Unmarried Ministers*. Each of these officials had married at a young age and each had had a wife extremely loyal. However, each minister had lost his wife, and thereafter each had remained unmarried as a kind of memorial to a dead bride. It is this kind of feeling that is representative of one of the most basic characteristics in Korean traditions. That characteristics is chastity, a loyalty based on love and respect.

This legend tells the story of why three ministers have remained unmarried widowers when asked by the king:

(1) The first minister's wife gave her life for her husband by plunging into the sea and vanishing due to superstition.

(2) The second one's wife fainted and died upon seeing her longed-for husband when released from prison.

(3) The third man had an unfortunate wedding night experience—he misunderstood that she had tickled his sleeve first, so he ran away. This bride died waiting for her husband's return.

The moral of these tales appears to be; don't jump to conclusions; too many misunderstandings are realized too late. Also, this legend stands as a symbol of the Korean woman's chastity plus revealing the Korean man's loyalty to a sacrificing woman.

In *The Nine-Head Giant* the husband is quite concerned

about his stolen wife and servant. He kills the giant and
rescues the victims. This "giant theme" seems to be popular
and typical of numerous stories in this group.

New Love in Modern Stories

The twentieth century marked a new era in Korean
literature. Interest in western culture, religion, modern sciences
and technology brought significant changes to the Korean way
of life. Of course, any change in the culture of a country
must effect its written novels and short stories, the area of
"Freedom of Love and Chastity" as evidence of a modern,
still traditional country—Korea.

At the beginning, one must realize that Koreans are emotional people; they love deeply, sincerely and passionately,
while they hate with a burning violence. This is quite evident
when we see that a Korean husband, wife or lover will become
quite violent because of the love or the hatred of another. It
should be noted that these violent actions are always directed
toward others, but often result in suicides also.

A good example of this is *The Thin Green Chrysanthemum*
by Su-gil An. In this story, the author has warned society
against the traditional custom of arranging child marriages.
He also brought out the foul practice of the eunuch system
where such women become the victims and suffer for their
entire lifetime. The story expresses the suffering subconsciousness between tradition and the new western influences. There
is a cry for freedom and resistance against tradition. Here,
Bunyi has expressed her resistance by committing suicide.

This story deals with the conflict of a young woman. Her
ordeal in life was severe to say the least. She was the unfortunate child of the past and yet attempting to grasp at the
future. Not only was she obligated to all the old sexual codes
but she was married to a eunuch.

Obedience to one's husband is of vital significance in
Korean life. It is because of this attachment of custom that a
eunuch would expect his wife to remain faithful. Another
facet of the arrangement was the betrothal of the female to the
eunuch at an early age through her parents. She therefore

would be brought up as part of the family and know no other life. Bunyi became very close with her mother-in-law. Bunyi also could feel akin to her mother-in-law because she was in the same situation as Bunyi.

Most of her young life had been spent within Ilgag gate in a mansion in Seoul. This gate was inside other gates as was the case in all eunuch's homes and no males outside were permitted in except the husbands. If the family had remained there, Bunyi would have stayed all her life a semi-prisoner. Finances were lacking, however, and she and the mother-in-law had been sent to farm in the country. It was at this farm she met her love Yi. He was a farmhand on the neighboring land and Bunyi would meet him often. They fell in love and they planned to eventually run away together.

In Korea such a happening is definitely frowned upon. The people believe in chastity at all cost. Bunyi knew this but remembered how it had been with Bag, her husband. He was vicious in bed and forced her to kick and beat his puny body. Bag was a masochist and very cruel. Her mother-in-law had had the same situation. Bunyi and Yi would run away together. She had known love and had exalted in it. Could she go back to that halfman who repulsed her so? She had news that Bag, her husband, and her grandfather-in-law were on their way from Seoul. What's more, Yi had changed jobs and would be leaving in the morning and asked her to come. If she did not, he would marry at his new place or so, he told her. All these thoughts ran through her mind as she tried to decide.

In Korea divorce is very rare and never entered Bunyi's mind. Divorce would cause dishonor on her husband. Especially because she was his only connection with any true life. He was indebted to her and she meant a great deal to him. To have a wife was a blessing for a eunuch. It was his equality before the rest of mankind kept him from being put apart by society. Was she truly free to have Freedom of Love? Her mother-in-law meant a great deal to Bunyi and she would have to leave her. She had been with her mother-in-law since she was eight years old and had become very fond of her. The thought of leaving the old lady whose husband was dead proved very upsetting to Bunyi. In Korea family ties are very strong and age means respect and consideration. Bunyi thought that to leave her mother-in-law to her husband and the senile old grandfather-in-law was very bad. The old lady was still a virgin and all she had in life was her daughter-in-law Bunyi. She would probably wither and die if Bunyi left.

This conflict raged in Bunyi's mind. To uphold the old code, to remain true to her husband and his family, to comfort her mother-in-law in her troubled years, to uphold everything she had been taught? Or should she leave this ancient arrangement and out into life with her lover? Should she try to live a normal life with children and sex? She needed advice and her mother-in-law offered it.

Her mother-in-law had been aware of Bunyi's illicit love and made Bunyi confirm it. She advised Bunyi to stay because she must. That Yi was only on a slight flirtation and would soon drop Bunyi rather than live with a married woman. The mother-in-law said that making love to a eunuch's wife was a novelty for Yi and that he would soon grow tired. Furthermore she said it was not Bunyi's nor her place to be happy but rather they had obligations. Bunyi did not know the world and the world was not for Bunyi's happiness. Bunyi was meant to be unhappy, said her mother-in-law; fate had made Bunyi a eunuch's wife and fate would keep her there.

Liberation was evolving in the country of Korea and women felt it. It was slow and showed only intermittently. Could woman grasp at Freedom of Love or must they respect traditional love of their ancestors? Her mother-in-law said liberation to farm was all she and Bunyi would ever get. Bunyi had found more in her meetings with Yi. Her desires were aroused and she wished to break the yoke of centuries. But the complexities of life and her ties with her family and past caused her to ponder and to cry.

Her final decision was one which is evident in many Korean stories. Bunyi cleaned up the house until it was spotless and then hung herself in the garden. She hung herself to avoid her problems and respect the past. She could not go living with her conflict. Perhaps she believed that after death she would find happiness.

The author has told a tale with both traditional and modern thoughts. The ending is traditional but her love affair with Yi is a show of modern resistance to the morality of the Korean part. Women are neither independent nor equal. In their subservient stage they can be very miserable. Should not selling of normal females to eunuch families be halted as truly unfair and unjust? Bunyi should have lived, and probably would have been very happy with Yi. The morality of Korea and the ancestor's rule of the present should be changed a great deal. The idea of selling children and pre-arranging marriages is very upsetting and we wonder how long this relic of the past will remain. The story is an example, however, it shows the ideas, customs, and traditions of the past as well as the modern trends in Korea. In fact the story exemplifies the conflict between the old and the new.

The traditional ideas are brought forth by the mother-in-law. Her father-in-law Dong-zi Gim is the actual representative of the old, however, he is mainly just discussed in the story. The mother-in-law is the character who discusses and portrays the traditional viewpoint. First of all, the rigid rules of chastity that were respected by all Korean women. In the story, it is mentioned that although the mother-in-law's husband had died many years ago, she had still to this date preserved her chastity.

Filial piety is also of course observed throughout the whole story. The mother-in-law and daughter-in-law, though they disliked the grandfather, listened to whatever he commanded. When it was ordered that they move to the country to till the soil, they listened. Speaking of grandfather, his mansion in Seoul represented the heart of the old. The women were kept in the innermost chamber of the mansion. They were not seen by anyone except the eunuchs whom they were forced to marry. Bunyi, the daughter-in-law, speaks of leaving the city and the mansion as "fleeing from a bird cage."

One of the most notable ideas of the traditional viewpoint is brought forth in this story. This is the fatalistic and pre-determinate viewpoint. We clearly can see this viewpoint being expressed by the mother-in-law. After she learns of Bunyi's hopes of leaving the farm, she explains in the following quote as to its uselessness:

"After your confinement behind the Ilgag gate it was rather to be expected that the freedom of this place should give you an idea like that. But what right have you or I to expect happiness in life? How could it come about that you were sold to this house unless you had been fated to a truly evil future? *One cannot escape from one's fate, I tell you.*"

The strength, brashness, and color of youth, independence and the modern way of life are exemplified in Yi, Bunyi's secret boyfriend. He was the "man strong in mind and body, a man who could carry her on his back across over high mountains...." He was the "...sturdy and vigorous Yi squatting there like a great rock as he tore out weeds by the roots...." The author might have meant the tearing out of weeds by the roots to mean the uprooting of the old and evil ideas of the past.

The "uprooting" would be in line with Yi's determined character and personality. He was, although respectful of his uncle, ready to throw off his shackles, leave the farm, and seek employment in Pazu. In between the old and the new, however, we find Bunyi. In her we find the conflict which develops in the story. Her main tie with the past is of course her mother-in-law who is really the only mother she has ever had. She loves her deeply and of course respects her and does not want to hurt her. Bunyi was sold to grandfather at the age of eight and was married to one of the eunuchs at the age of twelve. She hated this person she was made to marry and could not stand the miserable life she was leading.

When she and her mother-in-law moved to the country she was very happy. The old woman had said that this was really an "emancipation." The fact that she had left the past by leaving Seoul and her grandfather was sort of an emancipation. However, the emancipation was not as complete for her as Yi wanted it to be. Bunyi did not have the freedom of love. She was expected to remain chaste and loyal. Yi beckoned her away from this old idea of remaining chaste and her mother-in-law tried to keep the idea in her. She did not have the freedom to marry a man she loved the first time and now she wanted this freedom. Her ties with her mother-in-law, i.e. the past, caused her to be caught in the middle.

We find in the story that she has both a heart ache and a stomach ache. The heartache is caused by her yearning to flee with her lover. The stomachache, although attributed to indigestion, is caused by the uneasiness she feels within her. She is uneasy about leaving her dear mother-in-law. She has feelings for both Yi and for her mother-in-law. She has a great conflict. Yes, Bunyi respects the past in the form of her mother-in-law, but she is also afraid of the past. This fear is of her grandfather. He represents the worst of the past. Yi realizes this fear of the past when he tells her he wants to leave during daylight and sees that she is hesitant. He says, "He's just a eunuch and a beggar. Are you still so afraid of old Dong-zi? He's still got a stronger influence over you than anyone else, hasn't he?"

The subject of the freedom of love is of course one of the most widely discussed topics in modern literature. The author adopts it superbly to his story. He couples it with the transition and conflict of the past to the present. Also included in his discussion of the freedom of love is the popular use of suicide in the short story.

Bunyi, as was stated, has this so far unresolvable conflict between her ties with the past and her yearning to be completely free. While she was in the country with her mother-in-law, she was somewhat emancipated. However, she learns that her grandfather is coming to live with them. This she expresses will take away all of the little freedom she now had. What was she to do? The question of remaining with the past or fleeing to freedom of the modern day confronted her once again and now even more strongly. The conflict of course is settled by her committing suicide. It settles the immediate matter, but of course does not resolve the issue. She has not broken away from the past and she has not entered the modern era of freedom and independence. The author has presented the problem to us but has not let his main character answer it. This we are to do ourselves.

The story, *Memorial Service on the Mountain* by an authoress Zong-hui Czoe, is similar to *Green Chrysanthemum* in idea, in which a strong revolt is expressed against the arranged and unmatched marriage custom. More than custom, it was the sheer poverty and hunger which forced Zzogan's father to sell his daughter for a handful of rice. Perhaps the authoress expresses her distaste of traditional child marriages where the child is not consulted nor told of the circumstance of her marriage.

Even though Zzogan's parents were forced to sell their daughter, they did not know how to explain the situation to her. Zzogan's mother did not tell her the full implications of marriage and of the chores of the first meeting with her husband. That is why she got frightened on the first night. Zzogan became disillusioned about the abnormal qualifications of her husband, but she might not have suffered as much if her mother had indoctrinated her about marriage beforehand. In the orient, sexual matters are not explained nor talked about with the children. Hence, problems are created.

The traditional virtue of friendship and loyalty of Mr. Yun and Yi undermines the interest of Mr. Yi's daughter. An honest description of Zzogan's husband was not communicated by Mr. Yun to her father when the bargain was made. So here, the daughter became the victim of poverty and tradition. She expresses her suffering subconsciousness by burning the house she despised so much. She actually preferred to remain in jail than to go back to the husband.

The story opens shockingly with main character, Zzogan, in jail having a nightmare. From this point the authoress traces events which led to this fourteen-year old girl's marriage arrangement and her misdeed thereafter. It was learned that the marriage was arranged due to her family's lack of food. To get her for this thirty-year old, one-eyed creature, her starving family received rice and millet. Zzogan despised the ugly husband who adored her. Because she was so unhappy, the girl burned down their home and part of the village during the memorial service on the mountain. At the end of the story, then, the reader discovers why Zzogan was in jail in the first place. The ending, though abrupt, was satisfactory.

The readers may like the authoress suspenseful writing style, especially the stimulating introduction. The story moved rapidly and one could not put it down. The authoress revealed much about the Korean woman's role in this part of the world. She was able to create a deep understanding of the plight of Zzogan so that a reader had great sympathy for her. Reading this novel will awaken the readers to the fact that this type of marriage arrangement can bring tragedy to many people. It also created an awareness of the poor people's problems. This story, too, had value for gaining knowledge of rural Korean customs.

The Soil, a novel by Gwang-su Yi, taken from the book of the same title, is a story of change, change from past ages to a new society. The author is attempting to illustrate the trend from the ways of the characteristic ancestors to the modern western life. Through the thoughts and actions of the characters, we see ancient practices in direct relationship to the changing world. We notice the practice of separation of the sexes in Sung Ho's summer school. The shyness of the female, characteristic of traditional Korean women, is exemplified by Sun Yu's actions at the party given for Sung Ho. There is also a very traditional marriage view illustrated when Sung Ho mentions that he is not of sufficient social status to marry Zong-son.

Through Sung Ho's eyes we see the farmers living and working in the same manner as their father's, but opposed to this, we find the people very much concerned with the new way of life. The farms are no longer owned independently, they are controlled by companies, banks, or syndicates. We also see the new freedom of love between man and woman, when Sun Yu meets Sung Ho on the road. Social welfare is also placed in the reader's mind by Sung Ho's view of the poverty stricken people. Along the lines of social welfare, we see that the people are becoming increasingly aware of the need for education and their concern over unemployment.

The most striking example of transition is Sung Ho's movement from a rustic life in the village to the hustle and bustle of Seoul. The reader is faced with the increasing influence of the Western civilization on the Korean way of life, but there is a feeling that this change is not good. Throughout the story we see reflections by Sung Ho in which he says that the life of the people is far better without change. The village people are friendly and kind, whereas the people of Seoul are cold and are always in a hurry. It is with the feeling of regret that Sung Ho goes to Seoul to carry on his life as he must, but we see by his statement, "I'll come next summer" that he wants to return to the simple life.

This story illustrates life in Korea, a society of change. The people are torn between traditional viewpoints and viewpoints forced upon them by the western world. The conflicts result from hundreds of years of culture geared to a different way of life meeting the needs for survival in a small world of conflict. Korea had fallen behind the rest of the world industrially and it must now catch up in order to remain independent. Independence, a topic for many other literary works, is also emphasized in this story. We learn that Sung Ho's father worked for independence from Japan sacrificing his social welfare to do so. This illustrates the Korean desire for sovereignty.

Now speaking of *The Soil,* it depicts nature as a thing of beauty and the realization by human beings that changes in the world occurs very often for the worse. The leading character of the story is Sung Ho, a young man who is on his way back to his native village after an absence of two years in Seoul where he was a tutor for Zong-son.

There were three main themes which were quite obvious to the reader. They were either expressed or implied by Gwang-su Yi. The battle between a rapidly changing world and the ability of the young man's mind to contemplate the changes, the fond memories of the man in the real world where memories are a precious treasury, and the conflict of the urban society versus the rural society are the primary themes of the story.

The story of Sung Ho commences as he is on his way to his native village. On his way, he dreams of the memories of his past life and the people he loves. He visualizes the girl he once loved (and implied by the very thought of her that he still loves her) as the model of the pure society of the country, and the girl he met in Seoul as the model of the society of the city. The two girls from the basis of the comparison of the rural and urban social conflict. One is a village girl, reared in the ways of a farmer and close to the earth. Her values are implied to be the more practical, the more earthly values, not like the urban girl whose life is centered around the highly mechanized city Seoul. Sung Ho see the value of the closeness of the mind and spirit to the earth or soil. This realization is the basis for the title of the story. Nature had not changed for the farmer or the rural man, but Sung Ho who had left this society for the industrialized urban society had been influenced by his new environment. Now the mind of Sung Ho became critical of his environment. His longing for his native was intensified by the statements of Sung Ho concerning the sorrow he had for his family. His memory of his family was rather touching even though one realizes that here he is feeling sorry for himself not his family. The human conflict can be seen to be a secondary theme.

Upon his arrival back in Seoul, the dream world of his former village disappeared, and the hustle and bustle of the city appeared. The last paragraph of the story is one which describes the whole idea of the city and its impassive actions.

"When he got out at Seoul station, he felt as if he had awakened from a dream. The swarms of fussy taxis, buses like frenzied women, toy-like rickshaws, the crowds of cold people who seemed to spread an iciness around them."

The Story of the Villa Czangnang was written by Zin-o Yu.

The story centers around a man who after twenty-seven or twenty-eight years revisits the villa Czangnang for the first time since he was six. The description of the villa, the experiences he had on his first visit to the villa, and springtime at the villa were an indication of his strong fondness of the villa. At the conclusion of the story, the author put a question to the reader and to all of the human race. Could the villa Czangnang have some existence beyond the visible world, or was it just a dream wrapped up in clouds and smoke? He had indulged memories long enough, and now he slowly awoke to the harsh reality. It dealt with the conflict of the human being faced with problems though seemingly impossible to solve, dealing with advance of a new society replacing the old social structure.

Thus *The Soil* and *The Story of the Villa Czangnang* represent the contrast between human life in the past ages of decay and the new society. The latter is like the former. They both have as a basic foundation the nostalgic memories of a person who in the end suddenly awakens to the harsh world of reality.

The Open Door Policy in 1894 began the Movement of Modern Reformation in which literature filled voids for the people which the political situation caused. The Second World War completed the introduction of western thought into the Korean life. The novels and literature took on a new plot, with no fairy tale endings; they had psychological exactness and a new morality, one husband for one wife. They also expanded to include the thought of studying abroad and international friendship. The following modern Korean short story, *Thirty Years,* is one product of the effects history had on westernizing literature.

Thirty Years by an authoress Dog-zo Zang is the story of a man who falls in love with his best friend's betrothed but she resists his advances and puts him in his place. He runs away to America and makes a fortune and comes back to Korea. Driving his car one day, he knocks a man down in the road and finds that it is his old friend. He offers money to his friend and his wife but they refuse to accept. The authoress suggests that money isn't everything and that it can't bring happiness.

Even with all his money the man feels that he is alone in the world with only his material things. On the other hand, poor as his friend and his wife are, they have children and a love that won't die no matter what the circumstances. They are rich in the joys of simple living and loving. It is up to the reader to decide who is the richer of the two.

The authoress wrote this story after the Second World War. The main character is Mr. Zong-hun Gim, a Korean who had just spent thirty years in America. His grandmother, who raised him, allowed Gim to do as he pleased. Due to this his personality lacked breeding and self-control. As a lad his intimate friend was Gi-czan Bag. The latter supported Zong-hun Gim financially. They lived in the same village and both studied in Seoul. They both also felt love for Pil-lye but Bag was her betrothed. Gim told Bag of his affection when they argued about the importance of a feudal home. Gim didn't believe in a feudal home women were trained by beating when disobedient. Bag stood with the old ways even though a bit apprehensive on this subject. After the fight with his friend Gim went to present his love to Pil-lye. She only told him to leave the house. Fallen in love, crossed in love, and now at the darkness of disappointment he left Korea and came to America.

As the novel opens Mr. Gim has returned, after thirty years in America, a wealthy businessman and is placed ir ، high Korean government post. His contemporaries believe that his life is not what a modern Korean nationalist's should be. While driving one night he accidently struck a man and took him to the hospital. He was a poor man with three children whose wife lived in a refugee camp. The victim's identity revealed him as his old friend Bag. Mr. Gim was convinced that it was by the will of God that this had happened and therefore felt that it was his duty to aid these people. He thought only of monetary aid. He saw himself as the good rich little fairy who, after aiding his old friends, would help all other unfortunate Koreans. The next day he aproached Pil-lye and said, "I make this offer more as goodwill toward you than Bag." She was able to name the amount of money they would need but, as she had thirty years earlier, she now turned him down cold. She did not do this meanly or cynically, but with a determination which revealed her faith in her only treasures, her children and their future. As the short story is concluded an analogy is made as to how Mr. Gim feels. Around his old friend it was like a garden full of flowers and he was the whirlwind which had disturbed that peace. He was floating in the sky in the middle of emptiness surrounded by all pleasures and happiness of this world.

The main character of Mr. Gim was given most of its impetus by the authoress from the fact that he had spent thirty years in America as a successful businessman. In order to succeed in the business world one needs the profit motive which the character introduced into his philosophy in a capitalistic manner. It was such monetary thought of wealth which ensured his success in the United States but remained his great failure and weakness in his homeland Korea, where one is raised on idealistic principles. I believe also that the authoress wanted to show the importance of a child's younger years in developing a strong character based on such idealistic principles. Due to the fact that Gim did not acquire from his grandmother this self-control, he was easily indoctrinated with the Western philosophy of capitalism. This contrast was in the strong character of Pil-lye's refusal of his offer and his friend's strong adherence to the feudal social ways even though he questioned them.

The authoress by constructing the character of Mr. Gim as such was able to place westernism and its capitalistic motives in opposition to the values which the Korean had for centuries valued, such as his self-respect and great pride even when without a cent. We see this in the loyalty and faith Pil-lye placed in her husband and family. This loyalty expressed a nationalism because it did not honor or appreciate wealth that was made outside of Korea. A broader view could be expressed on the United States, a huge capitalistic country, with the smaller country refusing the aid of big brother not from fear but because it is not given without having to sacrifice loyalty and patriotism. Instead a feeling of servitude would prevail.

The authoress presented quite well her viewpoint and constructed the main character in such a way as to express not only her views but the feeling of the time. The authoress' writing was also influenced by political events. This was apparently written after the Second World War, when Korea, divided by the 38th parallel, had established its own government. Mr. Gim's fate had no fairy tale ending, plus the psychological exactness expressed in Pil-lye's character. There was also the attitude of a fairly free exchange between the international boundaries. Such writing could not have taken place when Japan occupied Korea. The 38th parallel was established after World War II and at this period in history the great battle of socialism versus democracy reached its literary highpoint. It is this conflict which makes me question the authoress' socialistic leanings since most of the subject is the rich versus the poverty and hunger stricken with the latter winning out.

An unrequited love, stymied by the conventions of a backward people who would still insist that they arrange a proper marriage for their daughter, and of a girl too stupid to realize the emotion she arouses in the best friend of her intended. The authoress at first seems favorable towards the leading character, Gim, and sympathizes with his inability to communicate his love to Pil-lye. He seems to be not so favorably towards Bag who seems to have everything. Yet later in the story when Gim has been blessed with good fortune and the reverse has been wrought on Bag, the authoress herself seems to change her attitude towards Bag and indicates that Gim for all his good fortune and success in America has not derived from life the basic rewards of a loving and devoted wife and obedient children. There are here of course basic tenets for discussion that would involve much more than this meager paper would allow.

In the story the reader realizes that in the Orient material welfare is merely one of several goals. Unlike the western world material accomplishment is not the sole desire in a person's life. Love and fidelity prove to be more valuable and enduring than temporary material gains.

The Dormitory Inspector and the Love Letters by Zin-gon

Hyon deals with a female superintendent of a girls' boarding school who is overly protective with her girls and thwarts all attempts of the girls in their search for love. The girls catch the superintendent late at night reading the letters she had withheld from the students. She is reading them in a man's voice to herself, accepting the compliments and the protestations of love contained in the letters and then answering the letters in her own voice.

To explain more in details a tight-laced spinster who is put in charge of a girl's dormitory in a well-known girl's school in Korea, Miss B is in charge of regulating the girl's social life as well as teaching at the school. Because of her own lack of affection, Miss B takes delight in false repression of normal activities of the girls at the school. The dormitory appears to be run in a military fashion. The girls are constantly under close scrutiny and their correspondences are watched and inspected by Miss B. If a girl happens to receive any form of a love letter, Miss B takes the student into her room for an interrogation. The student is asked if she knows the person who has sent the letter and she is also questioned about her relationship with that person. The students naturally believe Miss B would never be interested in a lover, but their ideas are suddenly changed by an incident which takes place later at night.

Strange sounds are heard by three girls in the dormitory, and they seem to be emerging from somewhere in the residence hall. Who can be making these sounds, and what do they mean? It is soon evident that the sounds are a conversation between two lovers, but who can they be? The girls decide that the situation warrants an investigation, so they silently move closer to the source of the sound. They are surprised to find that the conversation is taking place in Miss B's room. One of the girls opens the door just a bit, so that they can determine who is speaking in such a manner to their repressor. Lying on the bed, Miss B is surrounded by confiscated love letters. She imagines that the people who have written the letters are deeply in love with her. Miss B has created the hallucination in order to escape from a reality which is too much for a person in her position to cope with.

This story sheds light on a situation which is universal in origin. It is always the desire of those who are excluded from the affection to express their need in other than the normal manner. To deny love to others is to deny love to one's self.

The *Penance* by Mal-bong Gim is a cleverly written story. The husband is hiding in a small closet in his mistress' house and his wife is there on an unexpected visit. The man is torn between coming out of the closet and possibly losing the love of his wife or staying in the cramped closet where he could hardly breathe and where the pain of the cramped position was made worse by the insects biting.

The man waited a long time and did not come out of the closet till his wife left. He really loved his wife very much and didn't want to lose her. He heard her say how good she thought her husband was that he didn't visit with other women and this reinforced his love for her. The story is unique in that the wife punished her husband for his trans-gressions with other women and she didn't know that she was punishing him. I don't think the husband will run around with other women after this, so here is a case of a marriage being patched up without any bitterness, the wife will be much more loved by her husband and she will never know why. In studying this short story I shall consider the following charac-teristics; freedom of love, chastity, mistress affection, and democratic equality.

In days of previous centuries one would never show any affection or attachment to the opposite sex. However, in modern literature one does not find such a strong resistance of this subject. With the influence of the western world, freedom of love is also appearing. The story illustrates this point. Although Zong-hui's husband stated that he did not love Mi-za, still he had the privilege to do so. In ancient days one would not be quite so bold in expressing an attachment for one of the opposite sex.

Besides freedom of love there is a second characteristic of modern literature which the story illustrates. This second characteristic is chastity. In literature of previous centuries chastity was strongly stressed. However, in modern literature one does not find this as much. There seems to be a resistance in modern literature to the one-sided moral standard for women. *Penance* clearly illustrates this point. Mi-za in having an attachment to a man who is not her husband is breaking this ancient moral code of chastity for women. The story also points out how the man is not chaste either, for he has an attachment for a woman other than his own wife.

Besides these two characteristics there is a third one. This third characteristic is mistress affection. Marriages are often arranged by the family. Although the couple is intended to grow to love one another, this does not always happen. Therefore, mistresses are often found in Korea, although there is now a law which prohibits such actions. In the short story this characteristic is clearly seen, Zong-hui's husband does have a mistress which causes all the trouble and conflicts in this short story. His near exposure with Mi-za by his wife creates many complications in this story. The authoress' approach to the subject of having a mistress is quite "matter of fact." The authoress does not try to show that having a mistress is wrong or immoral. Rather she merely tells the story as if nothing was wrong with having a mistress. There seems to be no resistance or hesitancy in discussing this subject.

Besides the three previous characteristics there is a fourth. This fourth characteristic is democratic equality. This characteristic is an outstandingly modern one. Unlike ancient days when the wife was subservient to the husband, Zong-hui seems to be on more equal terms with her husband. She is so much of his equal that she expresses her displeasure when he refuses to go to the cinema with her. Furthermore, she decides that when he returns from his business appointment she will not be there. This does not appear to be the patriarchal type of home that existed in previous centuries. Rather, Zong-hui has and expects to have her way in many aspects of married life. She has gained with the coming of western ways to Korea, a democratic or equal basis with her husband.

Besides these four characteristics which are very evident in *Penance,* there are several general features which are common to modern Korean literature. Perhaps, the most significant of these features is the style in which Korean literature is written. The style of Korean works are not for technique's sake alone. Nor is the demonstration of certain technique the purpose of Korean writers. Korean writers are not concerned with a technique as much as a specific purpose. Korean writers are more concerned with ideas and concepts rather than a specific technique. This feature is seen in *Penance*. The authoress was more concerned with expressing the characteristics which I have discussed than a certain literary technique.

A second general feature that is common to most modern Korean literature is an attractive inner beauty. I feel that this relates back to the fact that Korean writers are more concerned with content than a technique or form. Their works relate this inner beauty in many ways. In closely studying this story one may observe that it too has this inner beauty.

Besides these two previous general features of modern Korean literature there is a third. This third general feature is a sense of humor. In reading *Penance* one can appreciate the humor of Zong-hui's husband being trapped in the closet. Although this situation is somewhat tragic, there is also some humor in it. It is not a type of humor that would cause the reader to laugh aloud. However, the humor is one that would produce a smile. Zong-hui's husband's tragic situation of queer discovery is a type of human comedy.

Therefore, in conclusion, one sees that modern Korean literature has certain common similarities. When illustrating further, in the story, we find the problems which can result from having a mistress. A man begins by prefabricating a story about another woman, and this snowballs into a situation which forces the man to finally realize the errors of his ways. What makes this story quite good is that it is a psychological study of a man in a difficult situation.

While this man is locked in his mistress' closet, we see opposing ideas of love and chastity passing through his mind. He thinks that having a mistress is perfectly all right, but still he will not step out of the closet. This leads one to believe that he really believes it is wrong. This belief is further strengthened when we view his hiding of these activities behind a front of ficticious business. The reason he believes his actions are wrong is because he loves his wife. His love is clearly shown in his actions at the end of the story, and supported by his actions throughout. The only feelings he has for his mistress are physical attraction and a sense of controlling something desired by others. As the man puts it, the mistress is but a toy of which he is tiring.

Chastity, which this story deals directly with, is becoming less highly regarded in Korea. This is seen in certain of the man's attitudes, but there is still a deep seated traditional view point that chastity is to be regarded. One notices this conviction when the man is trying to rationalize why he should get up and walk out of the closet. He cites certain men who have done the same thing he has, and because they were famous, this was supposed to make it all right. But, he still believes that it is wrong. This shows a victory for the traditional point of view.

An interesting situation arises in the story, the relation of man and God. We see the man in the closet trying to avoid notice, and his wife starts to open the door. At this time, the man needs someone to fall back on, and he immediately thinks of God; but he must fall back on a type of ancestor worship. A theme such as this is found often in modern Korean literature; it results from a system of changing moral and political values. Koreans today are having problems understanding the true meaning of life. This concept of a meaning for life seems to be not only present in Korean literature but also in world literature.

The Bridle by Sang-sob Yom is a story of an old man of sixty years of age who tries to escape from his authoritarian wife and his old age by playing the role of a young man. There are three main characters in this story; the old man, his wife, and the old man's concubine.

The old man is rather young looking for the age of sixty. He and his wife have been married for twenty years. During the early years of their marriage he found his wife easy to please, but in the last few years she had become quite intolerant and unreasonable. They are of above average means financially but this did not seem to please her. Her nightly nagging drove him from their bedroom to a separate bedroom only a year or two before. His leaving their bedroom provoked her even more. She refused to show the old man any affection. Her complaining and nagging dominated their whole relationship.

The old man started taking tonics, which is usually reserved for young men only. The lack of affection from his wife led him to look for affection from another woman. The concubine he took lived in one of his houses. She was a pretty thing in her twenties. She had a child by him. Only a year before the time of this story his wife caught the old man with his concubine. This scared the old man and he kept away from his concubine, but his wife's nagging drove him back to her.

The story begins with his wife looking for him because she knows he has gone back to the young woman. She finds them together in one of the five houses the old man owns and forces the young woman and her baby to move into the old man's room in their house. The old man is forced to move back with his wife. But the first chance they get, they run away from the old woman. A few months later the wife decides to check the houses owned by the old man to see if she can catch again. She finds nothing. But in the last house she checks the old man and the young woman are hiding where she does not suspect. The old man peeks out a crack and sees the great anxiety on the old woman's face. He finds her contemptible, but he knows that she does not hunt him for mere selfishness. He realizes that she can not help being so intolerant and unreasonable because of her mental and emotional state. He feels sorry for her, because he knows she still loves him.

It had been raining the whole day, which might have been a psychological reason (melancholy) for her going out to check the houses for him again. She had walked through the rain and mud to hunt him. Her clothing was wet and dirty. He felt a deep pity for his wife. He watched her walking through the mud again, after she left the house, through a window. This scene made him quite lonely and melancholy. He turned to help his concubine from their hiding place. She handed him their baby which he held as if it were his grandchild. A truly pathetic ending.

The Bridle like Penance is a story of man who has a concubine, but this is where the similarity ends. We saw in the Penance that it was wrong for a man to keep a mistress, but in The Bridle it appears to be right. The reason for this opposing point of view regarding the maintaining of a concubine comes from a similarity in point of view with respect to what a wife should be. In the Penance it is wrong for the man to have a mistress because his wife is sweet, kind, unselfish, and he loves her. But in The Bridle there is justification for the old man's action in the character of his wife. She is jealous, cruel, unthoughtful, and he does not love her, nor can he even bear being near her, as exemplified by his moving to the opposite bedroom. Zong-hui of Penance is the antithesis of the old woman of The Bridle.

In The Bridle the author illustrates a change in Korea, a change to a greater freedom of love and chastity. We see the traditional point, little freedom of love and absolute chastity, exemplified by the old woman. And we see the modern point of view taken by the old man and the concubine, Gesongzib.

In the Penance, the authoress is very humorous when she describes the adventure of Zong-hui's husband at Mi-za's home, where he was trapped in dingy closet. Throughout the story, the authoress brings out the commercial and wicked character of Mi-za. Perhaps the authoress is trying to uphold the traditional virtue of bashfulness and chastity of Zong-hui against the wicked and shallow character of Mi-za. It is Zong-hui's innocence and blind faith in her husband that impresses the reader the most. In the Orient, this particular virtue is considered most essential for a woman.

In the story of The Bridle, the author warns the wives of becoming too domineering over their husbands. She was almost dictating her husband's life. This resulted in first the separation of the beds and later on the husband transferred his love to the ministress, Gesongzib. It was an unconscious revenge against his wife. Here, the traditional virtue of innocence and obedience is broken, which results in the lower forms of love affairs and separations. Due to the mother's suspicious and wicked nature her son also became unfilial towards her.

In *Repentance* by Yong-zun Bag, a man leaves his first love, joins the priesthood and then marries another. His wife leaves him and he falls in love with the first love again. He is torn between serving God and running off with the first love and he chooses the latter. Can love be so strong that even God must take second place in importance? The author indicates that it is. The basic of Christianity surrounding *Repentance* seemed somehow alien to Korean literature. Yet probably it is a significant struggle of contemporary Korea. As they are probably more and more encouraged to accept the ways of Western civilization, embracement of an alien religion would be one of the more difficult aspects. One need only see a reversal of the situation to realize the difficulties inherent.

One need not look too far from twentieth century west to understand the difficulties arising from a mother and wife in the same home or the inability to communicate with either. Thus all through the story Byong-su is faced with decisions not unlike a counterpart in western society might face. Abandonment of old religious creed as well as old ideas and unacceptable ways of life and embracement of new ideas foreign to those principles on which they were raised is a problem with which they are becoming increasingly faced and which possess problems more complex than many would like to acknowledge but in a search for truth have to be resolved.

In *When the Moon Rises* by Song Gim, two people realize that they cannot be physical lovers even though they both love each other so much. The man is still married and custom and consciousness both must be preserved. So, they go their separate ways each longing for each other and suffering miserably for not being able to have each other. This is a tragedy because it bears out the fact that some marriages are made in error and never should have been in the first place. What a wonderful thing it would be if the two people in love could be together!

FRIENDSHIP AND GRATITUDE

When one compares the various social values and morals of the west and Korea, probably one of the most striking contrasts one encounters is in the area of friendship and gratitude. It is of utmost importance to an understanding of Korean societies. In the west, the traditional virtue in this respect is centered around the individual. Each man is expected to stand on his own two feet. One can observe this fundamental reality of westerner's life when one has dealings with other people. If one individual helps a second individual, the second individual must repay the favor. If he does not repay, the first individual will be insulted; or if the first individual desires no repayment for his help, then the second individual, not wanting to owe the first individual anything, will be insulted. Possibly it is inevitable that this outlook would exist in such a heterogeneous society as there is in the west. Nevertheless, westerners are only slowly moving toward a different position, a position, which is closer to the Korean outlook. A perfect manifestation of this entire process is the trend in the west today towards a more socialized society in which backward and underprivileged elements may be raised to a more favorable level of existence. In this connection, the Korean position with respect to friendship and gratitude is highly interesting.

Friendship and gratitude are noted in the moral of various stories. The one folk tale which depicted this theme the most was *The Great Flood*. The son of a tree was riding upon his father's back during a great flood like that of Noah's Ark in the west and he was able to save many ants, mosquitoes, and a boy of his own age. They found land and met a woman who had two daughters and together they farmed her land. The woman decided to give to the cleverest boy her natural daughter in marriage and to the other boy her foster daughter. The wicked boy spread millet on the sand and the son of the tree received aid from the ants he had saved to recover the millet. The woman decided to let fate decide for her and she put her daughters into separate rooms. The mosquitoes, however, told the son of the tree to go to the east room and there he found the natural daughter. The other boy then married the foster daughter and these two couples became the ancestors of the human race thereafter.

This is an attempt to explain the beginning of the human race. It seems that a great flood once covered the world and it also pointed up the fact that another human being was less loyal than animal or the insects. Gratitude for their saving was shown by the insects but not by the boy who was also saved. The moral is that who you receive gratitude from is not always the person you expect it from. The story, reflects the individual view of gratitude which has been held by Koreans, a view which stresses the virtue of giving. It is the kind of friendship and gratitude that is based on the pure desire to help without any thought of repayment. It is, to be sure, true friendship and gratitude. In this tale is shown the virtue of kindness to others no matter how insignificant they may seem.

The fables showing friendship and gratitude are very interesting. A tiger is often the main character. The story entitled *The Ungrateful Tiger* provides a good example for young and old of bewaring of wolves in sheep's clothing.

Human obligation is a theme in many Korean folk tales. *The Tiger Girl* and *The Police Marshal,* though different in subject matter, the theme is the same. The girl in *The Tiger Girl* is actually a tiger and because a man has fallen in love with her she must soon die. She gives the young man a chance to become a hero by saving the king's daughter, but he must kill the Tiger Girl. He carries out this obligation and true to her word the young man is given the princess's hand in marriage.

The Police Marshal is a story of a man who falls in love with a girl he sees washing clothes at a stream. He follows her to her house and finds that all the people within are dead. He buries them including the girl for she died when she entered the house. She comes back to him as a spirit and gives him information regarding law-breakers and he becomes the police marshal. As we see this story points out a significant moral obligation to duty and if the obligation is fulfilled the persons will reap great benefit from it.

General Pumpkin is a ridiculous story of a boy who had

an insatiable appetite for pumpkins. His gluttonous habit brought disfavor upon him from almost everyone. However, when his overeating, and the expelling of wind which followed, helped him to destroy a robber from the temple and later a tiger who had been responsible for a death, his memory was respected by his benefactors. Here is shown that people are remembered for the good things they contribute during their lifetime rather than for their unpleasantness.

The Curse on the Only Son is another example. A ninth generation only son from a line of only sons had been told by fortuneteller that his fate would be the same as previous ancestors. This meant that he would be eaten by a tiger when he became twelve years of age. The tale related how the lad was saved from this terrible fate by the daughters of the ministers Gim and Yi. The girls kept the boy safe in minister Gim's daughter's room throughout the night, not letting the tiger enter. Later the boy, with the help of the same girls, passed an examination for the Imperial Civil Service. He was offered and married both girls who gave him many children. This legend shows how a change of circumstances may often change fate.

The modern story of *The Wedding That Might Have Been* by In-gun Bang is the story of a love triangle between Dong-hun, Te-bong, and Nan-yong, with Dong-hun as the main character of the story.

Dong-hun and Nan-yong are two lovers who have planned to marry in the near future; but recently Dong-hun has noticed a change in their relationship on Nan-yong's part in which her visits have been less frequent, and she has been less punctual. Believing there is another man, Dong-hun has decided to question her about it the night if she comes.

Nan-yong arrives late having just left a nearby restaurant where she and another man had been eating. Dong-hun begins questioning her and an argument ensues, but is interrupted by the arrival of Te-bong, a childhood friend of Dong-hun, who is presently drunk. The two have grown up together with Te-bong, being constantly jealous until now, because Te-bong, who has accumulated wealth, believes he has won, since Dong-hun is a penniless author.

Te-bong having been properly welcomed, the three ordered from the nearby restaurant. The waiter gives a strange glance at Nan-yong and Te-bong, which is observed by Dong-hun. After their departure, Dong-hun's suspicions are confirmed by questioning the waiter. Immediately hatred and thoughts of revenge sweep over him until he realizes that he has lost his closest friend. This sadness sobers him, and he contemplates what action to take. Having decided to behave coldly toward the two and to devote his life to his work, Dong-hun and Nan-yong slowly drift apart to the point of not seeing each other, although Dong-hun's love remains constant.

Upon learning of their future wedding, Dong-hun visits a *giseng* house where he meets So-hong, who is in training to be a dancing girl, a profession she hates but is forced to endure. He frequents the house and becomes familiar with the proprieties of her profession. Upon Nan-yong's marriage Dong-hun asks to braid So-hong's hair, thereby proposing a temporary marriage.

They are accompanied on their honeymoon by So-hong's stepmother who fears their growing affection for one another. At the end of their stay, both endeavor to find a means of making their relationship a permanent one since custom does not allow this. Not having enough money, Dong-hun leaves to travel for many years. During those years So-hong's love for him increases; and, although now a first-class dancing girl, she remains faithful to him never allowing the evils of her past to change her principles (i.e. chastity).

A few days after his return, Dong-hun encounters Nan-yong, and by their conversation he learns of her unhappiness caused by Te-bong's unfaithfulness. Listening, he wishes to help her and when he hears of Te-bong's affair with So-hong, he takes her to the *giseng* house where he slaps Te-bong and sends him home. Dong-hun and So-hong are then reunited.

Such a story presents numerous aspects of Korean life. The author informs one about the meaning of chastity, the Korean attitude toward suicide, and Korean customs. Chastity is a very important part of a Korean woman's life as illustrated by So-hong. According to the custom of a temporary marriage, the girl enters into the relationship knowing that it is temporary and that there will be others later. After their marriage So-hong of necessity continues in her profession, but remains chaste to Dong-hun whom she loves. Suicide in Korea is an honorable act in which a man or woman sacrifices themselves for the benefit of something or someone. In-gun Bang brought this point into the story when relating So-hong's desire to commit suicide rather than love another man.

The most informative section was about the process and duties of a *giseng* girl. After losing her parents, So-hong was sold several times until finally the mistress of a *giseng* house bought her. Once in this house So-hong had no alternative but to go through the training period to become a dancing girl. The most striking feature about her life was the passage on the braiding of hair. If a man is pleased with a girl, he asks to braid her hair which meant he wishes to arrange a temporary marriage between them.

A forementioned facets of Korean life are minor points as compared to the main objective of the author which is to relate the importance of friendship as felt by Koreans. All nations view friendship in their own ways, but in the eastern cultures the word has a greater significance among the people which the author attempts to demonstrate. Throughout their childhood Dong-hun and Te-bong had been close friends despite Te-bong's jealousy of Dong-hun. Dong-hun realized the competition between them and Te-bong's change of character, but still he valued their relationship until Te-bong betrayed it. His betrayal caused feelings of hatred, yet it also produced a great sadness in Dong-hun, because he had treasured their friendship so greatly. This part of the story explains clearly the Korean idea of friendship which other peoples should consider.

The author was not only concerned with friendship and its betrayal but also with the differences between the traditional and modern views on the subject. Friendship in modern as in traditional times is considered an important treasure by the Korean people; however, centuries ago if a man were betrayed, he would continue his life without malice. Today the betrayed man seeks revenge against the woman and indirectly against the man by whatever means are possible, such as Dong-hun's temporary marriage. Having been hurt and not wanting a lasting relationship, Dong-hun found the idea of a temporary marriage to be his answer for resistance against Nan-yong.

In *The Pack Horse Driver* by Yong-mug Gye, friendship and honesty are the basic themes. Ung-pal, a naive farm workers, is deceived by his master, Czo-si. The simple, but honest Ung-pal is arrested when he attempts to take the money that is rightfully his. Thus sincerity is often unable to withstand the pressures of deception. It was Ung-pal's instinctive trust of his fellow man that led to his present situation. He had been falsely accused of stealing from his master, Czo-si; and now he was being arrested for trying to claim the money which he had earned.

After his wife had stolen his money and left, Ung-pal came under the influence of an even less reputable character, Czo-si, who tricked Ung-pal into believing that he would take care of Ung-pal's finances. Actually Czo-si kept Ung-pal's money and planned to marry Ung-pal to his servant, Sam-wol. In this manner Czo-si could keep possession of both his servant and Ung-pal's money.

When Ung-pal became apprehensive about marrying Sam-wol, Czo-si tried to force him into marriage, but Ung-pal was adamant. He wanted to marry an unattractive girl who would always be faithful to him. Ung-pal had chosen In-ne, but for obvious reasons, this match was unacceptable to his scheming master. Ung-pal resorted to taking his wages rather than asking for them. The master now had legal grounds to take action against Ung-pal.

Trust is a necessary element for living with others, but it is also a quality that should be expressed to only those who prove themselves worthy of it. The betrayal of friendship and trust is brought out in the story. The main character, Ung-pal, is a very gullible type of person. He trusted his wife who left him for another man, and this caused him to lose his property and become a wanderer. Even so, his faith in his fellow man was not changed just because one had caused him misfortune.

He trusted all men and thought that by doing so no one could speak ill of him. He believed that other men were honest because he was so honest himself. There is a lesson in this story in which it is good to have faith in others, but we cannot measure other human beings by our own set of rules and while it is good to trust others, one must be aware of having "blind faith."

Ung-pal was below average intelligence and so the man he worked for, Czo-si, realizing this, took advantage of Ung-pal but kept track of for him in a ledger book. He was supposedly saving them up for Ung-pal who might buy a wife. All Ung-pal was actually working for was the rice Czo-si gave him, but he worked so hard in the six years for his master, and he never disobeyed or doubted him once. Of course Czo-si never planned to give Ung-pal the money he owed him, but Ung-pal begins to pressure him for it because he wants to marry again and feels the amount saved up is enough to buy a wife. Czo-si doesn't want to relinquish the money so he conjures a plan to have Ung-pal marry Sam-wol, a lovely young girl who is a member of Czo-si's household staff. This way the money, he reasons, will be easily swindled from Ung-pal because he can tell him he used most of it for marriage expenses or the household Czo-si hides his cunning and real motive under an outward show of friendship and concern. Deceiving or being deceived is often the case in human being's relations with one another the world over.

Perhaps Czo-si's plan would have succeeded with no-one the miser, had Ung-pal not rejected his marriage to Sam-wol. It seems he trusted all men but not women who were beautiful and witty. He associated them with his wife, whom he considered the source of his every misfortune. He wanted to marry In-ne, a very plain girl, because he decided she would make a good wife and not be deceitful. Czo-si tries to talk him out of this with many arguments such as, In-ne is homely and if he marries her the town-people will blame Czo-si for picking him a bad wife. Czo-si goes so far as to set a wedding date for Ung-pal and Sam-wol. All of Ung-pal's objections are ignored and the date draws nearer. In desperation Ung-pal realizes that the only way he can get his money so that he may marry In-ne is to steal it from Czo-si while the latter sleeps. He does this but in his haste he takes too much money and in the end is arrested even though he wants to return it and keep only his just amount.

This is a tragic story not only because of its unhappy ending, but because of the injustice that is a result of man's inhumanity to man. It contains a tragic humor and ends on a sad note because Ung-pal accepts his fate without seeming to question it to help himself. If he had not had quite so much "blind faith" in other men, he would not have given Czo-si the temptation and easy means to betray him and Ung-pal wouldn't have let himself in for such extreme injustice. In other words, he should not have placed his property, love, and fate in another's keeping.

LOYALTY AND PATRIOTISM

Korea, long a victim of Japanese imperialism, is presently in conflict with two strong opposing forces. The Soviet regime and the U.N. forces in Korea have burst into open conflict. This struggle of Soviet and American rivalries is endangering world peace today and perhaps the days ahead.

On August 15, 1948, the people of South Korea left the hands of the American government to form the Republic of Korea. But future developments in Korea will depend largely upon the extent to which the two regimes move toward recon- ciliation or into deeper antagonism. Making Korea a turning point in international relations would be conceivable if an im- provement in the U.S.-Soviet relations takes place and unifies Korea. The international situation involved made a paradox of the liberation of Korea. Liberation extended the promise of the freedom for which the country had sought so long, and thus created a divided country which has become its despair.

After the liberation, August 15, 1945, many new hopes and ideas flourished for the new born land. Education and literature were rehabilitated with a tremendous advance. Elementary schools, junior high schools, senior high schools, and universities and colleges began to grow. With each new building, a new life began for those who had talent in science, education, literature, politics and many other fields of endeavor. Literature became the medium of social education. Common interest groups formed such as the Korean Poets' Association and the Korean Writers' Association and the Korean Center of the International P.E.N. Club, to provide intellectual stimulation and guidance for those with similar talents.

Korea should and must be united into one country. Many authors tried to show the ridiculousness and stupidity of trying to divide north and south simply by a political agreement. The point is brought out in many different ways. How can a country which is not divided naturally by a river or a mountain range be divided by the mark of a pen? The deep feelings of the people toward the armistice and the demarcation line are brought out in many forms.

The views such as a love for country and land, hatred of communist aggression, the want for revenge of fallen comrades, a hope for a reunified Korea and continued peace and cooperation seem to be the view of South Koreans and her allies in the free world. This love of freedom and dignity of man is one of many admirable Korean traits. These traits stem from Korea's rich heritage and ancestry.

The free world along with free Korea met communist aggression in the past from 1950 to 1953. This same action must take place to meet communist aggression such as this wherever it may occur. Korean literature is rich with the sentiments of self-determination and justice. I am confident that this just and rich heritage of free Korea will continue. Someday Korea may defeat the communists and regain their lost land, but in the meantime, they must not discontinue their vigil and ambitions.

The first folk story is that of Dan-gun, first king of Korea. The story relates how a bear and a tiger wished to become humans. A heavenly prince, who came to govern Korea, saw how the bear and tiger prayed for their wish. The prince was moved and gave to them twenty bulbs of garlic and a bundle of mugwort and told them to go back into the cave for one hundred days. The bear became a beautiful woman after twenty-one days. The tiger, however, could not tolerate the long wait and ran away. The bear, changed into a woman, eventually became the queen and gave birth to the first human King Dan-gun.

This story shows that chastity or purity of thought and behavior will bring a good life although one may have to suffer for a time. The myth recounts the story of how Dan-gun, the legendary father of Korea, came to be. The bear patiently endured weariness and hunger in order that she become a human being. It appears that this myth expresses the values of faith, trust, virginity, and courage to endure suffering in order to achieve those things which are most worthwhile.

Another myth tells that several thousand years ago there lived a king and queen in a small sea-side kingdom. This royal couple were good to their people but they carried a great sorrow. It seems that they had never given birth to an heir, though they were advancing in years. So they began to offer many sacrifices that they might produce a son. Soon the queen became pregnant, but she did not bear a child. Instead she remained in this state for some seven years, at which time she delivered an egg. The king, being greatly ashamed, made several attempts to dispose of the egg, finally casting it out to the sea. Eventually the egg was found by an old village woman and it set forth a boy. This old woman raised the boy as her own, sent him to school, and he eventually married the princess, becoming a king.

Now this story defies reason in many ways, yet, it holds a special meaning to the people of this small village. It gives these people a feeling of association with royalty and with the ancient history of Korea. The people of this village have even built a monument to the egg-boy as their legendary hero of sorts. This is a typical story in that, if not seriously questioned, it holds much delight for youngsters and adults alike.

The Rock of the Falling Flowers is a short folk tale that shows the deep devotion of the Korean people to their country...

especially the woman. During a struggle between the two kingdoms of Begze and Sinla allied with China, almost a thousand
years ago, the three thousand ladies of the court were left
alone in the ruins of the castle. In defeat they consulted together, and finding no honorable way of surviving this downfall of their country they decided to commit mass suicide.
Carrying out this design, the unfortunate ladies...all three
thousand of them...went to a nearby cliff and threw themselves over the cliff before the enemy troops reached the royal
palace. As stated before, this is a good example of the faithful
constancy of Korean women.

The Enchanted Wine Jug is the story of an old man who
owns a wine shop and sells wine very cheaply (with little
profit) to the people of the village. Once, long ago, the good
natured old man gave a traveller the last drink out of his jug.
For this unselfish act the traveller gave the old man an amber
gem with instructions to drop this in the wine bottle and he
will never be without drink. Realizing this to be so, the old
man opened a simple wine shop to seek out a meager living.
The old man, the cat and the dog were the only ones who
knew the secret of the ever present supply of wine, and each
kept an eye on the piece of amber, day and night.

One day catastrophe struck...the supply of wine became
exhausted. The amber amulet was accidently poured out into
someone's wine bottle and removed from its rightful owner
(the old man). The old man became very disappointed with life
and became very disheartened with himself and his shop. It
was at this time that the cat and the dog decided to search for
the amber gem and restore happiness in the old man's life.
They, the cat and the dog, now closer than ever went around for
months in search of the gem. They finally found the amber
stone with the aid of the rats and the little mouse, across the
river on the other side of town. After obtaining the jewel, the
cat and the dog were anxious to return it to the depressed old
man; all went well until they reached the river to return. The
dog gave the cat the gem to hold in its mouth while they
crossed the river (the cat, because it could not swim, was
mounted on the dog's back). What a sight this was, inter-

animal friendship, the dog swimming across the river with his cohort, the cat on his back. Everything was fine until they neared the home back of the river. A group of children seeing this amazing sight began to laugh at the animals. The laughter made the cat start to laugh and drop the amber in the river. Immediately, without thinking, the dog with the cat on his back, dove for the gem, dragging the cat along with him. When they both reached shore, the dog, angry with the cat's stupidity, attacked the cat, but failed to harm him as the cat safely climbed a tree. The gem was lost forever.

One day, a man was fishing and as he pulled out a fish the dog grabbed it and ran off with it to deliver it to the old man, who was poverty stricken now as all his savings had been spent on the necessities of life. As the old man was cleaning the fish, getting it ready to cook, slit open the fish's belly and to his astonishment found the amber gem. The old man placed the gem in his trunk among his finest clothes. When he later returned, after purchasing some wine for his celebration, he re-opened the trunk and to his amazement he found another suit of fine clothes exactly like the one in the trunk. The old man eventually became immensely wealthy. He carefully tended to his faithful dog, whenever in his remaining days molested a cat, and never lost an opportunity to attack every cat he saw.

It is evident from this Korean tale that it is classic among the culture in Korea. There is a moral present but with two major themes: Why cats and dogs are constantly at war with each other and the amazing faithfulness of the dog to his master. In Korea cats are rare, while dogs are abundant. This could also be explained by the essence of the tale revealed.

Loyalty and patriotism are not meaningless words to the Korean for they have been vitally intertwined in the country's cultural history. These words conjure to the Korean today the remnant effects of an oriental social order which has been invaded by western thought. The eldest of a Korean household is sure to remember the strict censure which was put on being loyal to one's master, the obedience owed the ruler, and the debt of ultra patriotism that was due to his land at every moment. An example is the short historical story *Death of Yun-Ssi,* Mrs. Sin, by Zong-hwa Bag, who held loyalty above love. She killed herself when her husband escaped death for his conspiracy against the usurper king. By doing this she took her husband's place and proved her loyalty to the former king.

The special interest of this story is the conflict between the ideas of Yun-Ssi and Sug-zu Sin. Yun-Ssi has patriotism as her highest ideal, she will be loyal to what she believes to be the right course of action while Sug-zu gives in to his urge for self-preservation and the love for his wife and sons. The conflict arises from the fact that a usurper king has taken advantage of his position to gain power. A plot by a group of royal retainers including Sug-zu Sin was discovered and the conspirators were to be executed. The royal retainers were loyal to what they thought were their obligations to the former king.

When Mrs. Sin, Yun-Ssi, heard that the conspiracy had been discovered by the usurper king, she assumed that her husband and sons would be executed, and she would become a servant in the palace. Mrs. Sin felt that she would rather die than support such an evil king; so she made preparations to commit suicide when she knew for sure that her husband had been executed. Yun-Ssi sent one of her servants, Yambun, into the street to see when her husband would be taken to be executed, but Yambun reported that all the royal retainers except Sug-zu Sin were executed. No one knew what had happened to him.

Later that evening Mr. Sin returned home. Naturally, Mrs. Sin was shocked to see her husband. He explained that he had decided not to go along with the conspiracy because he wanted to save her and his sons. He had failed to live up to her idea of a patriotic man. Mrs. Sin's shame for her husband was too much to bear, and so she committed suicide the next morning.

The loyalty of Mrs. Sin demonstrated by this short story of the past is characteristic of modern Korean literature. Loyalty and patriotism in literature is a drive for independence. Compared to western standards the level of patriotism displayed by Mrs. Sin would not be expected at all; however, Mr. Sin would have been expected to act differently.

One of the problems in examining this story for any westerner is suicide. Westerners have product of a mentally ill individual and then it requires much more courage to face life as it really is and try to affect a change than to commit suicide. The Korean view of suicide is much different from that. Suicide seems to play an important role in many of the stories.

Mr. Sin's actions are much easier for a westerner to analyze. He sacrificed his patriotic principles for the love of his wife and children and, of course, for his own self-preservation. It is important to note the inner conflict in his mind which is expressed in the story by the gloomy expression on his face. It is easy to understand this kind of personal mind, and the story expresses it well.

Sug-zu Sin's ideals turn out to be just the opposite as his wife's. The comparison of Yun-Ssi to the cold blue moon still shining amid black clouds clearly shows her resolute determination once she has decided upon death, while when her husband finally comes home he drops his head in shame. There never seems to be any question in Yun-Ssi's mind about what her obligation is. She knows it clearly. Nor is she gloomy about her fate. She chooses a white towel to hang herself with as if she had a preconceived plan of action.

The important point then for the story is the contrast between the resolute determination of Mrs. Sin to do what she thinks is her duty to the country and the uncertainty of the choice for personal protection taken by Sug-zu Sin and his shame. Mrs. Sin says she acts out of loyalty and chastity. She could not serve in the court of the usurper king, but that is precisely what weak willed husband is doing by not contributing to the conspiracy and carrying out his obligation as a royal retainer.

As was said earlier it is not difficult to understand that this short story was a product of the modern period. It would not be at all improbable that many cases similar to this in terms of the conflict of ideas and ideals arose from the Japanese and the short communist occupations of Korea. One living under such conditions would be much more sensitive to very powerful forces at work on the individuals to preserve their own life or those of loved ones at the expense of the nation as a whole. Only the courageous like Mrs. Sin can make the difficult decisions with pride and determination. It is the age old question of whether your ideals worth dying for, and if they are not, how can they be worth living for?

A Puppet by Sang-dog Czoe is the story of a young couple (unmarried) who fell sympathy for innocent animals who have been lured to their death by an animal which trained to deceive his kind. A Japanese hunting establishment has a rather unique method of hunting ducks. One domestic duck is trained to lead wild ducks to a particular spot where food is being distributed by a trapper. The ducks are unaware of his presence, so they crowd into the small area. When the hunter thinks that the puppet has delivered enough victims to him, he springs a snare which envelopes the trained duck as well as those who have followed him.

The decoy is separated from his innocent followers, and the wild ducks are roasted and eaten at a nearby restaurant. As the couple watches this form of deception, they become increasingly displeased with this underhanded methods of hunting, and they refused to eat their share of the catch.

The story illustrates that man sympathizes with those who are robbed of their freedom by the guile and duplicity of others. Not only does man sympathize with those less fortunate than himself, but also he will take steps to liberate those who merit their freedom.

Cattle by Yong-teg Zon has for its setting a small rural community just south of the thirty-eighth parallel in Korea. The main characters are the Honourable Hong, his wife, his son Yong-dog, his neighbor Zang-son, and the mother of Zang-son. The Honourable Hong has done much to help the other families in the village, and he is well-liked and respected. By careful planning, he and his wife have saved their money and have lived very modestly so as to have a prosperous farm and so they can provide well for their son, whom they love very much. They own cattle and hens, and the Honourable Hong keeps beehives on the side.

The story opens with the birth of a calf, which brings great joy to the family. The Honourable Hong takes very good care of the calf and its mother, because to him the cow has great value and is almost sacred. While the Honourable Hong and his family are admiring the calf, Zang-son's mother comes over to borrow some rice, because her family is not very prosperous, and their supply is used up. But the wife indignantly refuses to help her neighbor, and Zang-son's mother wretchedly runs away in tears. The Honourable Hong feels sorry for her, and when he sees Zang-son the next day he offers secretly to help him out.

At that time Zang-son begs his kind neighbor to get him a cow, because his own just recently died. After considering Zang-son's plea, the Honourable Hong agrees to help him, since he believes that it would be good for the community if every family could own a cow. When the Honourable Hong decides to give his new calf to Zang-son, his wife opposes him, because she is not as unselfish and kind-hearted as her husband, and she wants to keep the calf for their son, Yong-dog. They argue bitterly, but the Honourable Hong still gives the calf to his neighbors.

Some time later the Honourable Hong and his wife find further cause to argue. Yong-dog becomes sick, and each blames the other for his illness. So she leaves her husband and sick boy, and the boy finally dies, which makes the Honourable Hong very sad and repressed. But he still works hard and keeps up his hens, his cattle, and his beehives. Then one day reports are heard of a cow that wandered into a northern village and was killed by the people and used for meat. The Honourable Hong was hurt and angered at the thought of his own countrymen killing a cow for meat, especially when it was discovered to be Zang-son's cow that the Honourable Hong has given him.

In the meantime, the wife returned home, but she and her husband argued again. Times were getting hard, and the Honourable Hong was not as prosperous as he used to be, because much of what he produced had to be given to the government. There was a widespread state of poverty, and many people were leaving their farms and moving to the cities. The wife wanted to sell her cow and move to the city, too, but the Honourable Hong would not leave his farm.

One day noon the Honourable Hong heard a mob of people shouting and yelling. They were bringing a cow to his farm to kill it for its meat...a cow that had wandered down from the north. But the Honourable Hong would not allow the cow to be killed. He offered them his own cow instead, but when he went to get it from the stall, it was gone. He found a note from his wife saying that she was going to sell her cow and work in the city. Soon the Honourable Hong was forced to leave his cherished farm and country. He was never seen there again.

The story seems to present a critique of post-World War II Korea. Set in the village Oyoul, just south of the 38°N. demarcation line which separates North and South Korea, the story emphasizes the plight of Korean peoples in their present situation. In addition, it reveals the painful experiences of marriage. The tale also includes the universal question of how man should deal with his fellow man and the more recent issue of how people can best adjust to rapid socioeconomic change.

To focus attention on the tragedy of divided Korea, the author has chosen an incident involving cattle crossing the border between the two sections of the country. One cow from Oyoul has disappeared to the north. It is learned that the people of North Korea have slaughtered the animal, so the villagers of Oyoul, having caught a cow that came south, intend to retaliate. The leading character, Hong, has been gazing at the surrounding villages from a high vantage point, thinking that he could not distinguish south from north, when he hears the group approach. He asks what they are doing, and they explain. He strongly advises them against their action, reminding them that they are the same as those in the north. Hong cannot understand how these men could indirectly harm other man, and even more important, how one Korean could hurt another Korean.

Through the story, Hong has shown concern for his neighbors. He has bought cattle for the villagers who did not won any, remembering that he had received financial assistance from a friend before he had settled in Oyoul. That assistance had permitted him to start life anew on his farm where he had become quite successful. Believing that with cattle the other villagers could build a decent life for themselves, he had provided them with a chance to improve their lot. He alluded to the fact that the people of Korea had been oppressed, cheated, and robbed and never had received help; thus they had not been able to end their suffering. Against the wishes of his wife, he aided villagers. When these villagers were going to kill the cow from the north, he hurried back to his house to find his wife gone, took his money to give part of it to Zang-son, owner of the missing cow to replace the loss and left the village forever. Apparently he had found himself futile.

The marriage of Hong and wife, which ended in separation, has been the means by which the author exposes some of the opposing forces in Korean society, or almost any society for that matter. During their first ten years in Oyoul, the couple had decided to work hard on their land and to operate self sufficiently. The woman had tended the hens with great care, had saved eggs rather than serve them as food so that she could purchase a heifer, and had hoped that some day she could enjoy luxuries. Hong at first appreciated her willingness to sacrifice, but later was annoyed with her heartlessness. After ten years had passed, they had a cow which gave birth. Instead of keeping the calf for his growing son, Yong-dog, Hong gave it to a needy neighbor, Zang-son. By so doing, he prompted the first quarrel between him and his wife. He worked for the better interests of the entire community. His wife, on the other hand, considered only her well-being. Her sentiments were well expressed in these lines: "Even the government can't overcome poverty, they say, don't they? I can't do it myself, can I?" She embodies the modern concern for self-preservation and materialism while Hong represents the old traditions of loyalty to his country and idealism.

Another example of the differing attitudes in this marriage can be found in their treatment of animals. At the beginning of the story the wife had kicked the puppy away from her feet so that she could faster reach her hen's newly laid egg. Later as her life on the farm and with her husband grew miserable, she talked of selling the cow. She did not care that the animal which had served them well might be bought for meat. Hong, however, felt sympathy for the cow. He said, "A man often complains and does not do all he should, but a cow works silently and obediently...." Yet another instance of the conflicting values of Hong and his wife, this time on changing social and economic conditions, can be found in the story. Whereas the woman wanted to move to the city, either Czunczon or Seoul, Hong desired to stay in the country. He countered her newer position that favored commercialization, urbanization and industrialization, with his older one that valued love of nature and the land in particular.

The disagreements of Hong and his wife proved insurmountable. Because their son had died of pleurisy during the war, she no longer had a common bond in him. Hong was well educated, but she was not. Lacking traditional feminine patience, the wife could not tolerate her unhappy marriage and abandoned her husband and home. That she or he, upon learning of her departure, did not commit suicide signifies a new element in Korean life and literature.

In *Cattle* the author's manipulation of material results in what seems to be a very realistic appraisal of circumstances in modern Korea. Because he develops an antipathy toward the selfish woman, he also establishes an opposition to her philosophy. Since she generally stands for modernism, the author must disapprove of some current trends in Korea. Recognizing that these trends exist, the author strives to reconcile them with tradition, but is unsuccessful in his task. If he is not unsuccessful, at least he is inconclusive, for the principles of Hong certainly did not emerge victorious either. But that is the essence of realism.

Now speaking of the division of Korean, inspite of the 38th parallel line which divides Korea into north and south, the people still remain as one, or at least they should, according to the story. The cattle are completely unaware of the line, so they treat it as if it were not there. Like the Honourable Hong, the people of Korea should not turn against their own country-men just because they are divided by a mere line of latitude. When the people are blinded by this kind of hate they become irrational and senseless and incapable of intelligent reasoning. For ideology the Korean people hate communists, but they can not run away from the dream of unification.

In *A Bad Night* by Gwang-zu Gim, a middle income type fellow becomes drunk and is taken to the home of a prostitute for westerners. He is at a complete loss as to how to behave. All around him are events occurring that he knows nothing about. It is the world of the lower class. He is in a hurry to get back to his own world where he can feel safe and secure. There is a certain sense of foreboding in the room; he finds himself in the morning. This is a man with high morals who shouldn't have been subjected to the perversions of an unfamiliar atmosphere. He must have been very happy to get back home to his family. The woman was attacked by children of the streets who threw pebbles despisingly against her from the back, a manifestation of nationalism.

SENIORITY AND FILIALITY

The Koreans seem to have a great deal more filial affection than in the west. The elders carry almost absolute authority, because the elders must guide the children on life's paths until they are old enough to decide for themselves. Not enough children in the west listen to their elders, and conse-quently, the west has more problems with juvenile delinquents. The brothers and sisters in a Korean family are closer than in the west. They seem to share each other's problems more deeply than do western brothers and sisters. Age in brothers is also respected by the younger brothers. A man would not usually think of disapproving of his older brother's actions. There is an order of authority starting with the eldest male and ending with the youngest son.

Seniority is very important in the Korean household. The story *The Deer, the Hare, and the Toad* points out the respect the Koreans have for seniority. The animals in the story are trying to distinguish who is the eldest amongst them for the chair of honor at a banquet they were about to have. After their respective stories were told it came out that the toad was the eldest. The seat of honor was accorded to the toad.

In the story of *The Green Frog,* one can see the traditional Korean concern for the respect given to parents. The green frog was a disobedient son who always acted against the wishes of his mother. One day when his mother was near death, he was called to her bedside. She told him that she wanted to be buried by the river, thinking that he would thus bury her on the hill where she really wanted be placed. When the mother died, the son felt guilty and decided to follow the wish his mother had expressed. He buried her by the river and watched over her grave lest it be washed by the rain. And to this day whenever the weather is wet, it is said that the green frog croaks.

Thus filial piety is a most outstanding feature of Korean society. Furthermore, it is an important factor in the stability of other societies as well. In the west, however, filial piety has not played as significant a role as it has in Oriental societies. Thus as already mentioned above western cities are plagued with a significant problem of juvenile delinquency, which is to a large degree the result of the breakdown of family ties.

Sacrifice for parents is a duty held by the Koreans to be very important. They get the moral across to readers by writing such stories as *The Tiger and the Dwarf.* The dwarf's father was killed by tigers and the dwarf grew up with the responsibility of avenging his father's death. He practiced marksmanship for many years until he became very proficient at shooting. He endured many hardships and harrowing experiences but he did avenge his father's death and was rewarded by receiving the hand of a minister's daughter.

Sacrifice and superstition are noted in the legend, *Doryong Hong, the Filial Tiger.* In this story, Hong saves his mother from dying by turning himself into a tiger and killing dogs to make medicine to cure his sick mother. His wife burned the paper with the secret spell and he was then forced to remain a tiger. From then on, this tiger always ate up women wearing blue skirts.

Obedience is also very important to the Korean. The girl in the story *Yoni and Her Stepmother* depicts a girl who despite cruel treatment carried out orders given to her without hesitation. Nevertheless the girl was obedient and so she too eventually found happiness. In *The Bridegroom*, a toad, foster-son of a poor fisherman and his wife, wished to marry one of the three daughters of a rich man. At first rejected, the toad by using magic was accepted by the youngest of the daughters. Later the toad proved to be a handsome man with supernatural powers who took his bride and ascended to Heaven. This fairy tale helps one to see how first impressions are often misleading.

The story *The Two Sisters, Rose and Lotus,* as many others of the period, is filled with superstition and spiritual magic. It relates the story of two girls, Rose and Lotus, whose mother died when they were quite young. Their father's second wife who had three sons, was quite jealous of the two girls and her husband's affection for them. Through trickery, the stepmother brought shame on the daughter Rose. The father, Be, sent her away in the company of her stepbrother. When he said he was going to drown her in a lake, the girl voluntarily jumped in and a tiger sprang from the lake badly injuring the boy.

Later Lotus went to join her sister and the spirits of the unhappy girls remained in the lake until the wickedness of the stepmother was proven. After this the father retrieves the bodies of girls from the lake and buried them on a mountain. The cruel stepmother was put to death for her misdeeds. He married for the third time, now to a kind lovable girl, was blessed by twin daughters who were named Rose and Lotus, and grew to be like his former logical daughters.

Since the family is the primary social unit in Korea, the family relationships have a powerful influence on the society. Many Koreans feel a deep sense of responsibility toward

154 A GUIDE TO KOREAN LITERATURE

others in their families. They will make sacrifices to help relatives. Young people are taught to show respect for parents, grandparents, and older kinfolk. One of the stories that portrays this filial piety is that of *Gil-dong Hong.*

Briefly, this is the story of a mistreated son who rescues a sick father. Gil-dong Hong was the bastard son of the minister Hong. Like all illegitimate sons he was despised. After years of hatred he becomes a bandit. By studying strategy, he becomes a very successful leader of a band of robbers known as the "Saviours of the Poor." This group robbed the temples and government stores of their property. Their loot was given to the poor. The authorities made many unsuccessful attempts to arrest the leader.

Finally, the father and brother were imprisoned because of the bandit son's conduct. They were released when they promised to catch Gil-dong. Because of filial feeling for his sick father, Gil-dong offers to leave the vicinity if he is given provisions and a minister title. As agreed he sails to the South Seas where he establishes a Utopia on the island of Yugdo. This story abounds in the virtue of filial piety, a rare combination of loyalty and reverence, which demands that a son show respect to his father.

With regard to filial piety there is the modern story by Dong-ni Gim, *A Mother and Her Sons.* The mother had three sons. Two of them are disrespectful, but the third son is kind. When she is about to die, her two older sons treat her as though she were an animal. It is only from her third son that she receives the sympathy she deserves. The last theme to consider here is loyalty to a mother, but the descriptions of the two elder brothers who got married indicate a modern feature of individualism.

SOCIAL WELFARE

The Former Sports-Master by De-hun Ham is a story involving a man that was deprived of his job due to false charges made against his ideas. He was unable to find employment and was eventually forced to allow his wife to become a waitress, which was a disgrace. Throughout his life this man had attempted to maintain a healthy mind in a healthy body. It was through putting this idea into practice in his teaching activities as Sport-Master that caused him to lose his job. There is a deep philosophical overtone in this story. The author, De-hun Ham, is attempting to show that there is a definite social welfare problem involved in modern civilization. If conditions in modern civilization are such that they deprive a man of his livelihood, because he is doing what is right, and then forces his wife into immorality to avoid starvation, obviously something is wrong with our modern civilization that needs to be corrected. There is a basic problem in society, when it becomes easier for women to find work through immorality than for men to find employment while trying to do what is healthful and good. This, of course, is a serious problem in social welfare.

Sonata Appassionata by Dong-in Gim is a world literature classic. Philosophical and psychological questions of social welfare are entwined within this literary masterpiece. The social welfare concept of punishment by imprisonment for crimes against society is severely questioned. Is it not the loss that society suffers through the imprisonment of a great artist more costly to society in the long run than the burning of a few buildings or the rape of a corpse? This is the type of question that this story poses to its readers.

A great artist that comes along, perhaps, once in a generation, makes a tremendous contribution to society. According to the author, artists in society lose their raw creativity and expressiveness when they are forced to create by rules governing their art. Creativity and expressiveness would die out eventually if it were not for an occasional untrained artist of great talent such as the main character in this story.

It is the task of society to determine which is more important its truly creative and untrained artists, in whatever field of endeavor they may be. It would be wonderful if society could find some way to keep these artists from doing harm to others, but still maintain their creativity.

Perhaps, some of the psychological attitudes of society could be improved in order to prevent such chance happenings as an illegitimate birth, which leaves an indelibles scar upon a body whether he is a future artist or not. Perhaps if society could be improved the chance happenings of a crime could be reduced and the chances of great art being created could be increased. The author questions the validity of punishment for chance happenings. It is my opinion that society must question the use of severe punishment for infractions of its rules that happen merely by chance.

The Mind of an Ox by Mu-yong Yi is a symbolic story depicting the suffer of the Korean people. The story revolves around the day to day events in the life of an ox. He for the most part does not get easily angry or upset. It is only when he sees man's inhumanity to members of his own race in return for money from another race that he becomes upset.

He sees that his own beloved wife has been killed, and this fact grieves him deeply. The ox finally becomes so distracted that he rises up against the oppressor and kills him. This story was written during the Japanese occupation and carries a deep meaning for the Korean people as well as other oppressed people. The Japanese would not allow free literature to be printed that might cause the Koreans to rise up against them, so it was only through the use of hidden symbolism that writers could inspire their people without being imprisoned or killed. The ox in the story could represent the oppressed Korean people and the cruel men under the Japanese.

The patient ox could stand only so much cruelty and misery, and finally he attacked and gored his main oppressor. The author of this short story may have also been warning the landlords or the Japanese to stop their oppression, at the same time that he was urging his own people to rise up and overthrow the "devils." Japanese occupation was being accomplished with almost disregard of the social welfare of the Korean people. The author knew that for the good of Korea both socially and politically, the Japanese had to be eliminated from Korean soil. This is because the Japanese were choking Korea's political and social freedom.

Perhaps the author was also delivering a philosophical message to man. The message is that man takes too little note of the feelings of other people as well as of the feelings of animals. Man should try to be thoughtful of others to a greater extent than he is. The author indicated through symbolism the cruelty of the landlords or the Japanese to the Korean people. But this story also represents another conflict between man and his subservient animals. Perhaps this is the very reason that Yi chose to make the main character in the story an ox; not only to represent the cruelty of man to animals, but just as much the cruelty of man to his fellow man.

As the animal relates to the reader his previous life with other owners he is in fact relating the life of the Korean farmer. Late he tells of life under the Japanese control. Earlier times are related when the author writes:

> The second sale was the most fortunate for
> me. I lay down for three days to eat soya beans
> and the flies were kept away from me. I remem-
> bered the times clearly.

But then the author, in the guise of the oxen, goes on to describe the conditions later under the control of the another owner.

> From the time when I had come to my present
> owner Dog-czil, who was nicknamed 'yellow,' I
> had been worked extremely hard but fed very
> badly. In the summertime I could get enough
> grass to eat from the dykes and paddy fields,
> and so I had no particular complaint against my
> master, but no sooner had the grass turned
> yellow than his hand shook when he brought me
> hay.

The author, in effect, seems to be saying that in the summertime, the Korean people were able to forage food for themselves from the rice paddies, but in the winter, when the food was distributed, there was little left. As well may have been the case, the ox in the story, representing the typical Korean of the day, decided that he would test the farmer for whom he worked, and not eat food and refuse to work. He then realized, however, that such a course was imprudent, for in actuality, all Koreans, not only himself, were very poor and could not afford any better.

The passage in the story dealing with the owner of the ox being unable to pay for the rent on the home and having to mortgage it to a wealthy foreigner seemed to be a sad commentary on the plight of the typical Korean peasant at the time. Although all of the members of the family worked hard all day long in the fields, they were still not able to meet the demands of the high rents and were therefore obliged to sell the land. The author, through the narrative of the animal, reveals to the reader the poor health of the family members merely because of a lack of nourishment. The description of the members of the family having ravenous appetites but never enough to eat is indicative of the typical peasant of the time.

The whole situation of loneliness and despair of the peasant was summed up with the line ending the first part of the story. "I often gazed vacantly at the unfeeling mountains and rivers with the yoke on my neck." In the beginning of the second part of the story, the author says, however, that perhaps he did not have it any worse than most of the peasant families at the time. There also runs through these lines the principle of strong family ties. He writes:

> I did often consider myself to be in a way fortunate to have been sold to these people for it gave me a feeling of pride to have the duty of feeding the whole family. Although they fed me little and drove me the whole day long... I did not complain.

As the story progresses, the author presents a thinly guised attack on the cruelty of human to the animal.

My flanks were violently beaten and I put
forth all my strength.
"One step more, just one step more. Your
next step will feed me and the other nine of us."
I strained to the last sinew.
"That's the way, man! Whip me until I'm
stretched out stiff and dead. I'll die one way or
the another."

As the Japanese occupation grew longer, matters grew
worse and worse. The author says, "...the days when my
master's family could not cook porridge for me grew more frequent and the old master would sit on the step with his short
pipe and sigh more often."

Because of the indebtedness of the main character in the
story, and the typical Korean peasant at the time, he was
forced to sell his cart, his home and the last few remaining
vestiges of his means of livelihood. Just as the character, Dog-
czil, had reconciled himself to the thought of having to do
without the house and the cart, a Japanese approached and
wanted some goods hauled. Having to admit to the man that
he had become so poor and he had to sell his property to keep
alive, Dog-czil then flew into a rage of desperation, tearing off
the red labels from the cart and from the house. Since the red
labels indicated property was to be sold, and since it was
against the policy of the Japanese occupying forces to
remove such a label, the master was thrown into jail for
twenty days. This is another thinly guised testimony to the im-
prisoning tactics of the Japanese.

Although both the members of the family and the ox had
worked hard, the season's harvest amounted to very little. To
keep from going still deeper into debt, the farmer realized that
he would have to sell the ox. There was much crying in the
family, but the ever present Japanese wealthy land owners and
creditors were ready to collect for their unfairly accrued debts.
The apparent lack of mercy of the Japanese for the condition
of the Korean people is represented when the author tells of
the great crying of the family members, and, instead of allow-

ing the old peasant the last few minutes of pride, the wealthy ones insist that they hurry, lest they should be late for market.

As the story builds towards the climax, and the journey has ended in the market place, the author begins a commentary on the exploitation of the Koreans by the Japanese. He indicates that although he and his master have made the same long and hard trip to the village, they are not invited to eat and drink, as if they did not get as hungry and thirsty as did the Japanese. The ringing note of patriotism and fierce pride in his country and the feelings of intense scorn for the rich Chinese reaches its high point when the author, speaking through the ox, says:

> It was beyond my comprehension that these men could pour wine for the Chinese and ignore their own village. A sudden urge came over me to run my horns through their entrails and string them up like slices of meat on bamboo skewers and trample on them with my hooves.

The author could well have been alluding to the Koreans, who rather then suffer with their countrymen, instead took jobs serving the Japanese or Chinese, for their own protection. It made the author very angry to see these people feeding the Japanese or Chinese and helping them in every way, while their own neighbors and the people of Korea were getting no food and were starving to death. Throughout the story, the cruelties of the Japanese against the Koreans have been building up. They reach a real zenith, however, when the author, still in the guise of the ox, sees his former mate (Perhaps the author is seeing the body of his former wife mutilated) being killed and served up to the Japanese.

At this point, the ox swears revenge with the murderer of his sweetheart. This may symbolize the uprisings of the Korean people when they have witnessed cruelty to their own loved ones. At the time when the ox is mourning the fate of his mate, a trader slaps him on the thigh and indicates he wants to buy the ox. As the trader, the ox's master, and the creditors bicker about the price the ox will bring, the animal suddenly realizes that the trader is the butcher and intends to sell his body for meat. The thought also enters his mind that the trader or butcher is probably the same one who butchered his mate. Becoming incensed at this final of all insults, the bull changes and gores the butcher to death.

This scene might well symbolize the final resistance of the Korean people, springing from their own rising feelings of nationalism and patriotism, and is on indication that any people can be oppressed for just so long until they are forced to fight back. And so, Yi through his seemingly simple story not only gives the reader a moral about the kindness of man to animals, but also, if the reader is aware of his history and realizes that in November of 1933, the Japanese were occupying Korea, gives real insight into Japanese occupation tactics. All in all, the story is one of struggling and oppression of a people, who, through their own determination and a little outside aid, will once again become free and independent.

Korean Folklore

The written history of a people shows us the main currents of their politics and culture, but when we wish to discover the spirit of their daily life it is to their folklore that we must turn. Folklore is a vast storehouse of traditions, such as folk tales, folk songs, folk dance and drama, proverbs, riddles, superstitions, and even customs and manners. Of these folk tales are most widely known among the people of the country, and can most easily be appreciated by foreigners.

Modern Korean literature is a blending of the traditional features of our native life and the new currents of western literature. It deals with almost the same subjects as does modern European literature, whether in poetry, novels and plays, or in essays and criticism, but behind these common themes there are certain features peculiar to Korea, deriving from our language, customs and manners, and our geographical and political situation, which are not found in the literatures of other countries.

Although of course customs and manners have changed greatly through the ages, they still exert a great influence on literary production as well as on the daily lives of the Korean people, and many of their basic features can be approached through the tales included in my book. In some ways they are as full of primitive sentiments and mysterious superstitions as the folk tales of other nations, yet the main points suggested in the tales and the emotions which prompted them still predominate in the minds of our people.

Births, marriages and deaths are described in their genuine Korean traditional forms. Omens and dreams, auguries and divinations, charms and amulets all have a Korean flavour and are not identical with those of China. Many supernatural beings appear, but they do not behave in the same way as those in Japanese stories. For instance, Buddhist monks or priests are not always respected in the Korean tales which are told today, despite their possession of magical powers. This is due, as I shall show later, to the historical background of religion in Korea and its changing social status through the ages. Korean fairies, elves, goblins, ghosts, giants, monsters and other such creatures all have their own peculiarly Korean characteristics. Dragons, animals and plants behave in many cases in a Korean manner, and certain kinds figure in our stories more often than in those of other countries.

The geographical location of Korea and its political situation have greatly influenced on the literary taste of her inhabitants. Korea has played an important role in the history of the Far East as the bridge between the continent of Asia and the islands of the Pacific. So in her folk tales we can trace several intermingling currents from the surrounding countries of China, Japan, India, Mongolia, Tibet, Manchuria and Siberia. There are, however, some universal elements which can be found even in European stories. For example, Zu-mong Go, King of Goguryo, can be referred to the Greek myth of Perseus. Another story of the Perseus type is told in Korea in which a toad is the hero who saves a maiden from a serpent or a centipede by breathing its poisonous breath upon it, as the tortoise of China kills a serpent, or a scaly dragon, or the hero of Japanese folklore kills a serpent, or the knights of Europe rescue damsels in distress. Stories of the type of Cupid and Psyche (compare "the Three Stars" and "the Toad Bridegroom") and the Swan Maiden Tales (compare "the Heavenly Maiden and the Woodcutter") are also found in Korea, as well as in China, Japan, Siberia and Europe.

Some Korean tales are closely related to stories told in the neighbouring countries though they are moulded in a Korean style. For instance a tale resembling "a Stone Memorial to a Dog" was told in China from the fourth century A.D., as was recorded in volume 5 of the Sou Shen Chi by Pao Kan of the

Chin Dynasty. One of the same type of "the Mud-snail Fairy," called the Virgin Po Sui, is found in volume 16 of the Sou Shem Hou Chi by Chien Tao of the same dynasty. In the same way "the Story of the Virgin Arang" can be identified with the Chinese legend of the Maiden Chieh San, in volume 17 of the Chien Chih Yi by Mai Hung of the Sung Dynasty, and tales closely resembling our "the Green Frog," "the Man Who Wanted to Bury His Son" and "Three Corpses, Money and a Wine-bottle" have been told in China, as in volume 9 of the Hsu Po Wu Chih by Shih Li of the Tang Dynasty, in volume 11 of the Sou Shen Chi by Pao Kan of the Chin Dynasty, and in the Chang Shih Ko Shu by Chih Fu Chang of the Sung Dynasty respectively.

Turning now to Japanese legends, a story of the same type as our "the Sun and the Moon" is told in the island of Kyushu, Japan, under the name of Soba or "Buckwheat" (in the Legends of Japan by Mr. Tosio Takagi, p. 267). In Japan we also find stories of the same type as our "the Bride Who Would not Speak" (volume 75 of the Japanese book, Wakan Sanzai Zukai), and "the Mallet of Wealth" (Elves and the Envious Neighbour, in Lord Redesdale's Tales of Old Japan, p. 160). Moreover the tiger of our story "the Tiger and the Persimmon" is undoubtedly the monster called Toraokame or "Tiger-wolf" in a Japanese story of similar type (Takagi Tosio, Studies in the Myths and Legends of Japan, p. 450). This story may well have been introduced into Japan from Korea, as the old tiger is not found in Japan, and a modified form of the word wolf has been added. This type of story seems to be originally derived from the thief, the monster and the monkey of volume 5 of the Indian "Panch-Tantra," in which the central figure is a man-eating monster "Rakchasa." Therefore an Indian origin may be postulated for certain Korean tales. It is commonly held that "the Great Flood," "the Aged Father," "the Deer, the Hare and the Toad" and "Lazybones" are derived from the Buddhist Scriptures of India.

Then our "the Cat and the Dog" can be referred to the Mongolian myth, the story of Sharau (A Journey in Southern Siberia, the Mongols, their Religion and their Myths, by

Jeremiah Curtin, p. 201). In Mongolia too we find a tale of the same type as our "the Nine-headed Giant," and stories of the same type as our "the Young Gentleman and the Tiger" are found in East Mongolia, Japan, India and even in Tibet.

Korean folk tales can be classified in many ways. I divide these tales into five groups, myths, legends, fairy tales, fables and old novels. By myths I mean those tales which describe the creation of the world and natural beings. Legends include those tales which are derived from anecdotes about individuals which contain some historical facts. Fairy tales comprise innocent stories for children and fables those which point a moral. And finally I include summaries of many autobiographical novels written by early writers, because these old tales have been told among the people for so long that they have almost become popular folk tales and some of the authors forgotten. In any case they were originally derived from such material as gives rise to legends.

The tales can also be grouped under about fifteen main heads according to their subject matter or material. That is to say, tales dealing with the Heavenly Kingdom and other celestial matters, genii and mysterious priests, human beings and their activities, ghosts and devils, fairies and goblins, giants and dwarfs, magicians and geomancers, dragons and the kingdom under the sea, animals and birds, insects and worms, fish and shells, trees and grass, stones and mountains, rivers, lakes and seas, and stories about eggs. This list does not, of course, claim to be complete. Other types may certainly be found. All these types are often interwoven one with another and it is often difficult to draw clear distinctions between them.

In Korea we find almost every kind of myth, such as Creation Myths, Sun and Moon Myths, Star Myths, Flood Myths, Myths of Places of Rewards or Punishments, Myths of the Underworld, or Place of the Dead, Soul Myths, Hero Myths, Dualistic Myths of the Good God fighting the Bad God, Myths regarding Taboo, and Myths of Animals. The Myths of Korea are not, however, on the grand scale of the myths of Greece or some other western countries, but they are

elaborately designed stories, and more or less independent of
one another. They explain how the Sun and Moon originated,
as in "the Sun and the Moon," or came to have eclipses, as in
"the Fire Dogs"; they tell of the stars, as in "the Seven Stars
of the North" and "the Three Stars"; of mountains and
rivers, as in "the Mountain and the River"; why the ant has
such a slender waist, as in "the Ants and the Hare"; why the
bedbug is so flat and the louse has a spot on his back, as in
"the Bedbug, the Louse and the Flea," and so on.

In those myths and legends which tell of the foundation
of kingdoms and dynasties, eggs often play an important part,
and the heroes are born from them. Zu-mong Go, the first
King of Goguryo, was born from an egg, the founder of the
Sinla Dynasty was born from a big gourd, and the heroes of
Gaya also came from a box. Many Korean legends, fables and
old novels tell of the wisdom of magistrates, governors and
royal inspectors in solving legal problems. On the other hand
they also often tell of their wickedness and cruelty which bring
great suffering to the people. The civil examinations often
figure in the tales, since they formed the first obstacle in the
path of those who aimed attaining high rank in the government, or an honoured position in society. Another noteworthy
feature of the Korean legends is geomancy, which even
now exerts an influence on the popular mind. There are many
love stories which show how social conditions prevented social
contact between men and women, and other tales tell of the
sorrows of women kept in strick seclusion from the outer
world. The victims of the system are seen to form illicit associations contrary to the restrictions of the caste system. Many
fables, full of irony and humour, reveal to us the delicate
sensibility of Korean domestic life, in which charm is mingled
with tears.

The typical Korean goblin, called *doggabi* very often
appears in fairy tales. It usually takes pleasure in making
people happy, but sometimes it brings trouble to men. Some
people believe that the goblins are the spirits of good people
who have died but for some reason have not been permitted
to go to the world of the blessed, and so wander through this

world. And the Korean believes that ghosts are the spirits of those unhappy men or of wicked men who have been refused entrance into the other world and are waiting for their release from this world.

As in the folk tales of other countries animals have the power to transform themselves into men. Dragons, tortoises, dogs, bears, deer, hares, carp and toads are usually represented as good, and tigers, foxes, serpents, and centipedes as bad, although there are exceptions to this rule. The most typical animal is the tiger. Tigers must at one time have been very common in the mountainous Korea, and the tiger was commonly worshipped as the God of the Mountain, or the Lord of the Mountain or the Sacred spirit of the Mountain, because of its character, fierce, yet full of mystery. The tales of tigers can be divided into five categories; (1) the tales of its ferocity, as in "the Sun and the Moon," "Four Sworn Brothers," "the Ungrateful Tiger," "the Tiger and the Dwarf," etc., (2) tales in which it expresses gratitude, as in "the Tiger's Grave," "the White Eared Tiger," etc., (3) tales that tell of its marriage with men, as in "the Tiger Girl," and others, (4) tales of its revengefulness, as in "Doryong Hong, the Filial Tiger" and others, (5) tales that depict the tiger as a rather innocent, humorous animal, as in "the Three Sons," "the Old Tiger and the Hare," "the Young Gentleman and the Tiger," "the Tiger and the Persimmon," and others.

In a description of the main characteristics of the folk tales of Korea it is essential that a survey of the folk-beliefs of the Korean people should be included. The folk tales can also be classified under the six religious currents in Korea, Shamanism, Buddhism, Confucianism, Taoism, Christianity and Man-God religion.

Korean Shamanism, the typical form of which is called "Balg," is one of the basic elements in Korean folklore. It is a form of nature worship. The people of Korea attribute spirits to heavenly bodies and natural phenomena, such as the sun, moon and stars, the wind, clouds, rain, etc., and they also worship mountains, streams, caves, stones, animals, trees and other things. It is indeed a form of pantheism, but they believe that above all these there stands a supreme ruler, called "Hanunim." This name is compounded of two words meaning "Heaven" and "master," i.e., "Lord of Heaven," who figures in such story as "Dan-gun, the first King of Korea." The Korean people recognize him as the Celestial Emperor of the Heavenly Kingdom, who sends the sunlight and the rain, and strikes the wicked with lightning, or visits other punishments upon them, and rewards the good according to their merits, but they never worship him in the form of an actual idol. All other natural objects which are worshipped in personified forms are in the final analysis measured against this unrevealed higher standard of *Hanunim.*

Besides this Heavenly Kingdom and the human world there are three other regions, the Kingdom of Darkness that figures in "The Fire Dogs," the Underworld as in "The Nine-headed Giant," and the Dragon-Kingdom under the Sea. The guiding principle on which men are to act is that good deeds will be rewarded and evil punished. After death the good men will become good spirits and admitted to life in the Heavenly Kingdom, while bad men will be evil spirits, condemned to suffer in the Kingdom of Darkness or the Underworld. The Dragon Kingdom is conceived as a sort of underwater Utopia which men may sometimes have the good fortune to visit for a short time, as in "the Story of Zibong" or "the Mountain Witch and the Dragon-King." The tenets which guided the Korean people in their daily lives and their domestic virtues were based on these ideas, and from the time of the first King, Dan-gun, through the succeeding dynasties of the early period, the theme of political development was "to spread righteousness among the people." There were elements of democracy in the administration, although the kings wielded absolute power. Finally, it is worth noting that farming, which has been the basic industry of Korea for thousands of years and the occupation of 80 percent of the population, is closely bound up with Korean Shamanism. Shamanistic folk-beliefs have also been greatly influenced by chivalry.

Buddhism was introduced into Korea in 372 A.D., and soon achieved widespread popularity, for it had some pantheistic features which could easily be reconciled with the shamanistic elements of Korean beliefs. The Buddhist idea that the present life has been determined by the past and the future is being determined by the present is commonly found in Korean folk-beliefs. Moreover the government built many large temples throughout the country, and gave Buddhism an important national role as the principle of administration, and it became the mould of popular thought for about a thousand years. The negative and pessimistic elements of Buddhism, which had prevailed in the years following its introduction, were gradually replaced by an optimistic utilitarianism, as the faith became completely assimilated. Learned and virtuous priests exerted a powerful influence on the spritual lives of men and women, and many a time outstanding men retired to temples in the mountains for their literary and military education, a custom which enters into some tales.

Unfortunately, in later times Buddhism degenerated, owing to the luxury of temple life and the worldly ambitions of corrupt priests who meddled in politics. Under the Yi Dynasty, which came to power in 1392, Buddhism was suppressed by the government, partly for political reasons, when they attempted to give a new impetus to the national spirit. As a result it ceased to exist as an influential religion. So we find that priests and monks in Korean folk tales are often treated with disrespect and with great irony, as mentioned above. The tales called "Three Stars," "the Tiger Priest" and "the Two Brothers and the Magistrate" will illustrate this point.

Subsequently the new government gave great encouragement to the development of Confucianism, and for four or five hundred years after the decline of Buddhism it was the dominant religion of Korea. It cannot, of course, be properly called a religion, as it does not prescribe the worship of any god, and human activities begin with birth and end with death. It did, however, exert a powerful influence on the standards of political and individual conduct, and Confucian principles are an important element in many tales. Many tales interpret its ethical principles, the basic motives of human life, the "Five Principles of Conduct," loyalty to the king, filial respect for

one's parents, harmony of husband and wife, respect for
elders, and true friendship. Sometimes they are closely interwoven with Buddhist elements, whose imaginative character
appeals to illiterate woman, and so has resulted in their preservation to the present day. Confucianism is, on the whole,
deemed a man's religion, by reason of its learned background.
The ideas of virtue, justice, etiquette, wisdom and trust found
their way into our political thought, and popular customs
relating to birth, marriage, death, funerals, festivals and other
ceremonies were formulated according to the classical standards
of Confucianism, though in a modified Korean form.

Education and the civil examinations were standardized
on rationalistic Confucian lines, and all unorthodox elements,
whether of Buddhism or Taoism or anything else, were rejected.
Society was dominated by the gentleman, or *yangban,* or the
nobleman, whose privilege it was to receive the traditional
training. The ordinary people, especially those who were born
humble, were rigidly controlled by the caste system. It was
easy for those who suffered injustice, or who were exiled for
political or other reasons, to turn to a life of retirement in a
Buddhist temple. There they might ease their feelings of pessimism, or long for the supernatural exultation of Taoism, or
even plan adventures or revenge, as in "the Story of Gil-dong
Hong" and "the Legend of U-czi Zon."

Taoism in Korea did not develop as a distinct religion,
and there was no period when it flourished under official
protection, as Buddhism and Confucianism did. But certain
elements of Taoism, such as geomancy, divination, diagrams
and prophecy, exerted an influence on Shamanism, Buddhism
and even Confucianism and the Man-God religion, and appear
in many of our folk tales. Christianity was introduced into
Korea in 1653, and its ideals of love, humanity and eternal life
were a new experience for the people. When the new religion
established churches, schools and hospitals on the European
pattern, a large number of men and women turned to it. The
traditional acceptance of many superstitions gradually died out
among the believers, but the people in general still clung to the
customs and manners they had known for generations. So

Christian elements were not readily absorbed into popular folk tales, although it is possible that some stories of Christian miracles worked by Koreans may have been current among the native Christians. In other words, although in later times Christianity became the most influential religion among educated people, it never produced folk tales of its own that could appeal to the Korean people in general.

Finally in 1860 Ze-u Czoe founded a reactionary religious movement, the Dong Hag or "Eastern Doctrine," whose avowed aim was to save the people from the danger of exploitation by the western religion. In practice his doctrine combined the original ideas of Shamanistic belief with those of Confucianism, Buddhism and Taoism, as its founder himself declared, and even some Christian elements. It might be described as a kind of optimistic fatalism. The basic idea of this religion is that the present world is the result of the past, and the world of the future will be created anew from the present. That is to say the past ends with yesterday, and a new life will begin today, created by a new religion which will soon lead men to an ideal society. It does not aim at a life after death, but at a happy life in this world. The Saviour will come as the disciple of Heaven, the true absolute form of the Universe, and by His Salvation every man shall become a god in this world, and live in Paradise in this world. Czoe's followers insisted on the doctrine that "Man is God." On several occasions they fomented armed risings in various provinces to persecute Christians. They later formed an influential political and religious group to work for the independence of Korea against Japan, with the new title of Czondo Gyo, or Religion of the Way of Heaven, under the leadership of Byong-hui Son. This religion produced some historical anecdotes which can be found in the history of Korea, rather than in the popular folk tales.

These five religions, Shamanism, Buddhism, Confucianism, Taoism, and the Man-God doctrine have each given rise to a number of sects, each with its own individual title, in the same way as Christianity has produced sects. It is possible that they will in the future be the source of yet more popular folk tales.

Moreover, the situation of Korea since the Second World War may give rise to folk tales, for example on the subject of the 38th parallel, which could hardly happen in other countries. Already many stories of gallantry and suffering have been born of the conflict between north and south, a conflict brought about by the clash of world ideologies. As yet this new type of folk tale may not have become true popular folk tales, but I have no doubt that they will do so in time.

Korean Novel

EARLIER STAGES

By Korean literature, one normally mean those literary works written by Koreans in Korean, but in dealing with the Korean novel in this brief survey I may refer to some works written by Koreans in *Hanmun,* or classical Chinese, in order to help my efforts to trace the historical trend.

The two oldest extant books containing Korean stories, Samgug Sagi (Historical Records of the Three Kingdoms), written by Bu-sig Gim (1075-1151), and Samgug Yusa (Remaining Records of the Three Kingdoms), written by a Buddhist monk, Il-yon (1206-1289), are worth noticing. The former has for its sources early Korean records and Chinese history, and the latter is based on traditional accounts of the first King of Korea, Dan-gun, and many other historical, mythical, or legendary heroes and heroines. The latter is more important, especially for those who wish to trace ancient Korean stories. Poems are inserted in the stories as integral parts of them, and the stories may also be appreciated individually. This book is the first collection of our orally transmitted literature now extant, and at the same time it is the first anthology of written stories.

Unfortunately, these two books were written in classical Chinese, because, until the Korean alphabet was invented in 1443 by King Sezong in co-operation with linguists of the time, the Koreans had used Chinese characters as the medium for expressing themselves in writing.

But Chinese was not the language the Koreans spoke. It

differed in grammatical and phonetic structure. So some Koreans used an adaptation of Chinese writing, called *Idu* or "Official Reading."

These efforts were made in order to find an original style of writing for Korean literature, but *Idu* was mostly used for the recording of poems, which was comparatively simple, but not for prose literature, because the complicated descriptions of the stories could not be satisfactorily recorded with such a confused variety of characters. At that time the kingdom of Sinla unified the Three Kingdoms into a single country, diplomatic relations with China were greatly extended, many students were sent to the Tang court of China, and the Chinese influence was intensified. The above-mentioned Czong Sol and the famous scholar of the Chinese classics, Czi-won Czoe who was later called the pioneer of classical Chinese literature in Korea, were highly reputed. The kingdom of Goryo adopted Buddhism as its national religion to control the spiritual life of people, but on the other hand it developed the study of the Chinese classics, which gradually assumed more importance than Buddhism.

The prose literature at this time consisted mainly of literary essays, some of which contained legends or amusing stories. Books of stories may have been introduced from the Sung Dynasty of China, and some Koreans produced original stories, not mere records of the oral literature, though they were still written in the traditional style. And now foreign literature, such as the Chinese classics and Buddhist scriptures, began to be translated into the Korean language.

Thus novels had been developed as much as any other branch of prose literature. They had started first with the recording of folk tales, and then there had been experiments with original essays interwoven with legendary stories.

In the early Yi Dynasty (1392-1910) works on historical events, myths, legends, fairy tales, and fables were produced, such as "Funny Stories" by Go-zong So and "Villagers' Talk" by Hi-meng Gang, but these were not novels as we should define the term in modern literature. In the meantime, Si-sub Gim produced a book of stories, called "New Stories of a Golden Turtle." The complete edition can not be found now, but the one which has survived has five stories in it.

One of these, "the Story of the Peeping of Mr. Yi," is the romance between a brilliant young man, Mr. Yi and a pretty girl, Miss Czoe and the scene was set in Songdo (the modern Gesong):

"Their love was started by poems, but interrupted by Yi's parents. So Miss Czoe fell ill, being crossed in love. By the earnest request of Miss Czoe's parents, they were allowed to get married, and lived happily for a few years. But unfortunately they were separated by a sudden war, and could not find each other. After the war, Mr. Yi met his wife again at night in his deserted house, and they again lived in peace for some years. But to his sorrow his wife one day disappeared; it had been really the soul of his wife, who had died during the war and had transformed herself into a living being again for a few years."

This seems to have been an imitation of Chinese story Chien Teng Hsin Hua written by Ch'u Yu which was already regarded as a masterpiece as the beginning of the Ming Dynasty in China, and led to other imitations in Japan. The author of the Korean story was one of the six royal retainers, who disagreed with the newly ascended king, who had usurped the throne, forcing his nephew, Danzong to abdicate. This group survived, but another group of six active royal retainers were executed at this time. The author forgot worldly fame and retired into the mountains named "the Golden Turtle" as a priest, sometimes feigning to be mad. Though the story was practically an imitation of the Chinese story, and the book was written in classical Chinese, showing the influence of Chinese literature, it was here framed in a Korean background.

Another author worthy of note is Ze Yim whose pen name was Beg-ho or "White Lake." He was a young genius, who died at the age of thirty-eight. He wrote many poems as a poet of nature, wandering over mountains and fields, but he also produced two stories in classical Chinese, "the Diary of Sorrowful Castles" and "the History of Flowers." In the first, he personified the five human senses and the seven feelings.

For example, "Eternity" with an old man, thus trying to express his dissatisfaction with the world. In the second, different flowers are used to symbolize various kings, and he explains his political opinions through his descriptions of their glory and decay. This type of abstract personification was something new, but it was still far from real fiction in the modern sense of the word.

There was a movement to develop again quite independently the Confucianist literature, which had been influenced by the Buddhist literature during the Goryo Dynasty, and many scholars of Chinese classics, Do-zon Zong and others, strongly criticized the Buddhist literature.

During these years, almost all of the famous Chinese works of fiction, Sam Kuo Chih Cen I, Shui Hu Chuan, Hsi Yu Chi, Chin Ping Mei and others were imported into Korea. Among the Korean scholars of Chinese classics, who had been seriously influenced by the "Chu Hsi" philosophy which had been introduced into Korea at the end of the Goryo Dynasty, there was a current of thought which condemned such literary works of emotional richness. Scholars were divided into two groups, those who insisted on the importance of theoretical or conventional philosophy and abused the flowery literature, and those who insisted on the necessity of "Belles Lettres," while agreeing somewhat to the study of philosophy.

Leaving aside these conflicts, we may not overlook artistic appreciation among the people. The great scholars, Hwang Yi (pen name Toege or "Retired Stream") and Yi Yi (pen name Yulgog or "Chestnut Valley"), became highly reputed both in philosophy and literary authorship.

OLD FICTION

Just at the time of this growing consciousness of literature within the country, there broke out two great wars, one against Japan, called the Imzin War and the other against the Manchus called the Byongza Barbarian War which were, great influences from the outside on the political and cultural lives of the Koreans.

The first was lasted for seven years, during which the country was devastated, and the people starved, but when under the command of Admiral Sun-sin Yi, they were often victorious in the sea battle and the tide turned in their favour. After the war the people took stock of themselves, and in a spirit of democracy, social reform was launched.

The other war, in which they were defeated, had also a great influence on their spiritual life. They were spurred to cultivate a nationalism, which would stand up against any difficulty in the future. Thus the national spirit of the Korean people exercised a strong influence on the development of their national literature.

Now the people looked for epoch-making novels, which should be original and nationalistic, different from the vague imitations of Chinese fictions. The war tale, the first novel written in Korean, called "the Records of Imzin" by an unknown author, described those heroes who fought in the war against Japan, but it is rather a collection of supernatural adventures, than of historic facts. Other war stories, such as "the Story of Ung Zo," "the Story of Czung-yol Yu" and "the Story of Gyong-ob Yim" were more or less imitations of Chinese war stories.

Now we come to the two most important of the earlier pioneers of Korean fictions, Gyun Ho (?-1618), whose pen name was Gyosan and who is well-known because of his masterpiece, "the Story of Gil-dong Hong" and Man-zung Gim (1637-1692, pen name Sopo or "West Port") whose reputation was won by his "the Nine Clouds Dreams."

Ho was a brave and adventurous young man interested in the reform of the social classes. He had organized a group of hundreds of his followers, including many illegitimate sons. He had planned to start riots, getting his funds by robbing property owners or starting a salt business, spreading false rumours, and offering bribes to the government troops to gain suitable opportunities for his attack. But his scheme was discovered, and he was finally executed.

Into "the Story of Gil-dong Hong" are interwoven his

own life and political ideas. According to the social customs of that time, illegitimate sons were despised, and local officials had great stores of possessions taken illegally from the people. The hero of the story, a young boy called Gil-dong Hong was the bastard son of the minister Hong; he was not allowed even to call his father "father," or his legitimately born brother "brother," and he felt this to be unjust. He made up his mind to build his career in a very different way from that followed by his family. He studied strategy, became a bandit, and organized as its leader an underground party, Hwalbin Dang or "the Saviours of the Poor." By the use of magic and strategic skill, he robbed temples and local government stores throughout the country of their property, if it seemed to have been acquired unjustly, and used it to save people from poverty. The authorities tried to arrest him, but in vain. His father and brother, who had now repented of their former ill-treatment of him, were put in prison by the government in his place. They were released on condition that they should catch Gil-dong, but they could not succeed in this. Finally, Gil-dong, out of filial feeling for his sick father, proposed to the king that he would leave Korea, provided that he were offered some provisions for his group and the title of minister. This was at once granted, and so he left Korea, sailing to the South Sea, and established a Utopia on the island of Yugdo where he ascended to the throne. Later, relations between his country and Korea were friendly. (The full translation is introduced in FOLK TALES FROM KOREA written in English by the present author.)

In every respect, this story is considered generally to be the first Korean work of fiction and so may be regarded as epoch-making. Though the tale still contained many supernatural elements in its plot, its purpose and aim were realistic, and had never before been attempted, and the descriptions themselves were most exact and vivid. It shows some influence from the Chinese work, Shui Hu Chuan, but the plot and style are full of originality, and it was written in Korean. This type of story was later imitated by unknown authors in "the Story of U-czi Zon" (also introduced in FOLK TALES FROM

KOREA) and "the Story of Hwa-dam So." In the same period, another unknown author wrote quite a different style of fiction in "the Interpretation of Heavenly King," a psychological analysis which personified human nature, but this was not a significant piece which could gain popular interest.

The second of the two pioneers whom I mentioned above, Man-zung Gim, may be defined as the successor to Gyun Ho. He was a member of the Royal Academy. His father died before he was born, and he showed great respect to his mother, who was also learned, and taught him classics. He collected old historical stories and rare books, and wrote novels. His masterpiece, "Nine Clouds Dreams," is said to have been written to soothe his mother to be read by her while he was in exile and away from her. The following is the plot of the story:

"The Buddhist saint, Yuggwan Desa who came from the west, built a cottage and preached there. The Fairy Lady Wi accompanied by angels, came from the mountain and attended his lectures. The Dragon King under the water also took part in the gathering. One day, the saint despatched his pupil Song-Zin to the Dragon King to convey his thanks, and the Fairy Lady Wi sent Eight Angels to present flowery cakes to the saint. Song-Zin and the Eight Angels fulfilled their respective duties, and happened to meet on a stone bridge on the way back, where they made some jokes about their affection for each other. Then they were cursed, sent to the Yama, and ordered to be human beings. So Song-Zin was born again as So-yu Yang and the Eight Angels eight women in different places and with different careers—lady, dancing girl, daugther, princess, assassin, maid-servant, and so on. When So-yu Yang passed the Civil Service Examination as a young man and went on in the world, he met those women one by one, got married, and lived quite happily. Sometimes the nine of them gathered and talked of the mortality of human life, wishing to have eternal life in the future. Then, a strange monk happened to come there, and as they were talking, So-yu Yang recognized the Transmigration of the Soul, and found himself standing in front of the saint, his former master. So he repented his past mistake and apologized, and at the same time the Eight Angels came over and asked for the saint's instruction. Then the saint preached the Scriptures, and Song-Zin and the eight old women were awakened, and attained the way of Nirvana, returning afterwards to Paradise."

Thus, the whole plot is based on the empty dream of human life, which should lead to eternal life. Gim's mother became a widow while quite young, lost her eldest son, and her second son, the author, became an exile. So the author wished to soothe his mother with this work, and did not entirely reject Buddhism as the orthodox scholars of the time did, but rather tried to combine in his story the three religions— Buddhism, Confucianism, and Taoism. Similar types of fiction were produced by other authors whose names are lost.

Another masterpiece of his, "the Record of the Southward Expedition of Sa-ssi" is a domestic novel:

"Sa-ssi, a virtuous and intelligent woman, had no son for nine years after her marriage, so she asked her husband, Han Im to take a concubine, Gyo-ssi. Gyo-ssi was very jealous, and plotted to bring a false charge against Sa-ssi, which resulted in Sa-ssi's being sent away by her husband who was very much under the influence of his concubine. So Sa-ssi became an exile, but she was helped by a noble lady. The plot of the concubine was disclosed, and the husband repented his mistake, discharged the cunning concubine, and welcomed back his wife, and they lived happily thereafter."

This novel is said to have been written as an advice to King Sugzong who had chased away his honest queen and adopted a court lady. He wrote these two novels in Korean to promote the Korean language, but they were later translated into classical Chinese by other authors. He was also a capable critic; he wrote about Chinese novels, and explained also why he wrote such popular stories.

Another novel, "the Records of Encouraging Good and Feeling Justice" was written in almost the same period. This is also a domestic story. It describes the tragedy of the large family system, where a husband had three wives. This is supposed to have been written by Song-gi Zo, but it is written in classical Chinese.

These years produced many scholars of Chinese classics, who wrote various works in Chinese. The two schools, those of the orthodox philosophy and of Belles Lettres, developed each quite independently, but both exerted great influence on the literary life of the Koreans. These gradually came to be criticized by another group of scholars, who had been interested in more practical studies. They found fault with the futile arguments of metaphysical philosophy and visionary writings, and consequently insisted on the realistic researches of science. Thus, Ig Yi (pen name Song-ho or "Starry Lake"), Yag-yong Zong (pen name Da-san or "Tea-Hill"), and others tried to solve many practical problems.

This tendency was intensified as a result of the importation of Western civilization into China at this time. An Italian missionary had started preaching Christianity in China, after he had met the Chinese Emperor at Peking in 1602, and had translated books on astronomy, mathematics, and measuring; so much of the new civilization of the western world was introduced. A young Korean, Sung-hun Yi who followed his father when he was sent to Peking as an envoy in 1783, met a Catholic Father there, and became a Christian. Among the books he brought back were some on Catholicism, and so the Catholic faith was introduced into Korea together with the science of the west.

At the same time, the spirit of prose called for more novels. Zi-won Bag (1737-1805, pen name Yon-am or "Sparrow Rock") who visited Peking wrote his famous diary of the trip, Yolha Ilgi, in twenty six volumes. In it, he introduced western scientific knowledge and Chinese plays. He also wrote short stories, such as "the Story of Mr. Ho," which were realistic in style and written from a democratic point of view, full of vivid irony and humour, though unfortunately written in classical Chinese.

Many long novels were written in Korean by unknown authors. The most famous one is "the Story of Spring Perfume."

"The hero of the story, Mong-yong or Dreaming Dragon, who was well born, loved a beautiful young dancing girl,

Czun-hyang or Spring Perfume at Namwon in Zonla province, and gave his pledge to set up a home for the two of them on the completion of his studies. Suddenly, however, his father was promoted to a higher official position in the capital, Seoul, and he, being still a dependent, had to go there with his father, leaving Czun-hyang behind. Now a newly-appointed magistrate, who was evil minded and amorous, tried to make love to her. But she was chaste, and never yielded to his wishes. Being rejected by a dancing girl like this, his rage knew no bounds. She was whipped and tortured, and finally cast into prison. Her mother and her maid-servant, Hyang-dan, prayed to the stars to save her life. After three years, Mong-yong completed his studies, and became a Secret Royal Commissioner. By a special order of the king, he started on a tour through the country in the disguise of a beggar to see the real condition of the people. Now, Czun-hyang's mother sent a letter to Mong-yong by his former servant, Bang-za, who had been left in Namwon. Bang-za met, on the way to Seoul, a beggar, in whom, however, he did not recognize his former master. But Mong-yong got to know from Bang-za of the outrages committed by the new magistrate, and he secretly met in prison Czun-hyang, who was then awaiting the carrying out of the death sentence on the next day by the cruel magistrate. On the following day, which was the magistrate's birthday, she was brought to the banqueting hall, where she was to be tortured for the entertainment of his guests. Mong-yong came in at the critical moment, the magistrate was driven away, and so Czun-hyang's life was saved.''

This is a vivid description of love, local government, and the people of the time. Every Korean knows the story, and yet wishes to read it repeatedly. Many imitations have been produced, and there are scores of variations. Sometimes it is produced as an opera or a play, and the theatre is always crowded.

Another love story, "the Story of Un-yong," described in Korean the tragic love between a court lady and a poet. "The Story of Spring Perfume," which I have just described, is also a tragic romance, but it shows, in the main, the daily life of the people, and had a happy ending, while "the Story of Un-yong" is based on the Court Life in the palace, and ends with the suicide of the heroine, followed by that of the hero.

In both of these novels, we find the concept of romantic love, which had never been seen in the earlier novels. This suggests the theme of the modern novel, which was to follow in the next period, though there were still more fantastic romances, such as Ognu Mong, or "the Jade-Tower Dream" and others. Some other domestic stories, dealing with the relations between step-mother and step-daughter, or between wife and concubine, were produced in the same period by unknown authors. The most typical one is "the Story of Rose and Lotus," which is based on a legend in a collection by Dong-hul Gim:

"A village headman, Mu-yong Be, had two daughters, Rose and Lotus, but his wife died of an illness. He married a second wife, who was bad tempered. This step-mother became jealous of the two girls, because she had three sons of her own. She planned a false charge of abortion against Rose, catching a big rat, skinning it, and leaving it in Rose's bed. So Rose was ordered by her father to stay with her maternal grandmother. On the way there at night, she was thrown into the lake by her step-mother's eldest son, Zang-son, who had previously been instructed to do this by his mother, unknown to their father. Suddenly a tiger sprang out, and ripped off his ear, arm, and leg. The younger sister, Lotus, was very sad when she heard of the death of Rose. She went to the lake, and plunged into its waters to join her sister. After that, people who passed by the lake heard the cries of the two sisters, and whenever a new magistrate succeeded, he was found dead the next morning, killed by the appearance of the ghosts of the two sisters. Then, a strong man, Dong-ho Zong, was despatched by the King to the country to investigate, and he could hear the complaints of the ghosts at night. The trial of the accused parents was held, and finally the plot of the step-mother was unfolded, and the innocence of the father was proved. The souls of the two sisters were born again as the two daughters of their father, who married a new, good wife, and they were later married to the twin sons of a powerful man and lived happily." (Full translation is introduced in my FOLK TALES FROM KOREA.)

Filial piety is another theme of Korean novels. There are several written by unknown authors. The most famous one is "the Story of Sim-czong" in which a filial daughter sacrifices herself by plunging into the water to cure the lost sight of her father; she meets him again afterwards, and he is able to regain his sight.

Some fairy tales and fables were also told in novel form. The famous example of the first is "the Story of the Golden Circle," which tells of a monster in a cave and a hero who saved a princess from it. "The Story of Hung-bu" is a good example of the second; it shows the extreme contrast between a greedy brother and his innocent younger brother.

Many of these novels written by unknown authors are dramatized and often produced on the stage, and the stories of "Spring Perfume," "Rose and Lotus," "Sim-czong," and "Hung-bu" are known as the four greatest classical operas in Korea.

So, the prose literature, which had been developed later than the poetical literature, now became very popular among the people.

NEW NOVELS

After Christianity was introduced to Korea, it exerted a great influence on the religious, political, and cultural life of the Koreans. Europe and America tried to make treaties, first with China and Japan, and then with Korea. Dewongun began to massacre the Catholic believers, so a French warship came to the Ganghwa Island near Seoul, and the Americans came to Pyongyang with warships. Russia tried to enter from the north, and Japan and China wished to intervene in the internal affairs of Korea.

When the Dong-hag Dang or "Eastern Doctrine Party," which stressed a religious doctrine, "Man is God" Philosophy (a mixture of elements of Shamanism, Confucianism, Buddhism, and Taoism), launched a civil war against the western influences and the domestic corruption of the government, Chinese troops were sent to Korea to suppress them at the request of the Korean government. Then Japan also sent troops to Korea to put a stop to the Chinese intervention, and so the Sino-Japanese war broke out, after which Japan got control of Korea.

These difficult experiences opened the Koreans' eyes, and they sought to establish the movement of Modern Reformation in 1894. Thus, new schools were established, slavery was abolished, and the old civil examination was replaced by a new system of official appointments. Modern newspapers (Independence News, Royal Castle News, Imperial News, etc.) and magazines (Morning Glow News, Seoul Monthly, etc.) were published by the government, the Independence Club, and others for the first time in Korea. It was a national movement towards a new civilization.

In writing, they generally adopted the fixed style of Chinese characters together with the Korean alphabet to note the grammatical structure of their language, but some used the Korean alphabet only. The New Testament was translated into Korean by two American missionaries, Dr. Underwood, and Dr. Appenzeller. Gil-zun Yu, who studied in America, published his book, "What I Saw and Heard on My Western Journy," in the Korean alphabet only, and he even strongly insisted in his preface on the necessity of writing in this way. An American, Hulbert, was of the same opinion, and he contributed some publications. The modern pioneer of Korean linguistics, Si-gyong Zu and others proceeded with their ardent research work on the Korean language, and National Readers were edited under a new scheme. Many western books were translated into Korean, such as the stories of Napoleon or Washington, or the three heroes of Italy; histories of Switzerland, Indo-China, America, Rome, and Poland, "Gulliver's Travels," "Aesop's Fables," and other novels. At the same time, various phases of western culture, education, law, economics, sociology, physics, mathematics, commerce, engineering, medical science, etc. were introduced.

Meantime, three pioneers of the modern Korean novel, In-zig Yi (pen name Gug-czo or "First Blooming of the Chrysanthemum), He-zo Yi (pen name Yol-ze or "Happy House"), and Czan-sig Czoe published their own stories.

In-zig Yi was a journalist. His first novel, "the Voice of a Ghost" was epoch-making, and had a great influence on subsequent Korean novels, because of its new plot scheme and narrative description, what we may call the technique of the modern novel. The plot is as follows:

"The magistrate of Czunczon, Sung-zi Gim, took a country girl, Gil-sun, as his concubine. As a result of his wife's jealousy he was discharged from his post, and recalled to Seoul. He left behind in the country Gil-sun, who was already pregnant. Gil-sun's father took her to Seoul, and Sung-zi Gim arranged secretly a house for her to stay, where he visited her often. But his wife found this hide-out, and planned more mischief. She plotted to kill Gil-sun and her baby through a cunning maid-servant, Zom-sun. Zom-sun was a double-crossing girl, who, while having much sympathy for Gil-sun, on the other hand expected a large sum of money from Gim's wife for doing the murdering job. So she urged her lover, Czoe, to carry out the plot, and he finally murdered Gil-sun and her baby, after enticing them to a mountain. Gil-sun's parents came up to Seoul and visited their daughter's house, but she had already disappeared, because of the assassination. The villagers informed them that she had run away with a secret lover, but they happened to overhear a talk between Zom-sun and her lover, through which they learnt that their daughter had unfortunately been killed, according to the plot of Gim's wife and Zom-sun. At this, the parents were indignant, and wished to take revenge on them, so the father chased after Zom-sun, who had escaped down to Busan and there killed her and her lover, Czoe. He came back to Seoul, and killed Gim's wife, too.

Now there was a seamstress in Gim's house who had been regarded with jealousy by Gim's wife, when Gil-sun had come up to Seoul, and had been kicked out of the house. She had had to stay temporarily in Gil-sun's house. When Gim attended there, this seamstress became his mistress, too. When Zom-sun was planning the murder, the seamstress guessed the plot, so Zom-sun tried to turn any possible blame onto this woman, who had by now moved out of the house. Gil-sun's father, misunderstanding, blamed this seamstress, and wished to kill her, too, but when he came to her house, she cleared herself of any suspicion that might have fallen on her. Here, everything was cleared up, and Gil-sun's father advised Gim to marry the seamstress instead of making the mistake of killing her. So Gim finally married her."

This novel starts suddenly with a conversation of Zom-sun with Gil-sun, and then another with her lover Czoe. The description is in the Korean vernacular style, and the plot is carried on with a psychological exactness which had never before been found in Korean novels. The new marriage between Gim and his seamstress was the new morality, which had never before been allowed by Korean customs.

The next writer, He-zo Yi, produced several novels, and introduced several foreign novels in translation.

Czan-sig Czoe wrote four novels, but his masterpiece, "the Colour of the Autumn Moon" was the most popular. The plot is as follows:

"A Korean girl student, Zong-im Yi was suddenly attacked with a dagger by a rascal in the Ueno Park, Tokyo, Japan, while she was taking a walk under the bright moon. A young man who happened to be passing by came to her rescue. The rascal ran away, and the young man was taken for him by the police who rushed to the spot and arrested him.

This girl student was the only daughter of the Chief Attendant to the Korean king, and had been engaged long ago to Yong-czang Gim, the only son of Yi's most intimate friend, but they had been parted from each other when Gim had been appointed to be Magistrate of Czosan on the northern frontier with Manchuria. No news had been heard of Gim's family since the occurrence of a riot there, so Yi could not wait longer, but tried to marry his daughter, Zong-im, to another young man. But she could never forget Yong-czang even in her dreams, and refusing her father's offer, went to Tokyo to study.

The rascal who had tried to attack Zong-im was a Korean student, Han-yong Gang, who happened to know her in Tokyo; he had made suggestions to Zong-im that night in the park and threatened her with a dagger when she refused. Fortunately, she was not seriously injured. While she was receiving medical treatment in the hospital, she happened to read the newspaper in which her accident was reported. She was surprised to learn that the name of the young man who had saved her from the rascal was given as Yong-czang Gim.

The story of Yong-czang Gim since the riot in Czosan was a miserable one. His parents had been captured by the rioters, put in a bag, and thrown into the Yalu River. He himself had been saved by an Englishman named Smith. He followed this foreigner to England, and graduated from a university there. He had then come to Japan with Smith, who had been appointed to the British Consulate in Yokohama. That night he had been taking a walk in the Ueno Park, and had been fortunate enough to save Zong-im from attack.

So Zong-im was very glad to meet her lover and savior Yong-czang once again. They returned to Korea and married. While they were travelling on their honeymoon in Manchuria, they unexpectedly met Yong-czang's parents, whom they had thought dead long ago. So both families were reunited."

This novel is full of unexpected accidents, but the new customs of one wife for one husband, studying abroad, international friendship, and so on were quite new themes. The description was also in the modern vernacular style, and more realistic than in older novels. Besides these three novelists, there were more writers, such as Sang-hyob Yi and U-bo Min and up to the Independence Movement of 1919, more than one hundred novels were published by many authors.

MODERN NOVELS

The Russo-Japanese war ended in 1905 in favour of Japan. Japan became dominant in Korea, and annexed it on August 29, 1910. The Koreans were greatly shocked by this event. When their political careers were blocked, many of the young intelligentsia took to literary careers, while, at the same time, they tried with their underground nationalism to en-lighten the people through their literary productions and artistic creations.

In 1909, Nam-son Czoe (pen name Yug-dang or "Six Houses") published a new inspiring poem, "To the Sea, to Children" in his magazine Sonyon or "the Child," which was really the start of modern poetry or free verse in Korea. Later he turned to research works on Korean history, and became one of the best Korean historians of modern times.

Next, Gwang-su Yi (pen name Czun-won or "Spring Garden") started to produce novels, and, in cooperation with Czoe, edited their literary magazine Czongczun or "the Youth" from 1914 on. All his life he devoted to writing liter-ary works—poems, novels, essays, plays, criticism, and so on. But his main work was the novel. So his strong nationalistic ideals, his continuous efforts, his leadership, and his genius earned him the title of the Father of Modern Korean Literature.

He was a patriot, at one time exiled in Shanghai, and always appealed in his novels for the solution of some prob-lems, national, social, moral, or artistic. He was an idealist. His first work was a short story, "to Young Friends" as were his next two, "Gwang-ho Yun" and "Wandering." Then followed two long novels, Muzong or "Heartlessness," which marked a new epoch, and "the Pioneer." He insisted, in the face of the traditional conventionalism, on "new love" in these works. His later famous novels are "the Revival," "Soil," "Love," "the Life of a Woman," and others, includ-ing several historical novels such as "the Story of Ho-Seng," "the Prince Maui," "the Tragic Story of Danzong," "the Death of Cza-don Yi," "Admiral Sun-sin Yi" and "the Buddhist Saint, Won-hyo." He also wrote other short stories.

When the First World War ended in 1918, the spirit of self-determination prevailed through the world. On the first of March, 1919, the thirty three representatives of the Korean patriots, led by the late Byong-hui Son proclaimed a Declaration of Independence written by Nam-son Czoe, and started a public demonstration, which was followed by a similar movement in every town throughout the country. Tens of thousands were sacrificed in these demonstrations, but it resulted in the reawakening of the nation, and so the second period of modern Korean literature was begun. The number of pupils entering the schools suddenly increased to astronomical figures, and thousands went abroad (Japan, China, U.S.A., Russia, and Europe) to study. The novelists Dong-in Gim, Yong-teg Zon (pen name Nulbom or "Late Spring"), and Yo-han Zu (pen name Song-a or "Child Singing") edited a purely literary magazine Czangzo or "Creation" in 1919. They wished to be the successors to the new literary movement which had been initiated by Nam-son Czoe and Gwang-su Yi in the preceding period.

The first three early pioneers, In-zig Yi, He-zo Yi and Czan-sig Czoe had started the production of new novels, and showed that modern literature could be developed, but they had not consciously launched as a literary movement. The next two pioneers, Nam-son Czoe and Gwang-su Yi, started together a literary movement aimed at for the national enlightenment and they appealed to the nation on the basis of their ideals for a national reformation. But the young group of "Creation" began their periodical out of more purely artistic consideration, that is to say, they were prompted by internal forces. Though national ideals gave them a certain amount of inspiration, they did not preach them subjectively. They insisted on "realism" as the best medium of description. Just as Yo-han Zu was practising free verse in poems, as the real pioneer of modern poetry, they were not interested in the reform of social customs and manners, or the principle of encouraging the good and punishing the evil, but they tried to reveal human life as it was. At the same time, they did away with the use of all obsolete particles and unfamiliar expressions, even introducing the English use of the pronouns "he" and "she" into their novels, so that they might create an up-to-date style. But of the two, Yong-teg Zon was more or less an idealist in his subject-matter, though realistic in his descriptions (selected short stories; the Spring of Life and others. Novel; the Melody of Youth), while Dong-in Gim remained a pure artist for art's sake in dealing with his subjects (selected short stories; Life, Potatoes, etc. Novels; Young Persons, the Spring at the Unhyon Palace and others).

These two artists declared themselves to be pursuing realism, but they only meant that they were more realistic than their predecessors, and were not realistic in the truest sense of the word. The true realist was Sang-sob Yom who published his "the Green Frog in the Specimen Room" in the magazine Gebyog or "the Beginning of the World" in May 1921. He refers to a naturalist, who examined a green frog in a specimen room, and so tries to describe things as they are using the scientific method. But he had in his novels a gloomy colouring, sometimes disclosing the darkness behind reality. This means that he was fond of dealing with unusual characters and melancholy environments for his subject-matter, while his descriptions and style were faithful to realism (novels; prelude to the Independence movement, Love and Sin, Three Generations, When Peonies Bloom and many short stories).

In these and the following years, many magazines and newspapers were published, and the Korean writers were already much influenced by those of Europe and America, both by direct contact with the western literary works, or through Japanese translations or Chinese publications. As a result, all sorts of literary philosophies and "—isms" were introduced into Korean literary works.

In 1920 a magazine Peho or "the Ruin," and in 1921 a magazine Zangmiczon or "the Rose Village," were published by the "decadent" group. This group mainly consisted of poets, Og Gim (pen name An-so or "the Dawn on the Bank"), the poet and novelist Zong-hwa Bag (pen name Wol-tan or "the Moon on the Shallows." Novels; the Secret Melody in the Dark Room, the Daybreak, the Nation, Gyong-

ne Hong and others. Many short stories), Sang-sun O, the late
Sog-u Hwang (pen name Sang-a Tab or "Ivory Tower"), Pal-
yang Bag (pen name Yo-su Gim). This tendency towards
decadentism was caused by the political and economic situation in the period. After the Independence Movement of 1919,
which ended in failure, the literary men of Korea pursued their
careers actively in many ways, but their physical situations
were becoming worse and worse. The more they learnt, the
more they suffered, spiritually because of their intellectual
consciousness, and physically because of their worsening
standard of living.

Next, in the literary magazine Begzo or "the White
Tide," which was first published in 1922, some writers tried to
put a brighter outlook on these pessimistic elements, but they
still showed the sentimentality of twilight, or a nostalgic longing. This soon turned into a romantic movement. They wished
to let bygones be bygones, and tried to find new "White
Tides" to save them. It was intended to be a literature of
revival, as they tried to find unknown lands of mystery and
new dreams. The members of this group were the above-
mentioned Wol-tan, the late Sa-yong Hong (pen name No-zag
or "Dew Sparrow"), who also wrote a play about Buddha,
and the late poet Sang-hwa Yi and others, but the typical
novelist of the group was the late Do-hyang Na or "Rice
Perfume." He suggested the necessity of dreaming and the
vagabond's life in his novels "the Season of Youth" and other
stories. "Would That There Be No Keeping upon Embracing a
Star?" and "the Past Dreams Were Pale" were full of senti-
mentalism and mystery. Another novelist, better known as a
critic, was Yong-hui Bag (pen name Hoe-wol or "Thinking of
the Moon." Short stories; a Hound and others), and an
essayist, the late Za-yong No (pen name Czun-song or "the
Spring Castle") produced many belles lettres of this school.

But in September 1923, the critic and novelist Gi-zin
Gim (pen name Pal-bong or "Eight Peaks") threw out a
challenge against this romanticism with his humanistic or neo-
idealistic point of view, insisting on a literature for life (short
stories; Red Mouse and others). He wished to kick the ghosts

out from literature, and tried to build up the art of force. In cooperation with the above-mentioned Yong-hui Bag, he initiated New Tendency Literature, the socialistic literature in Korea.

During these years of decadentism and romanticism, the naturalism which had already been given a start was still being practiced by the realists, whom I mentioned above, Dong-in Gim, Yong-teg Zon, Sang-sob Yom, and the brilliant writer of short stories, the late Zin-gon Hyon (pen name Bing-ho or "Emptiness." Novel; the Equator, short stories; the Profile of Korea), etc. The last two writers were the most faithful to realism. So their novels enjoyed great success in 1924 and 1925. On the other hand, the literary magazine, Zoson Mundan or "Korean Literary Circle," which started in September, 1924, under the supervision of the "Boss" of contemporary Korean literature, Gwang-su Yi, and the editorship of a popular novelist, In-gon Bang (pen name Czun-he or "Spring Sea." Novels; the Incense Light of the Magic Metropolis, the Wandering Singer, etc., and short stories), produced many new novelists, such as the socialists, the late Hag-song Czoe (pen name So-he or "the Sea of Dawn." Short stories; Blood Stain, etc.) and Sol-ya Han (novels; the Dusk, etc., and many short stories), a woman novelist Hwa-song Bag (novels; a White Flower, etc., and short stories), and realists, the late Man-sig Czoe (novels; the Muddy Stream, etc., short stories and plays), Sang-dog Czoe (pen name Dog-gyon or "Lonely Cuckoo." Novels; the Lament in the Temple Room, etc., and short stories), Yo-sob Zu (novel; Trying to Grasp the Cloud, and short stories), and others.

These novelists all followed realism in their descriptions, but some of them ran to radical socialism for their subject-matter or ideology, and usually wrote of hunger or poverty. Then, in 1925, these socialists, the above-mentioned Gi-zin Gim and Yong-hui Bag, and the late Ig-sang Yi (pen name Song-he or "Starry Sea." Novels; Fury, etc., and short stories), Yong Song (novel; Before This Spring Goes and short stories and plays), and others organized the Alliance of Korean Proletarian Art in cooperation with the poets, the late Hwa

Yim, Hwan Gwon, Zog-gu Yu, and Czang-sul Gim, the novel-
ists, Gi-yong Yi (pen name Min-czon or "People's Village."
Novels; the Native Place, etc., and short stories), the late
Myong-hui Zo (pen name Po-sog or "Embracing Stones."
Short stories; River Nagdong, etc.), Nam-czon Gim (novel; the
Big River, and short stories), Hung-ob Im (short stories; How
the Watch-Dog Escaped, etc.), Bug-myong Yi (short stories;
the Nitrogenous Manure Factory, etc.), and a critic Gi-zong
Yun tended towards communistic literature, insisting on the
class-war, and denying the value of the other schools.

Now there were serious arguments between the "class-
literature" group, and all the other "non-class" writers
headed by the eldest novelist, Gwang-su Yi. Among the latter,
Dong-in Gim and Sang-sob Yom, the poet and critic Zu-dong
Yang (pen name Mue, or "the Endless"), the critic No-pung
Zong, the poet of the modern epic "the Night at the Border,"
Dong-hwan Gim (pen name Pain or "the Banana Man"), the
poets of Sizo, Un Zo, Un-sang Yi (pen name No-san or
"Heron Mountain"), Byong-gi Yi (pen name Garam or "the
Lake") and dozens of others strongly opposed to the literature
of class-hatred.

The Society for Research in Foreign Literature, which
started the movement for translating literature at home and
abroad conducting academic research into literatures of other
countries in 1926, and its associate, the Society for Research in
Dramatic Art, which was established in 1931, joined together
the arguments on the side of Democratic Nationalism or
Liberalism. Their members overlapped, historian Son-gun Yi
(pen name Su-sog or "Water with Stones"), essayist Zin-sob
Gim (pen name Czong-czon or "Listening to the River"),
poets, Ha-yun Yi (pen name Yon-po or "Lotus Garden") and
the late Yong-czol Bag, the late novelist De-hun Ham (pen
name Il-bo or "One Step." Novels; the Night before the
Typhoon, the Straits of Pure Love, etc., and short stories),
playwright Czi-zin Yu, producer Hang-sog So, critics, Hon-gu
Yi (pen name So-czon or "Night Spring"), U-song Son, and
Hui-sun Zo, a poetess, Yun-sug Mo (pen name Yong-un or
"Hill Cloud"), the critics and poets, Gwang-sob Gim (pen

name I-san or "Gratified Mountain") and In-sob Zong, the present author (pen name Nun-sol or "Snow Pine"), and others contributed much to the appreciation of foreign literature and dramatic art through their pens and on the stages as the Overseas Literature Group.

Another group of the Pure Art School, called the Nine Persons' Society, headed by novelists, Te-zun Yi (pen name Sang-ho or "Still Empty." Novels; the Flourishing of Youth, etc., selected short stories; the Broker, etc.), Te-won Bag (novels; a Day of Novelist Mr. Gu-bo, etc., and short stories), and Hoe-nam An (short stories; Smoke, the Devil, etc.), and the poets, Zi-yong Zong and the late Sang-yong Gim (pen name Wol-pa or "the Waves of the Moon), strongly criticized the left-wing literature through their magazine Munzang or "Style" for a few years from August 1933.

There were intellectual novelists Zin-o Yu (short stories; a Woman Worker, etc.) and the late Ho-sog Yi (short stories; the Sea Near Russia, etc.), a peasant novelist, Mu-yong Yi (novels; at the Daybreak, etc., and short stories), a socialist, Hyo-min Hong (novel; the Reformation of King Inzo, and short stories), humanistic novelists, Mu-gil Zon (short stories; Endless Love, etc.), In-teg Han (novel; the Age of Whirlwind, and short stories), and Yong-man Zo (short stories; a Job-Hunter at the Year's End, etc.), woman novelists, Zong-hui Czoe (short stories; the Unlucky House, etc.), Dog-zo Zang (short stories; Lullaby, etc.), Son-hui Yi (novel; the Woman's Command, and short stories), Gyong-e Gang (novel; the Problem of Humanity, and short stories), Sin-e Beg (short stories; Mother, etc.), Mal-bong Gim (novels; the Wild Rose, etc.), and the late Gye-wol Song, as well as critics, Ham-gwang An, Czol Beg, Ze-so Czoe, and Won-zo Yi. Generally speaking, these novelists and critics followed the road of neutrality or sympathizers. Far from such tumults of literary arguments, a surrealistic novelist, the late Sang Yi (short stories; the Wings, etc.) wrote his psychological stories and poems. The late Hun Sim and Sog-hun Yi tried novels for the enlightenment of rural life with "the Evergreen Trees" and "the Song of Twilight" respectively. One of the longest works of fiction,

Go-zong Yim, was written by Myong-hui Hong starting from 1928 for some years until 1936.

Among those novelists who made their debuts after 1935, Myong-ig Czoe (short stories; the Rainy Road, etc.), In-teg Zong (short stories; Labyrinth, etc.), and Zun Ho (short stories; the Diary of a Gold Night, etc.) were psychologists. Gu Hong (short stories; the Procession of Carts, etc.), Dong-gyu Yi (short stories; Nervous Debility, etc.), and In-hui Bang (short stories; the New Road, etc.) were ironical, witty liberalists; Yong-mug Gye (short stories; the Pack Horse Driver, etc.), No-gab Bag (short stories; the Wife, etc.), the late Yu-zong Gim (short stories; the Shower, etc.), In-he Sog (short stories; Sorrows of the Sea, etc.), and Gwang-zu Gim (short stories; a Bad Night, etc.) were humanistic, and Bong-gu Yi (short stories; an Elegy of Myong-dong, etc.), Dong-su An (short stories; the Street of Illusion, etc.), Zu-hong Yi (short stories; Wanmun Shop, etc.), and Bong-mun Zi (short stories; the Woman of Northern Country, etc.) practiced with modified ideas along the socialist's line, while Yong-zun Bag (novels; a Model Tiller, etc., and short stories), Gun-yong Yi (short stories; a Barber, etc.), and In-zun Czoe (short stories; an Ox, etc.) inspired farmers. Gyong-zun Hyon (short stories; the Sun of Heart, etc.), So-yob Gim (short stories; the Deserted Village, etc.), and Dong-yon Hyon (short stories; Ginsen, etc.) evidenced their socialistic attitudes. Dong-nyi Gim (novels; the Descendants of Hwarang, etc., short stories; the Sketch of a Witch, etc.), Song Gim (short stories; If the Moon Rises, etc.), and Bi-sog Zong (novels; Ethics of Youth, etc., and short stories) were promising writers. Ne-song Gim (detective stories; a Magician, etc.), started detective stories from 1937 and still maintains the best reputation among the readers of this genre. Yong-hul Gang who lives in U.S.A. had produced earlier an autobiographical novel in English called "Grass Roof," and others. Hyo-zu Zang and Sa-ryang Gim earned some repute in Japan for their short stories written in Japanese.

During these years, the Korean Philological Society and the Korean Phonetic Association, on many committees of which the present author served, contributed much to the unification of Korean spelling, with the cooperation of all authors, regardless of their sects or ideologies, and developed the use of the Korean language under the new scheme for their authorship, and eventually Chinese characters disappeared from novels and stories.

Thus their writing flourished until there occurred the Manchurian War in 1937, soon followed by the serious conflict between China and Japan, which finally led to the Pacific War between America and Japan in conjunction with the Second World War. During this, Koreans were obliged, even ordered, to write in favour of Japan, but they could not produce masterpieces along this line. Some went underground, while others pretended to write. However, more novelists made debuts even under such circumstances and could produce some literary works of their own. Among them were Dog Hyon (short stories; a Tortoise etc.), Yong-su Gim (short stories; the Snow-Cold Diary, etc.), Te-ung Czoe (short stories; Spring, etc.), Yong-sog Gim (short stories; Brothers, etc.), Ha-sin Gwag (short stories; Paradise Lost, etc.), Gye-zu Bag (novels; the Festival of Blood, etc., and short stories), Su-gil An (short stories; the Thin Green Chrysanthemum, etc.), Sun-won Hwang (selected short stories), So-ha Im (short stories; an Ox, etc.), and others. Woman novelists, Og-in Im (short stories; Lonely Shadow, etc.), and Ha-ryon Zi (short stories; Parting, etc.) also produced some favourite pieces.

AFTER THE SECOND WORLD WAR

After the liberation on August 15th, 1945, all the literary intellectuals seemed to be united into one, and they started a strong national movement with their pens, celebrating the independence of Korea. But soon they found the unexpected barrier of the thirty-eighth parallel dividing Korea, and two extremely different ideologies manoeuvering continuously under the influence of the international conflict. In south Korea writers were divided essentially into two camps, the Korean Writers' Association organized on the 13th of March, 1946 (later changed to the Republic of Korea Writers' Association which was the nationalist group, headed by Zong-hwa Bag, Hon-gu Yi and the poet Zi-hun Zo) and the Korean Literary Men's Alliance established on the 13th of Dec. 1945 which was the communist group, headed by Te-zun Yi, Zi-yong Zong and the late Hwa Yim. During the period of the U.S. Military Government, there were many arguments between the two groups, but by the time when the Korean government was established through the general election in the south (May 10, 1948), authors, as the people in general, had made their choice of location, moving or escaping to and fro across the line, though not quite freely.

North Korea is now behind the Iron Curtain, and no literary news is available from there, but in the south, all sorts of literary activities are being carried on, and more emphasis is made on the aspiration of national spirit, patriotism, and the thirst for the unification of Fatherland. There are several organizations for members of the literary profession; the above-mentioned ROK Writers' Association, the ROK Young Literary Men's Association which was initiated by the novelist Dong-nyi Gim, the critic Yon-hyon Zo and others, the ROK War-Correspondent Authors' Group (organized during the recent Korean War), headed by Gi-zin Gim and others. The Korean Center of the P.E.N. Club was established on the 3rd of Oct. 1954, and three representatives, Yong-no Byon (poet and president), Yun-sug Mo, the above-mentioned poetess (vice-president), and Gwang-sob Gim also above-mentioned joined its international meeting held at Wien, Austria, in June, 1955. In Sept. 1957, the present author succeeded its presidency, and led the Korean delegates to the 29th congress held in Tokyo, Japan. He made a lecture there on "The Influence of Western Literature in Korea" and invited 13 foreign writers to Korea.

Shortly before the recent Korean War, many new novelists made their debuts through dozens of daily newspapers and many magazines, as well as various publications; Zu-hyon Yu (short stories; Various Figures, etc.), Yong-gu Bag (short stories; Castle Czilzung, etc.), Gu-bom Hong (short

stories; a Father and His Son, etc.), No-hyang Gang (short
stories; Time and Tide, etc.), Yon-hui Bag (short stories;
Women, etc.), Song-pyo Yi (short stories; Groping, etc.), Yo-
an Czoe (short stories; the Village without a Doctor, etc.), as
well as the woman novelists, So-hui Son (short stories;
Upstream against the Stream, etc.), and Gum-sug Yun (short
stories; the Unfortunates, etc.).

Authors young and old composed many new patriotic
poems, plays, essays, as well as novels about the gallant Allied
Forces at the front and the people behind it, and also the
sorrows caused by the division of the country, and the villages
and towns deserted as a result of the recent bloody war which
suddenly began on that Sunday, 25th, June, 1950. The above-
mentioned novelist and playwright Yong-su Gim wrote a war-
correspondent's novel, "Seoul Once Red" in which he described vividly the horrible experiences of a woman in the
deserted Seoul during the second evacuation of the city in
1951. The Free Literature Prizes of 1954 were awarded to two
novelists; Su-gil An for his collected short stories, "the Third
Human Type" which dealt with bankrupt intellectuals who
evacuated from Seoul to Busan during the war and were engaged temporarily in miscellaneous jobs, and Sun-won Hwang
for his novelette, "the Descendants of Cain" which described
the members of a family and others in North Korea under the
new ideological regime, who carried out strategic divorces and
marriages without regard to social caste for the purposes of
maintaining their former properties. The same prizes were also
offered to two collected poems; "Pearl Harbour" of Dong-
myong Gim and "the Lyrical Exile" of Dong-zib Sin.

Among the new faces during the recent war and the
present armistice, Yi-sog Gim (short stories; the Lost Epi-
taph, etc.), Gi-hwan Bang (short stories; Destruction, etc.),
Gun-be So (short stories; Various Figures, etc.) are to be
noticed for their new subject matter. Soon after this new
cynicism modified by nihilism is often found in the works of
several young novelists. Czang-sob Son described the
abnormal sexualism of a prisoner in his short story "the
Human Animal," Han-sug Zong in his short story "a Cat's

Eyes and a Cat's Mind" dealt with psycho-analysis of a man's suspicion of his wife; Hag-song Gwag tried to visualize a graduate from a university, who degenerated and plunged himself into a group of beggars whom he preferred to the corrupt public life, in his short story, "a Shooting-Star," and Sang-won O gives us an example of political neuralgia of a young man in his "Crack." And Gwang-yong Zon warns in his short story "the Picture of Garbage Cans" the people of Korea not to lose their national pride by hunting food in the dust-bins of alien's troops. He does not preach, but describes the life of poor people near the front. These novelists indicate some of the sentiments which can be found among the people who are still suffering from the unsettled condition of the armistice.

It should be noticed that there have been some efforts among the writers to translate Korean stories and novels into English for the purpose of introducing their literature to westerners. Yong-te Byon brought out two publications after World War II, "Tales from Korea" and "Poems from Korea"; Ze-hong Sim printed his modified version of the old Korean novel, "the Story of Czun-hyang," mentioned above, under the title of "Spring Perfume"; Yong-no Byon published "Korean Odyssey" and others. The present author issued "an Anthology of Modern Poems in Korea" in 1948 and his "Folk Tales from Korea," which contains some old novels, was printed in England and America in 1952, and his translation of twenty modern short stories from twenty contemporary novelists, "Modern Short Stories from Korea," was brought out in Korea in 1958. "Korean Lore" and "Korea, Her History and Culture," published in 1953 and 1954 respectively by the Office of Public Information, Republic of Korea, and dozens of English publications including the ·periodical "Korean Survey" issued by Korean Pacific Press in U.S.A. are to be recommended to the readers who intend to get some background knowledge on Korean stories.

Korean Drama

MASK PLAYS

The Koreans have practised the art of drama since the very earliest days, and it seems that they must have used masks in their performances, but detailed accounts of theatrical performances in the histories appear only from the time of Three Kingdoms onwards, especially in the Kingdom of Sinla (57 B.C.-935), where the mask plays were greatly developed.

The mask plays of the Sinla Dynasty may be divided into three types, the sword dances, the five styles, and the Czo-yong dances. The typical sword dance is based on the story of Gwan-czang. Gwan-czang was a young general, fifteen years of age, the son of a Sinla general, Pum-il, and a hero of the famous Sinla ethic of art and chivalry for youths, the Hwarang-do. As second-in-command, he took part in a counterattack, together with his Chinese allies, on the neighbouring Kingdom of Begze (18 B.C.-660), and in the course of this, was killed by the enemy general, Gye-beg, and his head was sent home on a horse. His father held up the head, dripping with blood, and said that he was pleased with the loyalty his son had shown to the king. The details were later altered in the story, so that Gwan-czang became Hwang-czang, aged six instead of fifteen. A mask of his face was made, and used by the Sinla people in sword dances to soothe the spirit of the dead. This sword dancing is still performed on the stage by the classical dancers of Korea.

The five styles dance is mentioned by the famous Korean scholar Czi-won Czoe, who lived during the Sinla Dynasty, in

his poetry written at the end of the ninth century, and is included in the historical records of the Three Kingdoms, a
work of one of the earliest Korean historians, Bu-sig Gim
(1075-1151). The five styles are called Gumhwan, Wolzon,
Demyon, Sogdog, and Sanye.

The last of these, the Sanye, was the origin of the lion
dance, which is still performed in many parts of the country.
In the district of Bugczong county, in south Hamgyong province, the peasants put on masks of lions, tigers, and wolves,
and dance round the villages, begging for rice or money, on
the fifteenth day of the first month of the year, to the accompaniment of musical instruments. What they collect is used to
provide for the various public occasions and services, such as
marriages, funerals, memorial services, or the rebuilding of a
river bank after a flood.

Lastly there is the famous Czoyong dance. The origins of
this dance are recorded in the famous Korean history, Samgug
Yusa, "the Surviving Records of the Three Kingdoms," the
work of the Buddhist monk, Il-yon (1206-1289). According to
this account, the forty-ninth king of Sinla, Hon-gang (875-885
A.D.) went out one day on a picnic to the port of Geun (now
called Ulsan), but a thick fog came up, and the company lost
their way when they were returning by the seashore. The king
asked the court diviner to find out the cause of the fog, and
was told that the dragon of the east sea was responsible. He
therefore immediately ordered his men to erect a temple to
honour the dragon, and, as soon as the order had been issued,
the fog dispersed. Then the dragon came to the king with his
seven children, and thanked him for his kindness with singing
and dancing. One of the dragon's children, Czoyong, followed the king to his palace, and was later given a high post
in the administration. He married a very beautiful girl, but the
spirit of smallpox was jealous of her beauty, and, taking on
human form, got into the wife's room. Czoyong came back late
one moonlit night and found two people in his wife's room.
He did not get angry at all, but withdrew singing and dancing.
This so moved the spirit that it appeared before Czoyong,
knelt down and apologized. In consideration of his brave

generosity, it would never enter a house if it saw a picture of Czoyong there. So, from that time on, it became the custom to put a portrait of Czoyong on the threshold of every house, to keep out the spirit of smallpox and other evil spirits.

This was a Shamanistic belief, perhaps connected with the belief in the gate spirit of earlier ages, but now it was modified by elements of Buddhism and later developed into the mask dance of Czoyong, which continued to be performed through the following dynasties of Goryo (918-1392) and Yi (1392-1910). It was during the Yi Dynasty that it developed most, and, after many reforms, it was adopted as the court dance. Five masks, coloured blue, red, yellow, black, and white were used; the performers were six child-dancers, sixteen other dancing girls, and thirty seven musicians to accompany them, and the setting was a stage decorated with many flowers, including the lotus, one lantern, and white cranes.

In the early days of the Goryo Dynasty there was a mask play called Nanye, which used to be performed by custom on the last night of the year, with horrifying masks, to exorcise all the evil spirits of the year, and to welcome the new year. This performance originated in China and is known to have existed in the Chou Dynasty, but it is not known when it was introduced into Korea. However, by the middle of Goryo Dynasty, it had developed into the mask play known as the Sande play, which was sometimes mixed with the Czoyong dance described above.

During the Yi Dynasty, the Sande play developed into the typical Korean mask play under the name of the Sande-Dogam play. It was performed, for instance, when envoys came from China, a temporary stage being erected at the gate of Seoul to welcome the visitors. A special government official was appointed to supervise this dramatic performance reception. The name Dogam means, in Korean, "general director," and so Sande-Dogam play is the Sande play sponsored by the government, though it was performed elsewhere, and by other people than the official performers.

This play was a combining of all the mask plays of the past. Unlike the Nanye, which was performed in the palace once a year for the purpose of exorcism, the Sande-Dogam play was performed anywhere else but the palace, and at any time of the year, though sometimes elements of the Nanye or of the Czoyong dance were included in it, perhaps with purpose of warding all evil spirits off the foreign envoy, and ensuring that he reach Seoul as safely as possible. This was shown for the purpose of the performance given under King Sezong, the fourth king of the Yi Dynasty.

The Sande-Dogam play had twelve scenes. It starts with the service for feeding the evil spirits and ends with the witches' prayer, but the twelve scenes between this prologue and epilogue are quite independent, and we may suppose that the play was not a new creation, composed all at one time, but rather a composition of elements taken from earlier mask dances, an interweaving of elements from several periods.

In the first scene, two old priests, two young witches called lotus leaf and winking eye, an old man, and an old woman worship the gods with sacrifices of a cow's head or a pig's leg or the like, and of wine and fruit as well. In the second scene a young priest appears, bowing in prayer to god and dancing. In the third scene itch abuses him, and they both do a dance. In the fourth scene a monk and the itch have a quarrel though with many jokes, and do another dance. In scene five, lotus leaf and winking eye, who are both dumb throughout the whole of the play, do a humorous act to frighten off the priest and itch, and then dance together. In scene six, eight monks sing folk songs, and one of them, called Wan-bo, takes severely to task the degenerate monks, and calls on them to devote themselves to Buddhist prayers, but they will not take his advice. Here a Monk appeals to Wan-bo to save his son, grandson, and great-grandson, who have come to see the Sande mask play, and who are suffering from an attack of indigestion so bad that they can hardly breathe. Wan-bo sings "the Seagull's Words" and "the Backbone Melody," but fails to cure them. So the doctor, Zu-bu Sin, comes in to cure them by acupuncture, and upon their recovery all dance merrily together. In scene seven, a romping girl and a whore dance together. A monk, Top Hat, tries to tempt the whore, through the romping girl, with money, and the three of them dine together at a table, drinking and dancing. The monk then seizes a drum from the whore, and he and Wan-bo play around, making jokes at each other. In the eighth scene, itch and the monk are frightened by the sight of the old priest, and jump back from him. Wan-bo scolds the old priest for rambling out of the mountain temple, but the old priest takes no notice of him and walks steps to itch. Wan-bo, in co-operation with the other priests, reviles the old priest, who, however, just walks around with drunken gait, accompanied by two young witches. In scene nine, a servant Malddugi (meaning "stake") enters carrying a monkey on his back, and selling women's shoes. The old priest tries to buy some shoes for the young witches who are attending him, but he will not pay in cash. Malddugi gives up selling shoes, and gets the monkey to bring away one of the young witches for him. However, when he discovers that the monkey has committed adultery with the young witch, he goes back. In scene ten, the old priest appears with the young witches. Drunkenness insults the old priest harshly, and they quarrel, rivals in love. The old priest and one young witch are chased away, but drunkenness and the other young witch remain, and act out a love affair. The young witch becomes pregnant, and gives birth to a boy, who cries for milk, but his witch-mother will take no heed of him. Drunkenness also treats the baby roughly, and makes a great noise. In scene eleven, an old gentleman, the elder master and the younger master walk around accompanied by their servant, Malddugi, but lose their way in the evening twilight, and try to find lodgings. Malddugi happens to meet a friend of his, Soeddugi who fixes up the three gentlemen with a pigsty for a hotel. When he greets the gentlemen with insulting words, the old gentleman catches his own servant, Malddugi, and beats him instead of Soeddugi, who is forgiven. Malddugi promises a bribe of 19 *yang* 9 *zon* 9 *pun,* and so is spared further beating. Now all exit, except the old gentleman, his concubine, the young witch, and a young police marshal. When the old gentleman tries to have fun dancing with the young witch, the police marshal tries to stop him, at which the old gentleman gets angry and tells the police marshal off, but no one will listen to him, and the young witch herself prefers the police marshal to him. Much disappointed, he too exits, leaving the young witch behind. In the final scene, the old man comes in with the old woman, and suggests to her that they should now separate since they are already too old, and when he also suggests that it is time for her to die, she does so. Malddugi brings in his sister, the romping girl, and they lament the death of their mother, the old woman who has just died. The play ends with the witch singing prayers for the dead.

In short, the play starts with a religious service, then proceeds to criticize the corrupt priests and the *yangban* or gentlemen, and ends with the mortality of human beings and prayers for the dead. The religious service, which forms a prologue, serves the purpose of ensuring the safety of the particular theatrical performance. The next part, the criticism of corruption among priests, is not intended as an attack on Buddhism itself, but is a blow at such corrupt priests as Sin-don, Bo-u and Zi-zog who broke the commandments, and were the cause of much trouble in the royal family, or amongst the nation as a whole. For this reason the play had a great appeal both to those who were pro-Buddhist and those who were anti-Buddhist. When we consider the criticisms directed at the gentlemen, we must remember that the audiences for these plays were, for the most part, common folk, who would find fault with the class of so-called "gentlemen," the most influential section of society, who took every position of advantage whether of rank or of wealth, however unqualified they might be in character or intelligence. This last feature, then, gave the play great popularity, appealing as it did to the daily complaints of the majority of people.

Altogether twenty eight masks are used in the play, and one puppet. The masks were made of paper, wood, or gourd, and usually covered the whole face. Sometimes hair would be added, the nose turned up, or the open eyes be made to blink and roll the eyeballs, to suit the particular case. The plays were performed on temporary stages, or in the open fields, and no scenery or curtains were used, the scenes being separated only by short intervals. On the left side of the stage was a clothes box where costumes and masks could be changed. Usually there would be a six-piece band, consisting of drums, harps, and flutes, but three or five players only could be used. The most commonly used music for accompaniment is the dance-tunes known as Semaczi-taryong.

The actors and actresses may originally have been wizards and witches, but later ordinary people took part, and were known as Gwangde meaning "puppet players." On the whole they had a poor standard of living, but sometimes they were invited to the royal palace, or to some rich man's house to give a performance, and they were supported by grants from the government, from temples, or from hotels when they performed for a visiting foreign envoy. The government issued them special permits, stamped with a cicada in spring, and with a tiger when they went on tour round the country. In the twelfth year of King Inzo, 1634, the official status of the play was abolished, and its performance opened to all.

Some of the players, who were thus deprived of their livelihood, formed unofficial groups called Sadang-pe and may be termed vagabond-players, men and women who gave continuous performances of singing and dancing, sometimes acting bits of mask plays, or puppet plays here and there about the country like gypsies or wandering prostitutes.

Besides the Sande play which I have just been describing, there are two other schools of mask play, O-Gwangde or "the Five Buffoonery Plays," which originated in the country of Czoge in south Gyongsang province and its offshoot, Yayu or "the Outdoor Play," which flourished in the districts of Busan and Dongne.

The story goes that there was once a flood in the country of Czogye, and the villagers in the lower part of the country found a wooden box floating on the waters containing many masks and a strange book. Subsequently there occurred many disasters, which could not be prevented whatever method was tried, until finally they performed plays with masks from the box, according to the suggestions in the book. Then the villagers spread far the knowledge of these plays.

The number of masks used in the five buffoonery plays, or its derived form, the outdoor play, is about twenty but the number varies a little from district to district. Most of them represent human faces, but some are those of deities, or of animals such as lions, tigers, or dogs. The plot of the play is quite different from that of the last discussed, but its main points are humorous contrasts between the gentlemen and the common people, domestic love conflicts and criticisms of corrupt Buddhistic priests.

So the mask plays spread gradually to many provinces, and Bong-san and Sariwon in Hwanghe province, Bugczong in south Hamgyong province, Gesong and Yangzu in Gyonggi province, Andong in north Gyongsang province and Tong-yong and Dongne in south Gyongsang province have been famous as places for their performances. The dates and seasons for the performance vary according to district, some taking place in December or January, and some in May.

PUPPET PLAYS

Another type of old Korean play is the puppet play. There are two kinds, called Ggogdu-Gagsi, or Czom-zi Bag and Mansog-Zung.

In the Goguryo Dynasty (37 B.C.-668), according to the historical records, some Korean shrines used wooden dolls as idols in their worshipping, and later on a Chinese soldier who fought in Korea is said to have presented to his Emperor some Korean puppets of the Goryo Dynasty when he returned to China. These puppets spread to the neighbouring kingdoms, Begze and Sinla, and continued down into the Yi Dynasty. However, the Korean puppet play is thought by some historians to have had its origin in the Indian puppet plays as transmitted through and modified in China, and later to have been introduced into Japan, where it has continued to flourish until the present day.

The two Korean names for the puppets are, as we have

said, Ggogdu-Gagsi and Czom-zi Bag. Ggogdu is thought to be the Korean pronunciation of the Chinese word for "puppet," and Gagsi is a Korean word meaning a young married woman, so Ggogdu-Gagsi means "a puppet woman." "Bag" can mean "a gourd," or "wooden," and "Czom-zi" is a common title given to an old commoner, so that Czom-zi Bag means "a wooden man." These two names designate the two main characters for puppet plays, the third character being Dong-zi Hong, a man, naked and coloured all red. Any of these three names will indicate "puppet play" to a Korean.

Altogether, there are thirteen human puppets, and three animals, and they are usually from one to three feet in height. The play is coloured by Buddhist sentiments, and the main plot is comic in treatment, consisting again of criticisms of the gentlemen, corrupt priests, and government officials, with a domestic tragedy cleverly interwoven. The play is performed in the same way as a western puppet play, usually to the accompaniment of music, and with the words spoken through a bamboo tube. It was usually given in a temporary open-air theatre which was screened off by a white tent, on one side of which the stage was set up. Three sides of the stage were also screened with white cloths hanging from poles at the four corners. The stage was in two stories, the puppet play taking place in the upper part, and the manipulators being hidden in the lower while they used the fingers, spoke the words, and sang to the accompaniment of the band in front of the stage. The audience used to sit to right and left facing the stage and the band. With this style of performance the players used to go on tour, as did the mask players described earlier.

The other type of Korean puppet play, the Mansog-Zung, was performed on the Buddha's birthday, the eighth day of the fourth month by the lunar calendar. This is a silent play, where the players manipulate the puppets from a hidden position to the accompaniment of music, and, though no words are spoken, the audience can understand everything. There are five puppets used in this play, namely Mansog-Zung, a deer, a horned deer, a carp, and a dragon. The hero, Mansog-Zung, a man-puppet, represents a priest. When the strings attached to the body, arms, and legs are pulled, the arms can be made to strike the breast, and the legs to kick the head, and, since the head is made out of a gourd, and the body and limbs of wood, the puppet resounds continuously throughout the play. The deer and the horned deer, which are made of wood board, are made to fight on the right hand side of the stage by the pulling of one string which is attached to them both. The dragon and carp are both made of paper, and seem to be moving continuously. There is a lantern hanging over them, which swings to the left of Mansog-Zung. This dumb play is usually performed in the corner of a fence, or sometimes in the open market place at the same time as the Ggogdu-Gagsi described above.

Even to this day, the custom of hanging lanterns up on the eighth day of the fourth month by the lunar calendar is still preserved. In the Goryo Dynasty this festival was held in January, when everybody put on new clothes, and, after attending the temples by day, enjoyed the lantern festival at night, sometimes with the puppet entertainment as well. The lantern light symbolizes the virtue of Buddha, and Mansog-Zung is related to "the Lantern Light Buddha." Originally the puppet may have been a fixed statue of Buddha, but later modifications have led to the drama as we see it today.

There are two legends concerning the origin of the Mansog-Zung of this play, both tracing him back to historical priests. One was a priest of the Goryo Dynasty called Man-Sog, and the other another priest of the same dynasty called Zizog-Sonsa who had almost become a living Buddha as a result of his thirty years of facing walls, that is to say, devout prayer, and often secured an offering of *man* (ten thousand) *sog* (a *sog* equals to five bushels) from his followers until he was corrupted by the attractions of a rare beauty, Zin-i Hwang, the most famous dancing girl of the time. Zung simply means a Buddhistic priest.

These mask and puppet plays are the earlier drama-forms of Korea, and those who played in them were all called Gwangde, and used to tour everywhere. Another group of players did not use masks or puppets, but only sang songs, and were from time to time invited to sing in the palace, or for birthdays or marriages, or in processions held to celebrate distinctions gained in the Civil Examinations. In modern times, the name Gwangde came to be applied only to these singers and circus men, and not as originally to the performers in mask and puppet plays.

OLD PLAYS

Later, in the time of King Sunzo, a man called Owi-zang Sin (born 1812, in Goczang in Zonla province) composed some epic songs in operatic form, such as the songs of Czun-hyang and Simczong, and the rabbit melody. Since his time the Gwangde group of singers have sung these new dramatic songs, using simple gestures but having no theatre and no scenery on their stage. This was the beginning of the Gugug or "Old Play," or "Classical Play."

For about a hundred years this new style—the old play—continued without theatres, but in the year of Gwangmu the national theatre in Seoul, the Wongag-Sa, was built and managed under the control of In-zig Yi, a novelist, being supported by the palace office. The building was in the style of the Roman theatre, and could hold an audience of two thousand. The site is today occupied by a Presbyterian church called Semunan.

In this theatre were produced shows of singing and dancing by the official dancing girls, as well as comic stories or nonsense dialogues and the old plays like "the Story of Czun-hyang," "the Story of Simczong," etc., but the style of presentation was still primitive with a simple white back-cloth and little equipment on the stage.

At about the same time, a dramatic group called the Hyoblyul-Sa toured the country, performing semi-legendary tales, circuses, mask plays, and classical music, but it ceased in 1914.

In 1912, Sung-pil Bag built a theatre called Gwangmu-De in Seoul, where he produced classical music, circuses,

singing and the old plays—"the Story of Czun-hyang," "the
Story of Hung-bu," and others—for quite a long time. A
dramatic group called Gwangwol-Dan was organized on July
12th 1828, in which the actors Myong-og Yim and his brother
had great reputations, but the theatre was unfortunately
burned down in 1930. However, in the same year a new
theatre called Minado-Zwa was built near site of an old
theatre, the Gwonsang-Zang, and at first new plays were
produced there, but from October 3rd it was turned into an old
plays theatre, and from then on the performances consisted of.
the priests' dances, sword dances, classical music and other
songs, and also the old plays. Dong-beg Yi, the famous singer,
Miss Og-hui Gim and Ze-dog Go, the musician, earned great
reputations there. On November 2nd the same year it was
turned into an ordinary cinema.

Three other theatres, the Zoson-Gugzang, the Dansong-
Sa and the Umi-Gwan often gave recitals by dancing girls and
performances of the old plays. The Korean melody association, established in 1930, often performed old plays in the
Zoson-Gugzang in November, and the opera singers Czang-
hwan Gim, Dong-beg Yi, and Man-gag Song, and the dancing
girl singers Nog-zu Bag, Hwa-zung-son Yi, and Czu-wol Gim
were all the rage.

NEW STYLE PLAYS

In 1909 In-zig Yi, one of the pioneers of the modern
novel, produced his new plays, Solzung-me or "the Plum in
the Snow," and also Un Segye or "the Silvery World," both
in the Wongag-Sa, mentioned above, and this was the first
time the voice of the new play was heard. In 1911 Song-gu
Yim organized a theatrical group called the Hyogsin-Dan or
the Reform Party, together with his actor-colleagues Do-san
Gim, So-rang Gim, Song-hyon Yang, Yong-gu Yim, and
others, and the performances they gave in the Osong-Zwa and
later in the Dansong-Sa included "the Law of Laws," "the
Murder of the Sworn Brother," and "the Pistol-Robber."

These were called Sinpa Yongug or New Style Drama.

In 1931 a playwright, Beg-nam Yun, who had studied the new drama in Japan, took over the Wongag-Sa, a theatre mentioned above, and, organizing a group of actors by the name of Munsu-Song, produced "Buryogwi," "Zanghan Mong" or "Deep Sorrow Dream," "My Sin," and other plays. Gi-se Yi organized a group called Yuil-Dan or the Only Party, and produced plays in the Yonhung-Sa. The two groups just mentioned, the Munsu-Song and the Yuil-Dan, amalgamated under the name of Yesong-Zwa, or the Art-Star Troupe, performed Sang-ognu, or "Double Jade Tears," Tolstoy's "Resurrection," "the Lighthouse-Keeper," and other plays, but it was soon dissolved. There were many more such groups of actors, such as Gi-se Yi's Munye-Dan or the Literary Party, Do-san Gim's Singug-Zwa or the New Play Seats, and So-rang Gim's Czwisong-Zwa or the Gathered Stars Company, but except the Czwisong-Zwa these did not last long.

In 1921 the Korean students in Tokyo organized the dramatic art association, and toured throughout Korea. Producers He-song Hong and Su-san Gim, and authors Po-sog Zo, He-song Ma, and Czun-sob Yu were the leading members of this group. The plays they performed were "the Death of Yong-il Gim" and "the Last Handshaking." Though this organization, too, did not last long, it had a great influence on the new movement in Korea.

In 1922 Beg-nam Yun, mentioned above, organized the Minzung-Gugdan, or the Popular Drama Party, together with Zong-hwa An, Hyo-zin Na, Su-il Mun, Wol-hwa Yi, and others, and their productions included "Fate" and the "Eternal Wife." In the same year, Gi-se Yi organized the Yesul-Hyobhoe or the Art Association, which performed "the Tears of Hope." Both these groups, however, were dissolved after they made a tour of the country. When the Zoson-Gugzang was built, Beg-nam Yun formed the Manpa-Hoe or the Ten Thousand Waves Society, and, in co-operation with all actors of the time, he performed Victor Hugo's "Les Miserable," and "Louis the Sixteenth" and other plays, but the society was soon dissolved.

It will have been seen that there were many attempts by many groups for the new plays, but a higher standard of artistic achievement was reached by the theatrical organization known as the Towol-Hoe or the Earth and Moon Society, which was started in 1922 by producer, Sung-hui Bag, critic Gi-zin Gim, painter Bog-zin Gim, and journalists, So-gu Yi and Ul-han Gim, who had all studied in Tokyo. They gave their second performance during the summer vacation at the Zoson-Gugzang, and were later joined by painters, Sog-zu An and U-zon Won, producer Hag-nyon Yon, actors Beg-su Yi and So-yon Yi, actresses Wol-hwa Yi and Hye-gyong Yi, composers Se-min Bag, Ho-yong Czoe and Ze-yu Hong, among many others. Their repertory was "Bear," "How Did the Man Lie to the Woman?", "Love and Death," "Heidelberg," and "Susanna," including several European plays. Their artistic merits made them quite a sensation everywhere. They ran the Gwangmu-De theatre, and were joined by the famous actress Sim-dog Yun. They gave eighty seven performances altogether, but gradually lost their great reputation.

In 1923 Zong-hwan Bang, the best story-teller, organized a society for protection of childhood, called Segdong-Hoe, and edited a monthly magazine for children, Orini, and thereby initiated theatrical performances by or for children through the playwrights among his colleagues, Han-sung Go and In-sob Zong (the present author).

In 1929 a group called the Sanyuhwa-Hoe or the Mountain with Flower's Society produced Hyangto-Sim or "the Heart of One's Native Soil," written by No-zag Hong and in the same year they formed the association for the synthetic arts and the Hwazo-Hoe or the Fire Birds Society, but neither of these lasted for any length of time. The Czwisong-Zwa, mentioned above, however, was able to last through the thirteen epoch-making years among these organizations, during which time they were usually on tour. Their repertory included "the Eternal Wife," "the Buried Love," "Picture Postcard," "Wife," "the Love at the Pole," "Tears," "Wandering Men and Women," "Paradise Island," "Katyusha," "the Border,"

"Jean Valjean," "the Sick" and "One Night at the Hot Spring," but unfortunately it was dissolved in December of 1929.

The Towol-Hoe, a group described above, started operating again in November of 1929 in conjunction with a cinema in the Zoson-Gugzang. Its plays this time included "Fifteen Minutes," "a Joyous Life," "the Crescent Moon," "Sacrifice," "Fate," "the Street of Nangkin," "the Daughter of a Principal" and "Monday." Once, in 1932, it had the cooperation of the female stage dancer, Sung-hui Czoe, and later changed its name to the Teyang or the Sun.

Other short-lived groups of the time were Yongug-Sa or the Drama Research House, founded in the latter part of 1929, the Yongug-Sizang or the Drama Market in 1931, and the Dezung-Gugzang or the Popular Theatre, the Segug-Sa or the World Drama Company, and the Czonsa-Zwa or the Angle Theatre which were also founded in 1931. There were an opera-group, the Venus Opera Party which gave a few performances between 1929 and 1931, and the Minado Theatre which produced some social dramas at home and abroad.

He-song Hong, who had won a reputation as an actor in the Little Theatre at Tsukiji in Tokyo, returned to Korea in 1929, and organized the Sinhung-Gugzang or the Newly Risen Theatre which performed a Korean version of the Chinese story, "the Story of the Peony-Lantern," on November 11, 1930.

In December, 1930, the broadcasting drama association was formed by Sung-hui Yi and Yong-pal Gim and broadcasted some radio dramas. The famous humorist, Bul-czul Sin, produced comedies through his New Stage and Czon-hui Gang organized Zung-Oe Theatre in the same year.

NEW DRAMA

In June 1931 the actor He-song Hong and the playwright Czi-zin Yu organized the drama-cinema club and held an exhibition of drama and cinema for the first time in Korea.

Later in July they established the society for research in
dramatic art in co-operation with Beg-nam Yun, Hang-sog
So, Hon-gu Yi, De-hun Ham, Ha-yun Yi, Zin-sob Gim,
Gwang-sob Gim, Hui-sun Zo, Miss Yun-sug Mo and In-sob
Zong, the present author, through which they started to train
actors in an academy with lecture courses and in its Silhom-
Mude or the Experimental Stage, which, from 1932 onwards,
produced many European plays, such as "the Inspector" by
Gogol, "the Cherry-Garden" by Chekhov, "the Doll's
House" by Ibsen, 'the Lover" by Irving, "the Prison Gate"
by Lady Gregory, "the Sea War" by Goring, and Shakespeare's "Merchant of Venice" as well as Korean plays, mostly
those of Czi-zin Yu, such as Tomag or "a Thatched Hut,"
etc. This society made a great contribution to the dramatic
movement in Korea, because of the academic research and the
devoted efforts of its members, and it has maintained its
leadership in dramatic art ever since. Its members were scholars
of foreign literature, and they were criticized in some quarters
for the exotic nature of their pursuits, but the achievements of
pedantry and experiment were necessary to bring about the
enlightenment of Korean dramatic culture and to raise our
theatre to its modern level. This was called the Singug-Undong
or the Movement of New Drama.

Besides this direct work, the society inspired college
students with an interest in dramatic art, and, as a result,
Yonhui college gave performances under the sponsorship of
the present author who held a professorship there, of Tolstoy's
"the Power of Darkness," Ibsen's "the Lady of the Sea,"
Dunsany's "the Tents of Arabia," and Galsworthy's "Justice"
among others; Ihwa women's college gave some English plays;
the Zongsin girls' school gave Capek's "the Life of the Insects,"
the Severance medical college gave Shakespeare's "the Merchant
of Venice." "The Broken Bell," "the Wolf-Man" and "the
Scarecrow," all written by the present author, were given in
Seoul Kindergarten normal school and Behwa girls' high
school. Sunday schools had also their own performances.

Operetta and short plays were also produced by professional bodies such as the Samczon Gagug-Dan or the Three

Rivers Operetta Troupe, the X-Cinema Dramatic Dept., the Eastern Art Troupe and the Brother's Company. Most of the members of these were actresses, the most popular ones being Gyong-hui Zon, Hodosi Gim, Alice Yi, Gyong-sol Yi, Un-bong Sin, Pum-sim Na, Gye-sun Zi and Og Zon. There was also the Gu-za Be dancing party which produced operettas and short plays.

Another type of play which gradually appeared on the stage was the socialistic or communistic drama. Theatrical companies which performed this type of play were the street theatre formed in Degu in November, 1930, the people's theatre in Gesong in March, 1931, the drama factory in Hezu in the spring of 1931, the moving little theatre in the autumn of 1931, and the modern theatre in June, 1932, both in Seoul, the Dramatic Art Company in Masan in July of the same year, the New Creation in Seoul in September, the North East Theatre in Hamhung and the Tomorrow Theatre in Pyong-yang. Some years later the above-mentioned "Society for Re-search in Dramatic Art" regrouped under the name of Gugyon-Zwa or the Drama Research Company and applied western dramatic art to the performance of new plays written by native playwrights. There were two more influential groups, the Nangman-Zwa or the Romantic Company and the Zungang Mude or the Central Stage. Thus by 1940 about one hundred organizations which have commercial performances came to exist in addition to the three just mentioned.

After the war broke out between Japan and China, play and dramatic movements were tightly controlled by the Dra-matic Association of Korea which was organized in Dec. 1940 under the sponsorship of the Japanese government. The newly organized dramatic club, the Hyonde Gugzang or the Modern Theatre, which was practically the successor to the above-mentioned Dramatic Research Company, was managed by playwright and producer, Czi-zin Yu, critic and novelist, De-hun Ham, and producer Yong-sob Zu. The neutral groups, the Gugdan Gohyob or the Gohyob Dramatic Party, the Gugdan Arang or the Arang Theatre were associated with the playwrights Yong-ho Bag, Son-gyu Yim, Te-zin Gim and

Yong Song and a producer, Yong-il An. In July, 1942 the said
association was replaced by the Association of Dramatic
Culture which was also government-sponsored embracing
sixteen dramatic groups and eleven musical organizations
under its supervision through its annual dramatic contest. In
addition to these three groups, five more dramatic circles
joined in the contest. They were the Czongczun-Zwa or the
Youth Troupe, the Gugdan Song-Gun or the Dramatic Company Star-Group, the Yewon-Zwa or the Art-Garden Troupe,
the Hwanggum-Zwa or the Golden Troupe and the Gugdan
Teyang or the Sun Dramatic Party. Besides the above-mentioned playwrights, Hang-sog So, Se-dog Ham, and So-gu Yi
were known also as playwrights, and actors, Yong Sim, Il-song
So, Czol Hwang, and Hag Bag and actresses, Son-czo Gim,
Yang-czun Gim, Gyong-e Yu were highly reputed among
others. The contest was held at Bumin-Gwan or the Citizen's
Hall, Seoul, but the normal performances were usually given
at other theatres, most of musical plays at the Myongczi-Zwa,
the Yagczo-Gugzang, and the Hwanggum-Zwa. But the little
theatre, the Dong-yang Gugzang or the Oriental Theatre
devoted itself to the dramatic performances, being supported
by the above-mentioned the Youth Troupe and the Dramatic
Party Star-Group. Many of these groups went on tours throughout the country to give local performances. In spite of the
various difficulties they encountered at that time they succeeded
in polishing their dramatic talents and in stimulating organizations interest in drama for the people.

AFTER THE WAR

     After the Second World War, the big theatres were given
to the Koreans to control, but, for a while, dramatic performances did not flourish, partly because people's energies were
devoted so largely to the political activities, a privilege which
had been denied them, and also because it was difficult for
them to raise the funds to maintain successfully both the
buildings and the personnel at the same time. However, they

soon made a start on classical and modern drama and operetta. On the whole, introduction of historical plays enjoyed a remarkable success because of the interest aroused by the liberation in the stories of our ancestors who had fought for their country. Some playwrights, actors and actresses moved to North Korea, but many remained in the south, and are engaged in dramatic movements. The most significant figure among these is Czi-zin Yu, playwright and producer. The central government sponsored a national theatre and set up a committee to maintain and control the former Bumin-Gwan, the largest theatre in Seoul, which was designated as a national theatre. Yu and his colleague Hang-sog So formed a dramatic group to perform plays there. At the same time, the committee established an examination board for all who appear on the stage, including singers and stage-dancers.

In 1948 the students of the dramatic club of the Central university, Seoul, performed Shakespeare's "Hamlet" for the first time in Korea under the supervision of the present author who was then in charge of the Law and Art Dept. It was shown to the public at the Gugze-Gugzang or the International Theatre, formerly called Myongczi-Zwa, for three nights, together with an exhibition on Elizabethan drama in the gallery there. It was quite sensational. Soon after this a woman producer, No-gyong Bag, organized the Women's Theatre with her female colleagues, the poetess Yun-sug Mo and others, and well-known plays were performed solely by its woman members; Shakespeare's "Othello," Ibsen's "Doll's House," and others. In 1949 several colleges in Seoul participated in a dramatic contest which was held under the auspices of the above-mentioned committee led by Czi-zin Yu. The National university presented Shakespeare's "Merchant of Venice," the Goryo university Pirandello's play, and the Central university Synge's "Shadow of the Glen," and so on. The contest was held at the International Theatre and attracted the most crowded audiences of the post war period.

Some of Czi-zin Yu's plays were performed by his own dramatic group at the citizen's hall. "Sul-lang Won" and others were rewarded with the expected warm response. Since the recent Korean War the biggest hall has been used as the national assembly hall. But in spite of the damage to personnel and theatres, interest in drama seems to be still flourishing, for Koreans are fond of dramatic entertainment. Yong-su Gim, Yong-zin O, Zin-su Gim, U-czon Zin, and others are also known as playwrights.

Classical operas are still performed by *giseng* (the traditional "dancing girls") and *myongczang* or "famous singers," and by classical musicians. The classical music of the old palace, "a-ag," is still flourishing independently. Operetta is also quite popular among the people, and students now enjoy their dramatic performances, but, as everywhere else in the world, cinema, generally speaking, attracts larger audiences than drama.

Mask plays and puppet plays are often performed on special occasions such as local festivals, sometimes accompanied by folk music and folk dances in country districts. Occasionally there are also displays of dancing groups, circuses, or musical gatherings, specially arranged.

Korean Humor in Literature

The coming Congress of the International P.E.N. Club in Seoul is the second gathering of poets, playwrights, essayists, editors and novelists from all corners of the world in the Far East. Several hundred delegates from abroad and home will be here to discuss common themes.

The main theme of this Seoul congress is "Humor in Literature—East and West." But this does not necessarily mean only the examination of the difference of humor existing between hemispheres. Basically, we must admit that humor has universal traits which are derived from features of human behavior and psychology, expressed in witty style or ironical ways, tinted with jokes, satire or cynicism.

Technically, humor embodies and expresses, through simile, metaphor and symbolism, the surprise, distortion, incongruity, impropriety or exaggeration present in a situation or character.

Trying to define humor, however, is like trying to explain sex. Everyone has his own ideas on the subject. A joke may be one man's meat, but another man's poison. What sounds hilarious to one person may evoke nothing more than a polite chuckle from another. Sometimes a joke may appear to be trivial and nonsensical, yet it may express a profound truth. From this point of view humor is a very personal thing.

However, between these two extremes of humor—universal and personal—there is a third dimension, which is regional. This particular humor is deeply rooted in the minds, feelings, sentiments and traditions of people in specific areas.

It is sometimes almost impossible for people who are foreign to a certain region to understand its humor, and attempts by

aliens to interpret the various shades of meaning of humor embedded in the literature of another nation frequently fail. Cor-
rectly comprehended, however, humor in national literature
contributes to the understanding of other nations and represents a universal bond.

Now I will try to project the characteristics of Korean
humor, but complete coverage of all aspects of its diachronic
developments or its synchronic varieties is practically impossible.

Korean humor has many modes, origins and shifting
styles—witty riddles, twisted epigrams, proverbs of folly, sug-
gestive fables, funny stories, ironical ballads, nonsensical tales,
comic dialogues, sarcastic cartoons and so on. Every province
or period has its own variety, which suited the taste, attitudes,
moods and needs of the people at a given time.

It consists largely of topical, social and political satire on
Korean life. The late Dr. H.H. Underwood, born in Korea,
who spoke Korean as fluently as a native, stated that "No
other nation so much enjoys jokes and humor in their daily
life as Koreans do." Koreans are genuinely fond of laughing
about and among themselves. The explanation for this may be
geopolitical.

As one of the tribal groups of the Ural-Altaic language
family, the people of Korea were originally nursed in Shamanistic beliefs embedded in the vast continental plain of
Manchuria, but later confined to the mountainous Korean
peninsula which stretches to the south. Their views on life
were based on animism, human unity with nature and pantheistic Democracy.

But ever since the advent of the mythical founder and
first King of Korea, "Dan-gun," royal rulers have demanded
obedience and patience from their subjects. For example the
first phase of Korean history also imposed bashfulness and
shyness as well as chastity upon women as characteristics of
Korean womanhood.

According to legend, Hwan-ung, son of the Heavenly
King, descended to Mt. Tebeg in Korea and established a
Sacred City. Nearby, a bear and a tiger (both female) were
living in a big cave under a sandalwood tree. They ardently

desired to become human beings. The Heavenly Prince, while giving them twenty cloves of garlic and a bundle of mugwort, said to them: "Eat these and confine yourselves deep inside your cave for one hundred days and you will become human."

The bear and tiger entered the cave as instructed. The bear patiently endured weariness and hunger and after twenty-one days became a beautiful woman. The tiger, however, ran away, because she could not tolerate the long days of solitude in the cave.

Overjoyed the woman prayed that she might become the mother of a child. Her ardent wish was heard, and before long she became the queen and gave birth to a prince who was given the royal name of Dan-gun, or Sandalwood King.

The impatient tigeress, upon fleeing the caves, joined the God of the Mountain, "Sansin." Today they are worshipped by women in small Mountain-God pavilions erected in the corners of the gardens of Buddhist temples.

They pray to the images of the Mountain-God and the tiger beside him and worship both as symbols of supernatural beings and eternal life. These women, dissatisfied with the world, bring sacrifices to the altar of this duo of strange savageness.

Pious women of today also worship the personified images of "Seven Stars" at another small Buddhist temple pavilions.

Buddhism which spread to Korea from India by way of China long ago accepted these two Shamanistic symbols of Korean folk worship. Recent attempts by Buddhist organizations to eliminate these two Shamanistic pavilions, which are alien to Indian Buddhist philosophy, were in vain.

The strong influence of Buddhism strengthened the existing rules of obedience and patience through the theory of life cycles in which "good shall be rewarded and evil punished." While most of the classical literature tried to uphold this moral system, the orally-transmitted folk literature tended to ridicule the superficiality of these ethics as practiced in everyday life.

The two typical forms of early dramatic expression, the Korean puppet plays and the mask plays, for instance, humorously and satirically portray, among other things, corrupt Buddhist priests and government officials.

The actors were predominantly common folk, who found fault in society's most influential class which monopolized rank and wealth, regardless of qualification and in spite of lack of character or intelligence.

Later, Confucianism found its way from China into Korea and became a powerful influence. It established five ethical rules of stoic flavor; loyalty to the king, fidelity to parents, chastity of women, seniority and friendship. A great part of Sino-Korean literature and pedantic academism upheld the superiority of these five principles. Each of these doctrines indicated the existence of a differentiated social order. For example, women were considered inferior to men.

But many humorous folk tales illustrate the popular resistance against the pressure exerted by these stringent rules. This resistance was also evident in—for instance—the following humorous story of "Lazy Bones":

"There once was a man who was too lazy even to feed himself, and so his wife had to put food into his mouth with a spoon and chopsticks. One day she had to go away on a short visit. She cooked rice cakes and hung them on a string around his neck. "Those are for you to eat when you are hungry," she said. Then she left. Upon returning a few days later, she found her husband starving to death, with the cakes still hanging round his neck. He had been too lazy to lift his hand and put them in his mouth."

On the island of Cheju, for instance, many wives labor day after days as divers in the sea or workers in the field, while their husbands stay at home caring for the babies. Korean humor freely deals with the inferior social status of women.

"There once were three sisters. The oldest one refused to undress on her wedding night because she felt too bashful. The bridegroom thought she disliked him and got up and left the house, never to return.

When the second girl married, she remembered her sister's failure. So, on her wedding night she went to her husband naked, carrying her clothes under her arm. He was astonished that she behaved in such a strange manner, and he too left, never to return.

The third sister was very worried after these two failures, and on her wedding night she stood at the door of the bedroom and asked her husband: 'Shall I come in dressed as I am, or must I undress first and come in naked?' Her husband was so embarrassed by her strange question that, like the others, he too got up and left."

The rule of man's superiority led to the admission and sanction of the concubine, another target of Korean humor.

"Long long ago, an old man had a young concubine. He let her noticed the disappearance of the white hair and guessed that he was keeping a mistress. To prove his innocence, he asked his wife to pull some of the remaining dark hair. However, in her jealousy she pulled it all the hair out, so that he might no longer be attractive to his mistress."

Besides this humor, fiction and novels of old times were strongly motivated by satire interwoven with humorous scenes. The famous love story of Chun-hyang or Spring Fragrance, the story of a filial girl, Simczong, the adventure story of the Korean Robin Hood, Gil-dong Hong, the ironical story of good-natured Hung-bu and his older brother, greedy Nol-bu, the tale of a mischievous stepmother and her stepdaughters, Rose and Lotus, "the Liver of a Rabbit"; and others are good examples to prove the satire in Korean literature.

We have another variety of popular fiction filled with laughter. The story of Mr. Ho, the tale of Bijang Be, the story of *yangban* and others are well-known for their cynicism, ridiculing the follies of the so-called noble classes.

Among the modern Korean novelists who attempt humor, we should mention Zin-gon Hyon, the author of "Love Letters and the Dormitory Inspector." This modern short story deals with a female superintendent of a girls' boarding school who is very severe with her girls and thwarts all their attempts to find love. Late at night the girls find the superintendent reading the love letters she has confiscated from the students. She reads them aloud in a man's voice accepting the compliments and the confessions of love, and then answers the letters in her own gasping voice.

Another modern short story, "Penance," by the late woman writer Mal-bong Gim describes a husband who hides himself in a small closet in his mistress' house while his wife is there on an unexpected visit. The man is torn between leaving the closet and possibly losing his mistress and keeping his wife by staying in the cramped painful place where he can hardly breathe or endure the bitter attack by insects.

Those interested in the pursuit of Korean humor might also refer to the author's publications. "Folk Tales From Korea," "Modern Short Stories From Korea," "Plays From Korea," and "A Pageant of Korean Poetry."

When speaking of Korean humor, we must also consider the Korean poetry, called *Sizo,* which contain much naive and simple Korean humor. Here are a few examples:

> Holding a stick in one hand
>   And the thorns in the other,
> I tried to block the road of age with thorns
>   And beat away my white hair with the stick;
> But my white hair, taking precautions,
>   Pushed through a short-cut way.
>
> —by Tag U

> Candle light in the room!
>   Whom did you send away?
> Outwardly you shed tears
>   Not knowing that your heart is burning.
> The candle light, just like us,
>   Forgets that its wick is burning!
>
> —by Ge Yi

> Planning for ten years
>   A thatched cottage I built.
> Fresh air occupies one half
>   And the moon the other.

No room, however, for mountains and rivers
Which should surround it together.

—by Sun Song

The earliest poetry—of more than 1,000 years ago—called native songs of the Sinla Dynasty, showed primitive humor.

THE SONG OF CZO-YONG

Under the bright moon of the capital
I amused myself till late at night;
I came home to go to my bed.
Four legs were in there!
Two of them belong to me,
But whose are the others?
Mine I possessed before,
But they have been stolen now!

Humor is also often moulded into Korean folk songs. The second verse of the earliest folk song of the Goryo Dynasty (about 900 years ago), *"The Steamed Bun Shop"* goes like this:

When I went to the shop
    to buy steamed buns,
The old Mongolian shopkeeper
    took me by the wrist;
Inside and outside of the shop
    the rumor had spread
That there were
    four little clowns there!

Dorodungsong darirodiro darirodiro,
Darirogodiro daroro daroro.
    I would even go to sleep in his bed!
Wi wi darorogodiro daroro
    So tempting was that.

Many of our modern folk songs are full of humor and delicacy.

NILNIRI

You lay down and I too lay down;
Who will put out the light over there?
Why did you come?
Oh, why did you come?
You make me happy,
And then you leave again.

Nilniriya nilniriya,
Ninanonaniga I'm going back!

ARIRANG

Arirang arirang arariyo,
Arirang hill-pass I am crossing now.
If you run away leaving me behind
Your feet will get hurt within two miles.

The famous Korean troubadour Saggad Gim left us many improvised verses full of nonsense, irony, satire, jokes, etc.

Modern Korean poetry, however, is more intellectual in expressing poetical sentiment, sometimes reaching the level of modern complexity.

Here are some examples:

INVERSE PROPORTION

Is your voice silence?
If so, your unsung sorrow
   I do clearly hear—
Your voice is silence!

Is your face darkness?
If so, with closed eyes

Your face I do clearly see.
Your face is darkness.

Is your shadow brightness?
If so and when you are gone,
   at the dark window
Your shadow shines,...
Your shadow is brightness.

—by Yong-un Han

Now I should like to quote two verses (5th and 6th) from my own poem *"Mountain Climbing"*—a criticism of corrupt society.

Whose play is this? All the mountain is ablaze,
No flame is seen, but all is wrapped in smoky haze,
On the fire-signal mountain the castle ruins sigh
As a calf to its mother will make plaintive cry.
Although no pheasant in this forest flies.
A sound like gun shot is heard to rise.
Who in secret hunts beneath these summer skies?
From the widow's house there comes a laughing sound,
And the village clock which lacks a long hand goes
   around.

Credulous traveler, over this pass go not!
The village beyond the mount is a deserted spot.
"Czun-hyang" has hanged herself with a long swing rope,
"Bbengdog's Mother" wanders, cheating, with no
   hope,
Honorable Virgil in Hell's fiery blast
His walking stick away has cast,
And now eats candy whenever it is passed,
Oh, Hamlet! Your skull-philosophy to a museum
   bequeath,
And dip your sword into the cup of death.

"An Ode to White Flowers" by Yong-sang Yi gives one example of Korean War poems in which white flowers represent Korea, a pure and genuine nation.

It hailed a few days ago,
And the weather is the same today!
On the hill the season is busy bearing flowers!

The fresh green is overflowing,
The scene is bright.
Blooming in the sea of the red blood of fallen soldiers,
Why are the flowers so white?

On every peak,
In every valley,
The flowers in full bloom seem to be sad,
The tearful battalion commander
Kept silent.
Indeed!
Why are the flowers so white,
Blooming from roots dyed with blood?

My Chief Priest has run away to town,
I, though full of youth, have shaved my hair.

In the temple whose color was spoiled by bullets
Only the brass bells remained hanging under the eaves;
On the stone steps of the temple
I begin to smoke.
And white are also the flowers.
The clouds floating in the sky are white.
In the afternoon at the fighting front
All is quiet for a moment.
Indeed!
Why are the flowers so white
Blooming out of roots dyed with blood?

The sad humor of *"I am Not a Leper"* by Ha-un Han is

self-explanatory:

My father is a leper.
My mother is a leper.
I am the child of lepers.
But yet I am not a leper.

I am a life born of love,
Yet the flowers and butterflies
Between the sky and the earth
Cheated the sun and stars.

The people who feel pity over my life
Call me a leper who is human.

I have no family tree.
I try to understand in vain why.
Being a normal person
I am also a miserable man.

I am not a leper.
I am in fact a normal person, not a leper.

Another target of Korean humor is people who believe in the importance of the astrological animals assigned to their year of birth. There are twelve such signs. For example, a girl born in the year of the tiger finds it very hard to get along, because her character is comparable to that of a fierce tiger and she is said to be unsuitable for a good, gentle wife or mother.

1970 is referred to as the year of the dog. A humorous Korean myth explains why a dog lifts up one hind leg while relieving himself. When God created the world, he gave four legs to the kettle and three to the dog. The dog, however, complained, because the kettle can stand on three legs, whereas it is hard for him to move around on only three legs.

God heard the complaint, plucked off one leg of the kettle and gave it to the dog. The dog was greatly honored by this act and has ever after lifted up the holy leg so that it may not be spoiled while he relieves himself. This story is full of true Korean flavor, and yet it is one that can be universally understood.

In Korea, some people eat dog meat soup in the summer. A Korean student who had recently arrived in the United States was very anxious to do the same there. One day he found a can in a food store and cooked the meat in his kitchen. It tasted so good that he told a senior Korean student that Koreans and Americans had the same habit of eating dogs.

Not believing this, he was invited to the home of the junior student house who wanted to cook soup from the same can for him. The senior, however, spotting the can in the kitchen and seeing the picture of a dog and the label "dog food" began to laugh. He explained to the junior that this was not the meat of dogs but rather for dogs. The source of humor was the language barrier.

I will now tell a story as an example of the humor that has only regional appeal:

Before Columbus discovered America, a group of Chinese businessmen sailed to the shore of the American continent. Much to their disappointment, they found the natives, the American Indians, half-naked. At the sight of this, the Chinese businessmen turned back home immediately, because they realized at once that setting up laundry business would be a losing venture.

In the United States the audience usually breaks into laughter when they hear this story. In Korea nobody laughs at all because Korean women wash clothes themselves and no Chinese laundries exist. In the United States this business is almost entirely in Chinese hands.

I sometimes interpret that Christian story of "Paradise Lost" in a humorous sense when acting as chairman at Korean wedding ceremonies. Eve is blamed for her mortal sin of tasting the fruit from the forbidden tree, but I wonder where Adam was when she was tempted by the serpent. If he had been on the spot, his wife Eve might never have been tempted by evil. So Adam should be responsible for the lost paradise, because he had left her alone.

On the other hand, Eve also is responsible because Adam might not have left her, if she had been technically attractive enough to him. Thus both Eve and Adam must be responsible for the lost paradise.

This may be a synthetic illustration of myth as a source of humor which is neither regional, universal, nor personal. The essence of this humor, however, is understood by everybody acquainted with the original version.

During the Japanese occupation Korean writers were watched carefully by censors of the Japanese government. They often utilized humor in their sheltered hermitage to get around the tough censorship. Particularly the oppressed people of Korea tried to ease the feeling of external inferiority forced upon them and to preserve their national pride by means of humorous inspirations.

Thus in their daily life a great number of new jokes and humorous tales were created, the meaning of which was camouflaged by twisted interpretations.

Besides these categorical interpretations of humor, in Korea some personal names derived from the Sino-Korean calligraphy of animal status are the targets of humor. Greetings with pretended seniority, laughs at sexual analogies and other secret languages are also to be included in the list of Korean humor.

With the advent of movies, newspapers, radios and television Korean humor found new sources and additional ways of expression. In fact, humor and comedy have profited from the development of the mass media.

For the Korean public, they will get some information on the essence of foreign humor, and there are possibilities for our comedians and humorists in these new media to spread Korean humor in its national character and to interpret humor of universal, personal, regional, and synthetic nature for their readers or listeners.

While the creative sources of humor in the world, regardless of their origin, are practically unlimited, it seems to me that the way of expression has its limits. This applies especially to humor in literature and humor publicly expressed to an audience.

The main obstacle to free expression to my mind is a political one. Depending on the degree of totalitarianism of governments, humor in literature may arouse affirmative acceptance or may be interpreted as negative forgiveness.

Cynical criticism of a totalitarian policy is a most dangerous risk or an outright threat to its existence. On the other hand, the paradoxical catch phrases of totalitarian states can also represent a steady source of humorous amusement in freer countries. "Power is Justice," "War is Peace," or "Freedom is Slavery." George Orwell sketched these aspects in his memorable book "1984."

The humor is nourishment as well as inspiration for both spiritual and physical relaxation. The free people do not deny it in any form or shape and do not regard it as destructive to democratic ideology.

The humor of free Korea, I hope, will contribute its share to world literature as well as to the understanding of the people of this country. I hope that the delegates from all countries realize that the humor of the free world, by its very nature and uncensored means of expression, contributes to world peace.

May the discussion of the theme, "Humor in Literature— East and West," be fruitful and constructive!

March 20, 1970

Korean Literature During the 1960's

The history of modern Korean literature dates back to 1908 when one of its two pioneers, Nam-son Czoe, published in his magazine Sonyon or "Boys" his poem "To the Sea, to the Boy," the first vernacular poem in modern style. The 60th anniversary was held in 1968. It can be regarded as the biggest literary event of the last decade. The Korean Writers Society celebrated the anniversary with a number of colorful events, such as the symposium of writers, seminars for poets, recitals of poems, exhibitions of poems, theatrical performances and others, including various essays as well as criticisms in newspapers and magazines on historical evaluation of modern Korean literature. The important problem of the exclusive use of *Hangul,* the Korean alphabet, in literary works was also discussed and its immediate use was advocated by some poets and writers including myself. The anniversary brought an account of modern Korean literature throughout the past sixty years and raised new hopes and expectations for the 1970's.

The Korean War (1950-1953) was the most tragic event in the history of Korea after World War II and its direct influences on Korean literature extended to the middle of 1960. Inspite of numerous literary works on the war the expectation that great realistic war stories might be moulded into Korean literature was not fully realized. During the aftermath of this historical struggle the life of artistic intellectuals as well as the sentiments of the people in general were actually in chaos. There was not enough time and energy for reflection on their experiences and for their objective presentation or even to contemplate the future in proper perspective. In addition they had continuous political and social turbulences imposed on them from the very beginning of the 1960's. There was the Student Uprising in April 1960 which caused the downfall of Syngman Rhee's regime in the same year. After a few months, government by the Opposition Party the Military Revolution in May of the following year secured the rule of the military junta for three years. These three significant events in addition to the war-destructions encountered by the people prevented the birth of distinguished and important specific literature. The literary circle reacted to the Student Uprising with excitement, but spiritually did not regard the event enthusiastically as a citizens' revolution. Some were satisfied with simply writing epitaphs on the monuments of those who sacrificed their lives and passed through the years of exultations caused by the tumultuous development of the society.

However, in the latter part of the 1960's the so-called "April 19 Literary Generation" represented by participants of the uprising as Sung-og Gim, Czong-zun Yi and Te-sun Bag produced some memorable works different from those of the established writers. Sung-og Gim made his debut with his short story "Exercise of Life" where he presented the problems of the poor and tragic life of citizens. He also won the Literary Award in commemoration of the late senior novelist Dong-in Gim with his work "Winter in Seoul 1964." A young writer Czong-zun Yi also won the Dong-in Literary Award with his medium length story "the Crippled and the Idiot." Te-sun Bag has become well known by his memorable work "the Settled Place." The established writers of the earlier days, Su-gil An, Sun-won Hwang, and authoresses Gyong-ri Bag and Sin-ze Gang were still active in the traditional production of their novels, "The North Gando," "Trees Stood on the Slope," "War Front and Market," and "Waves" respectively.

However, those who made their debut in the first half of the 1960's were more distinct and outspoken in their struggle against injustice and in overcoming the tragedy of the Korean War. Bom-son Yi's Obaltan or "Bullet Misfired," In-hun Czoe's Gwangzang or "the Open Ground," Ho-czol Yi's Sosimin or "Petit Citizen," Gi-won So's "the Matured Embrace

in This Night," Gun-czan Ha's Samgag-zib or "the Triangle
House," Zong-in So's Wonmu or "Circling Dance" and In-
hun Czoe's "Voice of the Japanese Governor General of
Korea" are to be remembered. In the general depressing atmosphere of life some poets even achieved their merits by firm
determination. Du-zin Bag shouted loudly in his thirst for
social justice. Su-yong Gim protested bravely and Bong-u Bag
and Dong-yob Sin cried out in their young sentiments against
corruption for the purification of the society.

In the latter part of the 1960's, two most controversial novels
were published. Zo-son Czongdog-bu or "the Japanese Government General in Korea" by one of the established novelists of
middle-age, Zu-hyon Yu, and "Record of Bunnye" written by
a young author Yong-ung Bang. The former fictionalized the
chronological events in Korea during the Japanese control. It
was serialized in the monthly magazine "New Dong-a" and
has been much discussed both in Korea and Japan where it
was placed on the best-seller's list. Here readers could find
almost all significant events under the administration of the
Japanese rulers vividly described. The latter story has been
judged by literary critics as one of the greatest works since the
pioneer of modern Korean literature, Gwang-su Yi, wrote
his notorious novel Muzong or "Heartlessness." This young
writer had made his debut by contributing the work to a
quarterly named "Creation and Criticism." He won the second
creative writings' award sponsored by the daily newspaper
Hangug Ilbo. Several other writers contributed to literature
with their works. Song-won Hong with his "Soldiers' Village
on D-day," Ol-czon Zong with his "Rascals," Zong-in So
with "the Later Despatch" and Sang-yung Bag with "Bright
Daylight."

As a new feature of Korean poetical work, two long
lyrical poems or rather epics were published by two established
poets, one named "River Gum" by Dong-yob Sin mentioned
already and the other called "Diary of the Field" by Sang Gu.
Byong-hwa Zo was energetic in bringing out several books of
his own collected poems. Literature in the latter half of the
1960's shows several specific characteristics. Writers in general

gradually began to forget the tragedy of the Korean War and intensified their ideological approach of anti-communism in accordance with the strong efforts of the government in this direction.

Other authors corresponded to the sentiments and ideas of readers who are no longer interested in traditional analysis of the frustration and loneliness of individuals. They became therefore reluctant in dealing with the themes of big historical events or national anxiety and more absorbed in modern psychological descriptions of personal affairs. They also refrained from objecting against the prevailing social injustices.

Several significant controversial issues were discussed in literary circles. One was the development of obscurity in poetry. A poet Czun-su Gim and his colleagues tried to promote calm observation of the inner world of humans through their literary group magazine "Modern Poetry." Against this tendency the late poet Su-yong Gim and his supporters insisted on conscientious resistance against this effort through their group magazine "New Spring Poetry." Another issue was whether writers, poets, playwrights or critics should contribute to the promotion of social problems in their literary productions. Novelists Hui Sonu and Bung-gu Gim, poets Su-yong Gim and Myong-hwan Zong, critics O-ryong Yi and Nagczong Beg and others participated in the serious discussions.

The contrast between the individual contemplation of inner spiritual life and the renewed active participation in social affairs was caused by the two gigantic processes of modernization of Korea, one political and the other industrial. The former group intended to shy away from reality, but the latter circle aimed at the positive analysis of the drastic change of social life.

Other critics joined the debates. Ug Song, Zong-ho Yu, U-zong Gim, I-du Czon and Dong-il Zi in the first half, and Nag-czong Beg, Mu-ung Yom, Hyon Gim and Yun-sig Gim in the later period.

In the field of periodicals, the monthly magazines which were published before 1960 Sasanggye or "the World of Thoughts" and "Modern Literature" are still regularly issued.

During the 1960's several new publications appeared and contributed much to the development of Korean literature; two analytical magazines, both printed by daily newspapers, "New Dong-a" and "Monthly Chung-ang," two pure literary magazines, both printed with government subsidies, "Monthly Literature" edited by the Writers' Association of Korea, and "Women's Literature" edited by Women Writers' Association of Korea. The quarterly "Creation and Critic" is worthy to be mentioned. A dozen of other monthly and miscellaneous weeklies opened their pages to literary productions of poets, novelists, playwrights, essayists, critics, translators and others.

One more recent highlight of Korean literature is the 37th Congress of International P.E.N. Club to be held in Seoul from June 28 to July 4, 1970 under the auspices of the Korean Center. Headed by president, Czol Beg, and two vice-presidents, Miss Yun-sug Mo and Yong-ho Gim, the center extended invitations to all members of the world, including communistic blocks. This gathering of the world association of writers is one of the most valuable events for Korean literature. Delegates from Korea used to take part in its annual conferences abroad and 13 foreign writers were invited to Korea in 1957 following the 29th congress held in Tokyo, Japan. The 1970 congress, however, is the first opportunity for Korean writers in general to associate with authoritative writers of the world. The theme for the congress is "Humour in Literature—East and West," which was suggested by the Korean center. To contribute to the congress, the Korean center has translated classical and modern Korean literature for distribution at the Seoul meeting consisting of selected poems, stories and plays. The present author published "An Introduction to Korean Literature" in English and also may start translation of Samguk-Yusa or "Reminiscences of Three Kingdom," the earliest documents of literature of ancient Korea.

Korean literature has largely developed by its own creative capacity, but also lately shows the influence of foreign literature. Translation of foreign literature was very significant during 1950's and various literary thoughts were imported into Korea at random without apparent systems. From the 1960's on, however, writers became more cautious and tried to shape their individual characteristics. Korean publications of original world literature in the form of series, including the complete works of Shakespeare, are widely appreciated by the readers.

The reorganization of the ministry of culture and public information in 1967 encouraged various artistic activities in Korea. The ministry took a positive action in the field of literature and established funds to support creative writers. It adjusted the Award System to encourage the cultural and artistic pursuit of writers with an unprecedented amount of prize money, and also offered financial support to literary magazines. The ministry is also sponsoring dynamically the 37th International Congress of P.E.N. various academic associations of foreign literature such as English, American, German, French, etc., organized by Korean scholars are active in the pursuit of achievements through periodicals, meetings and public events.

The number of writers has much increased in the 1960's and many volumes of their works are found in every bookstore and library. But many literary men also have died during the decade. Six novelists; Mu-yong Yi, Mal-bong Gim, Yong-mug Gye, Sang-sob Yom, I-sog Gim, Gye-zu Bag and Yong-teg Zon; and seven poets; Sang-sun O, Yong-no Byon, Czi-hwan Yu, Zi-hun Zo, Dong-myong Gim, Su-yong Gim and Dong-yob Sin passed away.

Literature for children has been flourishing and profited from the increase of school children. Two brilliant story writers for children, He-song Ma and Yo-sob Gang passed away during the decade.

Dramatic activities once awakened right after 1945, but they could not flourish, because of the Korean War, which demolished theatres and dispersed players as well as producers. While plays and dramas were not prominent during the 1950's, theatrical performances have been a revival in the 1960's. The Korean Association of Drama and the Korean Center of International Theatre are active in the promotion of dramatic art. Playwright Bom-sog Cza, Yu-sang Ha and Hui-ze Yim distinguished themselves in the production of plays, and many young playwrights made their debuts recently through the rewarding systems of several newspapers.

1965: Gyong-za Ha (Dong-a), Hye-ryong O (Gyong-hyang), Gyong-sig No (Seoul).

1966: Ze-gyong O (Dong-a), Dong-yul Go (Gyong-hyang), Zin-ho Zon (Zoson), Gab-hi Won (Zung-ang).

1967: De-song Yun (Dong-a), Zi-hyon Gim (Seoul), Te-sog O (Zoson), Gil-ho Gim (Zung-ang).

1968: Il-yong Yi (Zoson), Ha-yon Zong (Seoul), Nam Gim (Dong-a), Czang-hwal Gim (Zung-ang).

Besides the National Theatre and the seniors' group, Sin-hyob (started in 1950), the Wongag Theatre (now burnt) and the Drama Center (supervised by playwright Czi-zin Yu) were inaugurated in 1957 and 1962 respectively. Now we have about 30 comrade players groups, such as the Zezag-gughoe (started in 1956, producing 31 plays), the Experimental, the Mountain and River, the People, the Freedom, the Open Ground, the Bridge and others.

From 1967 we saw a new movement for independent producer's system by producers, Yong-ung Yim, Gyu Ho, Zong-og Gim, Se-yong Na, Dog-hyong Yu, Sung-gyu Yi, Yu-zong Gang, Hyon-yong Gim, and others. They tried to abolish realism, seeking for a new technic in abstract expression on the stage, so that they might interest young intellectual audiences, including the small indoor stage, Cafe Theatre.

On the other hand during the 1960's there was a revival movement of traditional plays, such as Korean puppet play and mask play, to meet the upheaval of nationalism among the people. And during the decade we lost several prominent figures.

Two senior producers: Sung-hui Bag (1901-64), Czol Hyon (1891-1965).

Two playwrights: Zin-su Gim (1906-66), Gwang-ne Yi (1908-68).

Three players: Sung-ho Gim, Hwan Zo, Og Zon (actress).

Classical Music and Dance of Korea

THE EARLIER DAYS

According to the various data of Korean history at home and abroad, the geographical boundaries of Ancient Korea extended far up to the north across the present bordering rivers, Yalu and Duman. Its territories covered the whole of Manchuria including the Liaotung peninsula in the south-west of it. The ancient Chinese traditionally applied four synonyms which meant "barbarians" to the descriptions of their neighbouring aliens on the four sides, east, west, south, and north, i.e. Dong-i, Soyung, Namman, and Bugzog. Among these Dong-i, or the East Barbarians, was the name generally used in the ancient histories of China to refer to the tribes of the Korean people who inhabited in this vast area of the Far-East.

The history of Korean music and dance begins, traditionally, with the reign of the first King, Dan-gun, who is said to have ascended the throne in the year 2333 B.C. He worshipped *Hanunim,* Lord of Heaven, and regaled the gods of the earth with music and dancing. The people, too, are reported to have celebrated religious festivals with wine, songs, and dance (Zuri-mu, Zimo-mu, etc.). Evidence that the Korean people had their own native style of music in ancient times may be gleaned from a statement in the old Chinese book, Hou Hanshu (5th century A.D.), that Korean musicians visited China during the Hsia Dynasty and danced to their own music at its court (2117 B.C.).

The kingdom of Buyo (1286 B.C.-?), which occupied the second period of Korean history, was established in Manchuria, its northern capital being located somewhere about one thousand li (about four hundred kilometer) to the north of Liaotung. The people of Buyo held the festival of worshipping Heaven in the twelfth month every year with wine, music, and dancing called Yong-go or "Welcoming-Drum."

One of the Korean tribes, called Ye, had also a festival for worshipping Heaven in the tenth month called Muczon or "Dancing-Heaven" in which they served wine, accompanied by songs and dancing like the people in Buyo.

In 1122 B.C. an exile from China named Giza, who established a kingdom in the north-west of the peninsula, brought to Korea books of literature, music, medicine, science, divination, and various handicrafts, and the people were instructed through translations. Their rough dispositions were tamed by the musical pieces of Sogyong-gog or "West Capital Melody" and Dedong-gang-gog or "the Melody of River Dedong," which he composed. Here it is to be noticed that some Chinese influences were made on Korean music from the earlier days.

In 925 B.C. King Songdog personally observed farmers in the fields to appreciate their industry, and also established a Royal Academy called Yanghyon-won to facilitate the teaching of the six arts—ceremony, music, archery, horse-riding, calligraphy, and mathematics.

In 703 B.C. King Agsong composed himself fifteen pieces of music which consisted of verses and tunes, called Agzang. Furthermore history tells us that in 642 B.C. King Czonlo while sailing on the river Bullyu enjoyed music called Yongson-ag or "Music for Welcoming of Genii" performed by an orchestra, and a dance called Yongson-mu or "Dance for Welcoming of Genii," performed by court ladies.

The same history source indicates that an alien musician from the north imported music in 298 B.C. and the courtiers advised the King Samno not to accept the barbarians' music from the north by which they generally meant "Mongolian," but the king was generous enough to receive the alien with many gifts. This means that Korean music had some contact with Mongolian elements.

Thus the ancient Korean music and dance so far can
analysed as a basic structure of native currents influenced
two alien elements, Chinese entering from the west a
Mongolian from the north. There is one more influence whi
was felt much later. That is from India.

THE PERIOD OF THREE HANS

From 250 B.C. onwards one reads of ceremonies perform
to the accompaniment of singing and dancing, as for exampl
"the Sowing of Seeds" in the fifth month and "the Autun
Harvest" in the tenth in the district of Mahan, one of tl
Three Hans (250-57 B.C.).

The other two Hans, Zinhan and Byonhan, played
musical instrument called "Pil" by which perhaps was mea
a flat harp probably of 25 strings.

But the first instrument which appears in the history
Korean music in a more concrete form is an upright wester
type harp called Gonghu. In one history, Hedong Yogsa, the
is mention of a Korean lady called Yo-og who sang her ov
poem to the accompaniment of this instrument. One ear
morning her husband Gwag Izago went to the riverside
board a boat, and saw a white haired old man, seemingly ma
and drunken, plunging into the river, and the old man's wif
who was chasing after him trying in vain to stop him, follo
her old husband into the water, singing a mournful son;
Hearing this story from her husband, the lady deeply touche
and composed a musical poem as follows:

Though urged not to wade the river,
He nevertheless plunged into the current,
And down under the deep water he died.
Tell me, my darling! What shall I do?

This is the first musical song to appear in our history, an
it is called Gonghu-in. It is written in Chinese characters wit
four syllables in each line. This instrument must have been on

he popular instruments at that time, and it can be assumed
t Korean music was already flourishing two thousand years
.

DER THE THREE KINGDOMS

Now coming to the days of the Three Kingdoms, Goguryo
B.C.-668), Begze (18 B.C.-660), and Sinla (57 B.C.-935),
ean music and dance were greatly developed in conjunction
t the culture in general, which was marked by vigorous
inality and rich diversity.

iic and Dance of Goguryo

One of the most famous ancient instruments, and one
:h is still extant, is a six stringed flat harp called Hyon-gum.
years ago, at the time of King Zangsu of Goguryo, a
n stringed flat harp was brought from Chin in China, but
people did not know how to play it. So the king pro-
ned to the public that those who could master the instru-
t would be richly rewarded. One of the then Ministers,
ag Wang, examined it and suggested that the instrument
was not suited to Korean music, and he himself created a
lified version of the instrument, and then composed 187
pieces which he himself played on it. It is said that the
ic was so touching that cranes flew near and danced to the
tiful rhythms. Hence the harp came to be called Hyonhag-
or "Black Crane Harp." Later the second syllable was
ped in the popular speech and it was called simply Hyon-
. Korean melodies are much more delicate than those of
ta, and they require a more deliberate technique based on
native characteristics. San-ag Wang realized this and
ted the development of new instruments and tunes. He is
ured now as one of the three greatest musicians of Korea.
inally, during the reign of King Shun in China, this harp
five stringed, but King Mun and King Mu of Chu Dynasty
hina added one more string each, this making a seven
ged instruments as it is even today in China.

According to various historical records, the people of Goguryo seem to have played 20 different types of instruments; 7 kinds of harps (flat harp played with a bow, 3 different kinds of Gonghu, mandolin-shape, and flat plucking harps of 5 strings and 7 strings), 7 wind instruments (harmonica shaped, 2 clarinet-shaped, bamboo bundle pipe, reed bundle pipe, flute with a protruded hole, and flute of 13 holes), and 6 percussion instruments (waist drum, turtlehead drum, 2 more different drums, iron plates, and blowing shell).

In a book of Chinese history, Suso, one finds some names of dances and songs, such as Ziso-mu and Ziso-ga. Other books also suggest the existence of the song Hwangzo-ga or "Yellow Birds' Song," and of other songs as well as dances.

In 1936 some excavations of old tombs and graves were made at Zinban-hyon, Andong Province, Manchuria, which was the old capital of Goguryo, and some of the wall pictures there depicted dancing and the blowing of trumpets, as well as group dancing to the accompaniment of an orchestra.

Music and Dance of Begze

The third son of King Zumong of Goguryo, Onzo, seized Miczuhol (now called Inczon, near Seoul) from Mahan, and his elder brother Bullyu occupied Wirye-song (present Gwangzu district, south of the Han river). After the death of Bullyu, Onzo established the kingdom of Begze, including the district of Miczuhol at first, and then extended its territory to the south-west of the peninsula.

Speaking of the music and dance of Begze, one of the three kingdoms which was thus established by the descendants of Goguryo, various records prove that their artistic level was remarkably high. Japanese histories in particular contain lots of facts regarding the influences of Korean music and dance on those of old Japan. A Begze scholar named Azigi was despatched to Japan and the then Japanese King Ojin put his prince under him to study Chinese classics. Next another Begze scholar Wang-in was invited to Japan to teach Confucianism. These two scholars paved the way for the subsequent appearance in Japan of many Korean scholars of classics, divination, calendar, medical science, and pharmacy, as well as musicians like Dog-samgun, high Buddhistic priests, and all sorts of technicians and artisans, such as tailors, seamstresses, weavers, smiths, brewers, crockery makers, saddle makers, painters, tile makers, and others.

The Statute of Taiho of Japan which was enacted in the 2nd year of Taiho during the Era of Emperor Monbu contains descriptions of Koma gaku, that is to say, Goguryo music, Kudara gaku or Begze music, and Siragi gagu or Sinla music, even specifying the number of musicians. During the Nara Dynasty Begze music flourished, while in Heian Era in the year of Taiho under the Emperor Heijo the number of musicians in the Gagaku office was fixed by 4 Kudara (Begze) musicians, 4 Koma (Goguryo) musicians, and 2 Siragi (Sinla) musicians. Furthermore in the paragraph regarding the 20th year of Emperor Suiko in volume 22 of the Nippon Shoki, the oldest history of Japan, one can read that the Begze musicians Malmazi, Gizungbang, and Dalmaui opened a music school in Sakurai village of the present Nara prefecture, and instructed Japanese children in music and dancing, and that Shinkan and Saibun were the most distinguished among the disciples. Those masks which were used then are preserved still in the temple Horyu, Nara prefecture, and some of them are those for the Czoyong dance which were fashionable then throughout the Three Kingdoms. This dance, one of the most famous Korean dances, originated in the Sinla Dynasty will be described in detail later.

The only poem of Begze now existent, called Zong-ub Sa, is a musical verse to be sung accompanied by instruments and dancing. This is an old folksong with a refrain of the Begze Dynasty, and was probably first sung by an unknown of the time. This is the first poem written at a later date in the Korean alphabet. This is the story of the poem: A pedlar did not come back home until late at night. His wife climbed up a hill-pass and waited there, fearing that he might be injured or robbed, and wishing that he would dispose of his goods somewhere and come back safely.

THE SONG OF ZONG-UB

Oh, Moon! Rise high,
And shine far and wide!
Ah, *ogangzori*, oh, *darongdiri*.
Are you on the hill-pass of Zonzu?
I fear you will be treading wet roads!
Ah, *ogangzori*, oh, *darongdiri*.
I wish you would unload your goods somewhere!
I am walking late at night.
Ah, *ogangzori*, oh, *darongdiri*.

One of the most well-known books on Korean music, Aghag Gwebom or the Handbook of Musical Study, gives a detailed description of this poem, as well as the dancing and music accompanying it, under the title of Mugo or Dancing Drum. It requires 16 musicians and 8 dancing girls. The latter dance while singing the poem, circling around drums which they strike with two sticks each. Meanwhile the musicians accompany them. The music starts with a slow andante, then proceeds to moderate speed and finally ends with quick steps.

The instruments used in Begze, according to the Bugsa or the History of the North, volume 94, paragraph for Begze, were drums, bugles, western style harps, harp played with a bow, bundle-pipe with 17 tubes, flute with a protruded hole, etc.

The Sinla Dynasty

Coming into the Sinla Dynasty, one of the Three Kingdoms which occupied the southeast of the peninsula, one must notice that music was quite flourishing among the people according to a paragraph from the Samgug Yusa, one of the earliest records of ancient Korea. The lines indicate the wealth and peaceful life of the people. This kingdom finally unified the whole peninsula under its highly advanced civilization and military strength.

Sinla had an excellent social system called Hwarang-do or the Morality of Flowery Generation. It was a sort of social

ıb where young men of character and bravery could join
gether to cultivate their minds and bodies with music, dance,
:rature, chivalry, and excursion. They often made trips
:ough the country to carry on musical or dramatic per-
'mances, so that they might train themselves as well as inspire
: public. The leader was supposed to be man of personality
d well qualified with musical talents. This was first called
onhwa or Original Flower, and then Hwarang, or also
ıgson or Genii of the Country. This leader was originally
ected from among beautiful girls, but later was invariably a
ndsome boy who was well trained in literature and musical
ncing as well as in chivalry.

The Hwarang youth were royal to the king, filial to their
rents, sincere in friendship, not retreated in war, and
ective in killing, as the five principles of their virtue re-
ired, so that the people esteemed them highly and many of
:m were singled out by the government authorities for high
ıking posts, both military and civil.

One of the typical instruments still existent in Korea is
)ther flat harp of 12 strings, called Gaya-gum. One thousand
ır hundred and eight years ago there lived a King Gasil of
: kingdom of Gaya (situated in the present Goryong County
trict of Gyongsang north province, along the Nagdong
'er) who was very fond of music and claimed himself to be
expert. He found the 25 stringed harp of China not suitable
Korean tunes and restyled it into one of 12 strings, calling
: new instrument Gaya-gum after the name of the country.
en the king ordered a musician named Urug to compose
ʌ musical pieces. The musician composed 12 new ones, but
: kingdom of Gaya then was at low tide, so he proceeded to
neighbouring kingdom of Sinla with the new harp, accom-
ied by his disciple Imun. In March 551 King Zinhung of
la -heard about this musician when he was journeying to
ngsong (present Czongzu of Czungczong north province)
l summoned him to the palace to perform music there with
disciple. They played two new melodies Harim and
nzug, and the king and all the courtiers applauded excitedly.

He trained more musicians under him, among whom were

three distinguished students, Gyego, Bobzi, and Mandog. In accordance with their respective talents, he taught "Gaya harp" to the first, songs to the second, and dancing to the third. These three disciples joined together in the revision of the 12 compositions which they had learned from their instructor and rearranged them into 5 pieces, for they found their senior's music to be complicated and obscene, and wanted to make them more tidy and refined. At first the teacher was angered by the revision, but when he heard them performed he admitted that the revised pieces were better—pleasant but not luxurious, and sad but not sentimental. Thus he achieved much for development of this harp and of the music of Sinla, composing 185 pieces altogether. He is also called one of the three greatest musicians of Korea.

Another musician named Bo-go Og, who had trained himself at Unsang-won on Mt. Ziri for 50 years in playing the harp of 6 strings, Hyon-gum, mentioned above, composed 30 new pieces and taught them to his student Myong-dog Sog, who passed on his knowledge to his disciple Gwigum. But this last named musician also took refuge in the same mountain and did not return to the world of men. Fearing that the music of 6 stringed harp might thus die out, the king appointed Ihan-yunhung, Magistrate of Namwon county, and ordered him to learn the harp from the hermit musician. So the Magistrate despatched two clever young boys, Anzang and Czongzang, to the mountain for this purpose, but for three years the hermit refused to disclose his secrets to the young men while instructing them. The Magistrate and his wife visited the musician on the mountain and appealed to him to relent for the sake of the young generation, and the hermit finally taught the two boys three melodies, including Pyopung or Whirling Wind. One of these young musicians later instructed his sons, Sugsang and Gugzong, and the latter composed 7 pieces. Thereafter many players of the 6-stringed harp established themselves as musicians.

Another musician of the 6-stringed harp was called teacher Beggyol. He was so poor that one new year's eve his wife was much worried about their poverty and consequent inability to greet the new year in the customary fashion. But Beggyol played his harp in imitation of the sound of a pounding mortar, as if he were preparing rice-cakes, by which he meant to comfort his wife. Thus this instrument of 6 strings was very popular among the people.

Another instrument which was quite unique in Sinla was a large flute played sideways called Manpasig-zo or "the Flute for Easing Myriad Waves." The origin of this flute is described in detail in volume 32 of the Samgug Sagi, the earliest written history of Korea by Bu-sig Gim. It says "in the Eastern Sea suddenly a little mountain emerged and its peak resembled a turtle's head. On the top a bamboo grew, and it was divided into two in the daytime, but at night the two united into one. The king had it cut and a flute was made from it, and the name Manpasig-zo was given to it." This happened in the reign of the 31st King Sinmun. One day the king received a report from a marine officer Pung-czong Bag concerning the appearance of this hill in the sea which was lingering to and from facing the Gamun temple, and asked the divination officer Czun-zil Gim what it meant. The latter explained that the late king had already become a dragon in the sea in order to protect Korea, and that the spirit of general Yu-sin Gim had now descended for the same purpose, so that this was an omen promising their benediction on the Sinla Kingdom, and the king was advised to proceed to the sea to receive their grace. So the king ordered his men to investigate the mountain in the sea and everything was proved to be true. When the king visited the place, the two bamboos were united into one at noon, whereupon ensued a great storm lasting for seven days. On the 8th day, when the storm abated and the waves were calm, a dragon received the king and presented a jade band. The king asked about the meaning of what had happened, and the dragon answered that the bamboo might be compared to two hands which made a sound by clapping, and advised the king to make a flute from it as a national treasure. The dragon added that the late king and general Yu-sin Gim agreed to offer this gift to the country and despatched the dragon himself to present it to the king. So the king was glad and thanked the dragon with the gift of five coloured silk and golden jade. He ordered his men to cut the bamboo for the suggested purpose. When the bamboo was brought in the mountain and the dragon suddenly disappeared, and the king returned to the palace and had a flute made from the bamboo. It has been said that the flute made enemies run away in war, the sick well, rain fall when the weather was too dry, the skies clear in the rainy season, the wind stop when necessary, and waves calm in storm. Hence the flute took its name from one of its attributes, and was preserved as a national treasure. It was once lost during the reign of King Hyoso, but miraculously was recovered, and the name was enlarged to Manmanpapasig-zo or the Flute Easing Myriad and Myriad Waves and Waves.

Three kinds of flutes originated in Sinla, one large in size, one moderate, and one small. The large one was quite similar to the above-mentioned legendary flute in its size and shape, and indeed seems to have been a frank imitation of this national treasure. It was often made of jade or bamboo, and such a flute of jade is still preserved in the museum of Gyong-zu, the ancient capital of the kingdom. There are 124 musical compositions for the large flute, 145 for the moderate size, and 298 for the small flute.

There were many other instruments in use in Sinla. For example, one of the musical dances mentioned above, Czo-yong, employed 20 different instruments: 9 harps, 4 blowing ones, and 7 striking ones. (Two harps of 2 strings, 4 harps of 4 strings, 2 round harps of 6 strings, one 7-stringed harp played with a bow, one 15-stringed harp, one 12-stringed harp, two flutes with 7 finger-holes, three clarinet types of 8 finger-holes, one upright flute of 6 finger-holes, six large flutes of 12 finger-holes and 1 vibration hole, four thin waist drums of 2 heads, one round drum on a stand, one large drum, one especially large drum, one set of 16 steel plates instrument, one set of brass cymbals, one set of 6 clapping boards.)

This musical dance, a type of mask play, is based on an old story of exorcism. The son of the Dragon of the Eastern Sea, named Czoyong, visited the capital of Sinla, Gyongzu, and was offered a high government rank and received a pretty wife. The God of Plague, desiring Czoyong's wife, transformed himself into a man, stole into the house at night, and got into the woman's bed. Czoyong came back late in a moonlit night and found them there. But he went out of the house singing the song translated below, probably written in 879, the fifth year of King Hon-gang. Then the God of Plague, returning to his original form, went to Czoyong and knelt in front of him, apologizing, "I desired your wife, but you are so generous and patient that I am really touched. I will never enter your room if I see only so much as your portrait there." Since then people have drawn the face of Czoyong and pasted it at the entrance to their rooms to keep all evils away from their houses.

> Under the bright moon of the capital
> Amusing myself till late at night,
> I came back home and saw my bed.
> Oh, there were four legs there!
> Two of them belong to me,
> But whose are the other two?
> Mine were mine before,
> But they have been stolen now!

This is one of the 25 surviving poems called *Hyangga,* which were written down in *Idu,* a system whereby Chinese characters were adapted to the agglutinative structure of the Korean language using both the ideographic and phonetic principles. The actual verses now in accompaniment of this musical dance are different from this. There are three poems commonly used and they all command the bright and flourishing reign of the king and the virtuous administration of the government as well as the peace of the world. Then they express the happy life of the people because all calamities have disappeared.

5 Czoyongs, the heroes of the musical dance, put on flowery hats and five different coloured masks, white, black, yellow, red, and blue. The stage is decorated with one lantern,

two bundles of lotus flowers, more flowers, and two cranes, white and blue. There appear more characters, four dancing boys decorated with flowers, three dancing boys each on the left and right who carry decorated sticks and flags, umbrellas for dignity, 16 dancing girls and musicians—the total number on the stage is 88 (28 boys for carrying decorative tools, 5 Czoyongs in masks, 4 dancing boys, 16 dancing girls, 37 musicians, and 2 conductors).

The meaning of the verse to be sung is to praise the mysterious power of Czoyongs; their broad foreheads which predict their long life, their huge eyes full of benevolent love, their ears strong enough to receive wind, their beautiful noses which can smell 5 perfumes, their mouths full of gold within, their teeth like white jade, their chins symbolizing wealth, their shoulders carrying 7 jewels, and their long sleeves full of happiness.

This musical mask opera has 4 scenes, the prelude and the epilogue are the same, a circling dance to musical accompaniment is performed by the following players; 3 guiding boys with stick, flag, and umbrella, 1 dancing girl, a boy carrying flowers, a white crane, a blue crane, and 5 Czoyongs. In the second scene they assume a square fixed positions, and play music and dance. The third scene consists of dancing by the masked Czoyongs, in which the blue, white, red, and black take the four directions of east, west, south, north respectively, while the yellow stands in the center among them, and they all dance in these positions.

King Hon-gang whose reign produced this Czoyong dance seems to have been greatly interested in dancing. Once he went on an excursion to Posog-zong, a little park where scholars, men of letters, and poets used to gather and sit along a tiny circular stream artificially made for a special kind of poetry competition, and would hurriedly compose poems, while a cup of wine was floating slowly on the stream. each earning thereby the reward of drinking the cup of wine. (The historical remains of this man-made stream may be seen even today in the suburb of Gyongzu above-mentioned, the ancient capital of Sinla.) The God of Mt. Nam emerged in front of the king, but the other participants were not aware of the appearance of the God. The king then danced in imitation of the feature of the God. This dance was later called Sangsim or Dance of Sangsu, a name which has reference to the impression of the God of Mt. Nam.

It is also said that when the above-mentioned king had a party at one of the palace buildings, the Dongye-zon, the Goddess of the Earth, appeared there and performed a dance called Zibeg.

One of the three representative dances of the Sinla Dynasty, which include the above-mentioned Czoyong, is the dance of Hwang-chang-nang, from which the sword dance originated. The typical sword dance is based on the story of Gwan-Czang. Gwan-Czang was a young general, fifteen years of age, the son of Sinla general Pum-il, and a hero of the famous ethic of art and chivalry for youths, the Hwarang-do already mentioned. As second-in-command, he took part in a counterattack on the neighbouring kingdom of Begze, and in the course of this, was killed by the enemy general Gye-beg and his head was sent home on a horse. His father held up the head, dripping with blood, and said that he was pleased with the loyalty his son had shown to the king.

The details were later altered in the story, so that Gwan-Czang became Hwang-Czang, aged six instead of fifteen. A mask of his face was made, and used by the Sinla people in sword dances to soothe the spirit of the dead. This sword dancing is still performed on the stage by the classical dancers of Korea.

According to the old records there were several other Sinla dances. The Five Style Dances are mentioned in the five poems written by the famous scholar of the time, Czi-won Czoe, each of which concerns one of these five styles—Gumhwan, Wolzon, Demyon, Sogdog, and Sanye. The last of these, the Sanye, is the origin of the lion dance in Korea. In 689 King Zongmyong proceeded to Sinczon and appreciated 7 different musical dances there; Gamu, Hasinyol-mu, Sane-mu, Hangi-mu, Sangsinyol-mu, Sogyong-mu, and Mizi-mu.

Those who were well acquainted with the theory of music

and instruments were called Agsa, those with instruments on Aggong. Among those last group the musicians played har was called Gumczog, singers Gaczog, and dancers Muczo Musicians of Sinla were skillful in three harps; Hyon-gum strings), Gaya-gum (12 strings), and Bipa; three bamboc (large flute, moderate size flute, and small flute), large drum and clapping boards.

Goryo Dynasty (918-1392)

Korean music and dance were greatly developed in th dynasty by two significant influences: Buddhism as the na tional religion and the wholesale import of Chinese classic music. There were two big Buddhist festivals; Yondung-hoe (Lantern Light Festival in spring and Palgwan-hoe in winter And once every three years was held a national festival calle Begzwa Dehoe or One Hundred Seats Festival, where thirt thousand priests were in charge of the memorial services an over one thousand musicians took part in the performance: Koreans also played various games on such occasions, and th king himself joined in the appreciation of carnivals boastin of such attractions as a lofty lotus-adorned platform, an models of dragon, phoenixes, elephants, horses, carts, an ships.

In 1114 and 1116 during the reign of King Yezong th classical music of Sung, China, called Desong A-ag was intro duced by two Korean envoys to China, Zi-sung An and Za zi Wang. The Sung Dynasty of China had revived the ol Chinese classical music which had fallen somewhat out o popular favour, and been in low tide sometime. The Chines Emperor offered some music instruments to Korea. This newl imported music called A-ag as well as the music called Dang ag which had been imported earlier came to be used at th morning audiences with the king, at various memoria services, and at royal entertainments.

There were four special Royal altars. Wongu was fo worshipping Heaven (the 8 angle tower in the back garden o the present Chosun hotel is the remain of that of the Y Dynasty), Sazig or Bang-gu for the Earth (a remain is stil found in the Sazig park, Seoul), Temyo (or Zongmyo) for Royal ancestors (one still exists near the Zongno 4th street, Seoul), and Munmyo for Confucius (one in the Song-gyun-gwan university, Seoul). These two types of music above-mentioned were performed at these shrines, two different arrangements called Dung-ga and Hon-ga being practiced on alternate occasions.

Dung-ga; one set of 16 bells, one set of 16 jade-stones, one hollow sound box, one tiger's backbone, two clapping boards, harps (1 string, 3 strings, 5 strings, 7 strings, 9 strings, all one each), two flat harps of 25 strings, four flutes with a protruded hole, four bundle pipes of 17 tubes and 13 tubes, two ocarina-shaped, two harmonica-shaped of 16 tubes, one conductor-in-chief, one technician of instruments, and four singers.

Hon-ga; three sets of 16 bells, three sets of 16 hunging jades-stones, two drums, one hollow sound box, one tiger back-bone, fourteen harps of 25 strings, harps of 1 string, eleven harps of 3 strings, twelve harps of 5 strings, fourteen harps of 7 strings, fourteen harps of 9 strings, fourteen-bundle pipes of 17 tubes, fourteen-bundle pipes of 7 tubes, sixteen flutes with protruded holes, fourteen ocarinas, fourteen flutes of 13 roles, one drum on a stand, one conductor-in-chief, twelve singers, a musical technician, 48 civil dancers, 48 marshal dancers, four persons carrying decorated flags, two drums with long handles, two single hand-bells, two double hand-bells, six bucket-shape bells, two long tubes, two small drums, and two upright oblong drums.

Besides these the native music was also well appreciated by some of the Goryo Kings. King Myongzong ordered his musicians to use native music and dancing at the summer services in addition to the foreign music. King Czung-yol was fond of music and dancing for his own amusement, and his princess advised him in vain not to indulge in them too much. He even appointed official dancing girls from among the Shamanistic sorceresses as well as from local dancing girls.

There were two kinds of musical poems; the musical verse called Agzang which were written in the form of Chinese classical poems, and poems in popular forms called Siga, which were usually composed in Korean vernacular style. The first one usually praised the glory of the country and appreciated the achievements of the rulers, while the latter for the popular sentiments.

Yi Dynasty (1392-1910)

The first King Tezo established Confucianism as the national religion. Establishing a new shrine for royal ancestors, he had the ceremonial music revised by the musician Do-zon Zong. Zong composed musical poems dedicated to the king and also imported more music from the Ming Dynasty of China. Gun Gwon, one of the scholars of the Royal Academy called Song-gyun-gwan, composed three verses dedicated also to the king, Czon-gam, Hwasan, and Sinmyo, in praise of the royal birth, the establishing of the capital at Seoul and the founding of the new shrine for royal ancestors respectively. ·

In 1402 the Government Office of Ceremonies presented musical compositions to King Tezong, and in the same year a local governor Yun Ha presented two musical verses, Gun-Czonzong and Su-Myongmyong. There was a tendency to use classical Chinese music, popular Chinese music, and native Korean music, for Royal Shrine, morning audiences with the king, and Official Banquets respectively. But there was much discussion regarding the suitability of three different types of music for various occasions.

King Sezong (1397-1450) who was a scholar himself and well known for his key role in the creation of the present Korean alphabet in 1443, contributed a great deal to the encouragement of many phases of Korean culture, including music. Not only was he a player of 6 stringed flat harp himself, but he inspired one of his musicians, Yon Bag who made two new sets of 16 L-letter shape instruments using stone newly discovered in Namyang, Gyong-gi province, Korea. Yon Bag also fixed a new musical system of scales. He presented his opinions on music over 30 times to the king, travelled to China more than ten times for research in music, and classified the classical music of his time into three categories; A-ag, by which he meant that of classical Chinese origin; Dang-ag, the popular music of China; and Hyang-ag, the music of native Korean source, including Buddhist elements.

King Sezong was not satisfied with the tendency at the time to play classical music of foreign origin at memorial services, so he himself studied the theories of classical music and created a genuine Korean style, such as Winter A-ag, New Year's A-ag, and A-ag for Elder's Banquet in August and September, together with accompanying musical verses. Among Dang-ag already mentioned, these of the Sung Dynasty were predominant and some of them are still preserved in Korea, though none of them survives in China. But these were more or less Koreanized and gradually absorbed into Korean native music. Some of the native music contained Buddhist elements; two such representative pieces are Yomin-lag composed by King Sezong, and Yongsan Hoesang, which accompanies the mask dance of Czoyong already mentioned. The crane dance is played by over 80 performers, consisting of musicians, dancing boys, dancing girls, and girls who sing musical verses which end each line with "namuamitabul," a refrain of Buddhist sutra.

The musical verses to be sung for musical dance such as Zong Deob, or Bo-tepyong were too long, and by order of King Sezo were simplified by Hang Czoe. For example, in this way were created 9 selections for memorial services for Royal ancestors; Hyonyezang-gimyongzi-gog, Gwiinzi-gog, Hyonggazi-gog, Zibnyonzi-gog, Yunghwazi-gog, Hyonmizi-gog, Yong-gwangzi-gog, Zongmyongzi-gog, and Dehonzi-gog, Gigan Byon composed some poems called Nayon-gog by order of King Sezong. Among many poems that praised the honour of the king and glory of the country is the famous Yongbi Oczon-ga, a collection of 125 poems composed by the members of the Royal Academy during the reign of King Sezong.

Dancing of the Yi Dynasty, generally speaking, consisted of the so-called Bob-mu, which employed a sort of mechanical action without the deep philosophical implications of the dances of the preceding ages.

Munmu required 38 dancers and two more persons carrying 2 vertically long flags called Dog, each bearing the design of a flying dragon. The marshal dance employed the same number of dancers, but they were aided by 10 more persons. Two of these stand with a pole each having three clusters of decorative hanging threads called Song, 8 of them stand, 4 each on the left and right, one side holding four different kinds of bells with handles and the other side four different instruments, called Ung, Sang, and Dog.

Botepyong requires 36 dancers, and 6 persons in the first scene. Zongdeob also employs the same number and arrangement in the first scene, but the latter is more gorgeously decorated with 7 crimson swords, 2 white swords, 2 yellow swords, one blue sword, 4 white spears, 4 yellow spears, 4 blue spears, 7 black bows and arrows, 1 white bow and arrow, 2 yellow bows and arrows, and 2 blue bows and arrows, and furthermore are surrounded by flags and horns, all in 5 colours each, white, yellow, blue, crimson, and black, and 5 yellow flags with a black turtle, a white tiger, a yellow dragon, a blue dragon, a crimson phoenix. There are also one large horn, one large gong, one large drum, and a large flag, all in yellow. These are accompanied by 2 different kinds of orchestra especially arranged in accordance with the particular requirements. The second scene uses a curved row in the front, only the positions of dancers being changed to an arrangement called Gogzin-do. The 3rd scene is a rectangle arrangement, called Zigzin-do, the fourth scene is a pointed front arrangement called Yezin-do, the 5th is a full circle arrangement, called Wonzin-do, and the 6th scene a square arrangement called Bangzin-do. In these five scenes other than the first entering arrangement, 2 swords, 4 spears, and 2 bows and arrows, all in yellow, dance in the center being circled by other performers. Thus this requires 71 dancing girls in total, 36 holding various arms and 35 being decorated as mentioned above.

This is one example of a formal dance. There were many other forms. For example, Gumczog is performed in 3 scenes by 12 dancers bearing a golden measure, 2 bamboo poles, and one embroidered tapestry, circled by 2 guiding sticks, 8 poles of 7 clusters of threads, 2 dragon fans, 2 phoenix fans, 2 sparrow feathers' poles, and 2 cocktail fans. Gasongmyong has 2 groups of 12 dancers, each group carrying fans, poles and umbrella-shape covers. Songteg employs 16 dancers in 2 groups of 8; Yonhwa-do or the Lotus-Flower Platform is performed by 12 dancers in 2 groups of 6; Suyonzang by 16 dancers with only 2 decorated poles; Poguag by 32 dancers near 2 gate-shape stands in imitation of a ball-throwing game; Gogpa by only 2 dancers with 2 bamboo poles; Bongneui by 16 dancers surrounded by harps, flutes and decorated poles, Abag with 2 clapping bundles of wooden boards, Hyangbal by 8 dancing girls who dance to the decorated cymbals; and Gyobang Gayo requires one hundred singing dancers.

Other types of dancing are represented by theatrical performers in Hyonsondo or Offering of Genii Peach; O-yangson or Five Sheep Genii; Su-borog or Receiving Treasure; Zisonmudo or the Picture of Earthly Genii's Dancing; Gun-czonzong or Showing the Heavenly Garden; Su-myongmyong or Receiving of Bright Life; Ha-hwang-un or Bearing Royal Grace in Mind, Mundog-gog oɼ the Melody of Literary Virtue, and others. In these demonstrations the formal dances are not emphasized, but all the procedures are of course performed to the accompaniment of appropriate musical compositions.

WOMEN MUSIC

It is to be noticed that the majority of dancers in Korean classical dancing were female. Now speaking of the origin of dancing girls in Korea, it should be remembered that the old Hwarang-do of the Sinla Dynasty, as mentioned already, was a special system in which some fair girls of noble family were selected at first as the leaders of the groups. But the existence of woman musicians as well as dancing girls as a social system was started from the Goryo Dynasty.

There was a medical office called Teui-won under the direct control of the premier for the purpose of serving the royal family, and there were the woman doctors and nurses in charge of the health of the queen, princesses, and other female members of the royal family, because the male doctors were not permitted to take care of them. These girls were also required to study music and dancing as well as composition of poetry, calligraphy, and drawing pictures to amuse the royal ladies at their banquets, while male musicians and dancers were in charge of those held for the king, princes, high ranking officers and honourable foreign guests. But later on the above-mentioned court women-physicians or nurses well trained in music and dancing were required to attend the banquets for male members of the royal families or foreign envoys, and they were called Yoryong. There were at one time 730 girls for this purpose in the government offices, 260 belonging to the great music office, 170 under the control of the orchestra office, and 300 for the municipal office. Their music was called Yo-ag, which included various games in the court. They were sometime invited to the banquets of the high class people outside of the palace, then being called *Giseng* as they are even today.

In the Yi Dynasty this system of *Giseng* was much enlarged. Those belonging to the royal medical office mentioned above were called *Yagbang Giseng*, those worked in the royal mourning clothes office *Sangbang Giseng*, those employed in the military uniform office *Gongzo Giseng*, and those in charge of making pills of the welfare office *Hyeminso Giseng*. Hence these girls put together were called *Sa-czoso Giseng* or the dancing girls of the four offices, and they all attended the royal banquets in the palace.

Then by and by the local government offices adopted this system and trained many dancing girls called Gwangi or official dancing girls, and the central government often summoned these girls in the prefectures when they needed additional performers in the capital. Generally speaking, their moral standards were very high and they were proud of being chaste. But their positions after the end of the Yi Dynasty, when the women's medical office was abolished, became degenerated, because the women's music no longer existed within the palace, and accordingly they served as hostesses or entertainers in high class restaurants or at social gatherings. Yet they intend to maintain their tradition of chastity. The famous story of Czunhyang and the historical heroine Nongye are still their spiritual models who sacrificed themselves for true love and patriotism respectively.

PRESENT CONDITION

After the decline of the Yi Dynasty the classical music was preserved in the classical music of the Yi House-Hold under the leadership of the well-known musician Hwa-zin Ham, while the traditional style of classical dancing was kept alive to some extent among these dancing girls.

After the 2nd World War the Korean government newly inaugurated supported the classical music office in order to maintain the museum of instruments and the musicians who had been trained there. The recent Korean War did not damage these national treasures, and they are still being practiced now as a part of the continuing development of this priceless cultural heritage. There are also several groups of experts who are instructing the classical music and dancing in their private institutes for those who are interested in them.

POPULAR MUSIC AND DANCE

There are 6 kinds of popular music; peasant music, folk opera, witch music, local folk songs, ballads and nursery rhymes, and modern popular songs.

Festivals for sowing seeds in the spring and autumn harvest in the days of the Three Hans have already been explained. Even today peasants in the rural districts sing seasonal songs when they cut wood on the mountains, weed in the fields, or take care of their cattle in the meadows. For example, in the south-east villagers engage in the weeding of the rice fields of each house collectively, and they proceed directly from the fields to the house of the owner when they

finish the third and final weeding, decorating themselves with
ivy, flowers, or other leaves of the grasses in the fields, and
singing and dancing to the accompaniment of noisy music
played with gongs, large or small, drums, pipes, flutes, 2
stringed violins, large bamboo trumpet, etc. Sometimes the
employee of the house rides on an ox leading the way. Thus
they show their happiness together in the garden of the house
until they are served with wine and supper. A comical character, called Kite-Hunter, joins in the procession performing
the role of clown carrying a net on his back to make the
audience laugh. Some of the musicians in the group make the
long paper tapes fixed to their hats whirl miraculously in the
air by the skillful movement of their heads while playing music
for the dance.

Folk opera originated in the Hwarang-do of the Sinla
Dynasty mentioned above. Since this system was abolished
and the new system of civil service examination called Gwago
was started in Goryo Dynasty, these men of arts and chivalry
gathered together as troubadours and toured the country,
singing, dancing or often performing some puppet plays. They
also dramatized some of the Korean legends or stories of
romance and performed them on the stage in the form of
opera. Their program often included some sort of acrobatic
circus. They were called generally Gwangde by which was
meant players, or actors, or actresses, and those groups consisting only of men and handsome boys were called "Nam-
sadang."

Another group of these troubadours, that comprised of
official dancing girls, degenerated into witches or sorceresses
called Mudang and were engaged in Shamanistic music and
dancing to the accompaniment of their own special musical
sutras and brass band.

Every province has its local folk songs. For example,
various versions of Arirang are sung to different musical
arrangements. Dancing girls of a certain district are expected
to be skillful in a certain type of music or dance; for instance,
those of Seoul are better trained in Nore-garag or Short
Pieces, those of the south-east in Yugzabegi, those of the

south-west in operatic pieces, those of the north-west in Susim-ga or Laments. The people of Sariwon are well-known for their mask dances, called Talczum, dancing girls of Zinzu are well reputed for their sword dance, those of Songczon for lion dances, and so forth.

Ballads and nursery rhymes are sung by the people, mostly by women of the country and children throughout the country. Every province has its own way of reciting at home or in the fields while at work or play.

A great number of modern popular songs have been produced. They are more or less westernized but the basic tunes are still Korean. Besides these all sorts of western and other foreign music, classical and popular, even including jazz or mambo, are appreciated in Korea, as are all modes of dancing and musical instruments imported from abroad.

There are several colleges of music, both under government control and private management. And high schools and middle schools, as well as primary schools and kindergartens teach music. There also several organizations for research in old classical music and dancing as well as in native operas. It might be said that dancing girls, *Giseng,* are the principal preservers of the traditional music and dancing of Korea.

CLASSIFICATION OF KOREAN MUSICAL INSTRUMENTS

Finally some explanations should be made on the classification of Korean musical instruments. According to my investigations, the total number of Korean instruments, excluding all western instruments, is 82. They may be grouped as follows:

(I) 13 different kinds of stringed instruments—
Flat Plucking Harps: 6 strings 玄琴 , 12 strings 伽倻琴 , 25 strings 琴瑟 .
Standing Plucking Harps: large 竪箜篌 , moderate size 臥箜篌 , and small size 小箜篌.
Mandoline Shaped Plucking Harps: 4 strings 唐琵琶 ,

5 strings 鄕琵琶.

Guitar Shaped Harp: 4 strings 月琴.

Flat Harps Played with a Bow: 7 strings 牙箏, 15 strings 大箏.

Small Violin Shaped Instrument: 2 strings 奚琴.

Flat Harp Striken with a Slender Wand: 25 strings 洋琴.

(II) 25 different styles of wind instruments—

Flutes: 13 holes in 3 sizes; large 大琴, moderate 中琴, and small 小琴. 8 holes 唐笛, 7 holes 管, 6 holes 笒.

Upright Blowing Flutes: 3 holes 籥, 5 holes 短簫, 7 holes 洞簫, 6 holes 㔔.

Clarinet Style: 4 different 8 holes instruments.

Bag Pipe Shaped Instruments: having 7 pipes 竽, 13 pipes 和, and 17 pipes 笙.

Harmonica Shaped Instrument: having 16 holes 簫.

Trumpets: 4 different horns 大角, 螺, 喇叭, 角. .

Instrument in the Shape of the Leaf of a Tree: 草笛.

Ocarina Shape: 塤.

One More Different Style: 壎.

(III) 44 different styles of percussion instruments—

Bells: single bell 特鍾, 16 bells in a frame 編鍾, 2 clapper bells 鐃, 鐸.

Stones: single stone 特磬, 16 stones in a frame 編磬.

Steel Plates: 16 pieces in a frame 方響.

Brass Gongs: 6 different styles 大金, 小金, 鉦, 鑼, 哮哼囉, 雲囉.

Kinds of Cymbals: two different styles 響鈸, 銅鈸.

3 Wooden Boxes: 柷, 應, 犢.

1 Bundle of 6 Clapping Wodden Boards: 拍.

1 Wooden Instrument in the Shape of a Tiger's Notched Backbone: 敔.

1 Crockery Bowl Shaped Instruments: 缶.

16 Single Drums of Different Styles without Handles: 建鼓, 晋鼓, 朔鼓, 羯鼓, 節鼓, 座鼓, 龍鼓, 中鼓, 教坊鼓, 齊鼓, 擔鼓, 雅, 相, 舞鼓, 杖鼓, 應鼓.

Drum Clusters: 2 drums connected 路鼓, 6 drums connected 雷鼓, and 8 drums connected 靈鼓.

Drums with Handles: single drum 鞀, 2 drums connected 路鞀, 3 drums connected 雷鞀 and 4 drums
connected 靈鞀.

Shakespeare in Korea

If I had had much earlier communications directly with the authorities of this Congress, I might have prepared more concrete data and could have delivered an accomplished contribution. My talk here at the present moment is just to show you Korea has its own scene of Shakespeare and also there are a number of Shakespearians in our country.

We assume that Shakespeare was introduced to Korea by the later period of the 19th century through British and American missionaries, but the actual translation of works of Shakespeare was done in the 1920s. Mr. Chul Hyeon translated both Hamlet and the Merchant of Venice into Korean and published them in two volumes separately. I presented one copy each to the library in the Memorial Theatre of Shakespeare at Stratford-on-Avon, England, when I visited one Saturday morning in early September of 1936 on my way home from the Fourth International Congress of Linguists held at the University of Copenhagen, Denmark, where I attended as the official delegate from Korea.

Since the above-mentioned publication of Shakespeare, journalism often referred to the works of Shakespeare in various ways, quoting those lines from them which seemed to be necessary for the purpose of interpreting some truth of life in the form of sayings, aphorisms, or intellectual philosophy. Elementary schools and high schools enjoyed stories of the works of Shakespeare in their abbreviated forms, the former in Korean and the latter in English. And then in 203 colleges and universities in Korea as of 1969, they taught Shakespeare with the original texts in English. Thus some quotations, such as "Frailty, thy name is woman" or "To be, or not to be, that is the question", etc. were spoken even among those people who did not know their derivations. Students as well as professional dramatic groups often performed Shakespeare's dramas on their stages and got good responses from their audiences.

Moreover, many of the plots of Shakespeare's plays have analogous similarity with those of a number of Korean folk tales, legends, historical anecdotes, or old fictions. For example, King Lear, Romeo and Juliet, Macbeth, Othello, the Merchant of Venice and others can be referred to equivalent themes in some of our traditional works, though their settings, characters, and descriptions are different from each other to a certain extent. This might be one of the reasons why our readers become familiar with the universality of Shakespeare and could appreciate his works with much interest.

Particularly one of the most famous of old Korean novels, called Chunhyang-jeon, or the Story of Spring Fragrance, has somewhat the same structure of Shakespeare's the Merchant of Venice. This story is often performed on the stage in the form of Korean classical opera in its own style of versification, which had been written by an unidentified author. The main theme as well as the process gives almost the same dramatic effect as in the Merchant of Venice, with its escalation of curiosity, disappointment, catastrophe of the court, and happy ending as a tragi-comedy.

The ring is replaced by a mirror broken on purpose into two parts at the time of parting after engagement, but to be identified later for reunion. Shylock is represented by a brutal, amorous magistrate, and Portia can be compared to a secret royal commissioner who is the bridegroom, now disguised as a beggar, but acts later as the judge of a trial in the court. Then the intention of cutting a pound of flesh and the idea of blood not to be shed are symbolized by the poem in which the disguised judge warned the merciless magistrate not to suck the blood of the oppressed people. This selfish magistrate and other corrupt officials are finally punished, followed by the happy reunion of the imprisoned bride, named Spring Fragrance, and the Royal Commissioner, the bridegroom himself, named

Mong-ryong Yi.

Time does not allow me to deal with the whole stories in detailed comparisons, but I can say such universal communication of ideas and literary techniques as well as the dramatic effect can be traced in the works of two different nations. As I explained above, these two works, the Merchant of Venice and the Story of Spring Fragrance, might be excavated from a comparative literature's point of view to find some clue for the possibility of interrelated influences, or to admit them as the theme of approach, or to take them as the examples of universal happenings without any direct or indirect contact between them whatsoever.

Now turning to the activities of scholars of Shakespeare in Korea, we organized in 1964 the Shakespeare Society of Korea and its members are well coordinated in the pursuit of their purposes. These are the annual memorial celebration of Shakespeare on his birthday, periodical publications, such as the Shakespeare News and the Shakespeare Review, the teamwork in bringing out guidebooks on Shakespeare and editing of textbooks with Korean notes.

Recently two complete sets of Shakespeare's translated works have been published, one by a lone professor and the other by a number of specialists who jointed together one or two works each.

In conclusion I can tell you that Shakespeare has secured great popularity even among our people, and we expect an international contribution to Shakespearian studies through close contact with colleagues at home and abroad. This congress will, I am sure, prove such a vision be realized.

Thank you very much for your kind attention.

(A speech delivered at the International Cooperation Committee of the World Shakespeare Congress held in Vancouver, Canada, August 20-28, 1971)

Spotlights of 1970's

REVOLT OF MODERN LITERATURE IN KOREA

Traditional literature in Korea down to the 19th century had been centered around the love of peace, tranquility of mind, and acceptance of social order. The primary religion of Korea, Shamanism, suggested close identity of human to nature and to this was added the self-satisfied human life of circling quietude from Buddhism. Then Confucianism tried to doctrinate our people to accept the status quo with the five morals of ethics, and also some influences of Taoism were imposed on their life with the idea of supernatural utopia. These religious principles had formed the foundations for the traditional literature of Korea, and they gave to it a sense of subjugation to circumstances.

But coming into the 20th century, the so-called New Literature started. This new literature aimed at the emancipation of individuals who had been suffering from the traditional conditions of life as well as the oppression under the imperialistic Japanese occupation of the land. Romantic lyricism in poetry and naturalistic realism prevailed during the first half of the 1920s, giving new hope of nationalism to the nation and visualising the miserable conditions of the oppressed people. Now in the second half of the 1920s Marxism emerged in Korean literature as a strategy of class war against the Japanese capitalism. Though there was a certain amount of struggle between the above-mentioned right wing and this new left wing of proletarian literature, both of them were promoted for resistance against the alien ruler. Their strategies were antagonistic toward each other, but their aim coincided to revolt against the common enemy.

In the 1930s, among such tumults of literary arguments, translation of western works increased. They tried to introduce those masterpieces of the Western world to the nation in their genuine form, and many of them were performed on the stages. During the same period there were also several movements of pure art for art's sake, such as modernists, imagists, surrealism, pastoral literature and others. But these can be considered as escapists, and were an indirect revolt against reality.

With the start of the World War II the Japanese authorities banned the use of the Korean language in schools and also adopted a very tough policy on the writing of creative literature in Korea. The result was that many writers stopped writing, took refuge outside the country, or went underground as a non-violent protest.

Since the Independence of Korea in 1945, two different groups of literature sprang up—one in support of a free and democratic Korea and the other as an apologist for communist doctrine. Here again as in previous history, we had a deep antagonism between two literary groups and their division was made complete by the political division of the country at the 38th parallel.

The Korean War started in 1950 and the truce treaty was signed in 1954. The post Korean war literature lasted until the early 1960s and tried to reveal descriptions of the war and its tragic consequences. But after the war the life of intellectuals was actually in chaos caused by the almost continuous political and social turbulence. In the south the Student Uprising in April 1960, the few months of Government by the Opposition Party, and then the Military Revolution in May of the following year greatly influenced on many writers.

Those who made their appearance in the first part of the 1960s were outspoken in the struggle against injustice, and in overcoming the aftermath of the tragedy of the Korean War, they also cried out their sentiments against corruption in society. In the latter part of the 1960s several young writers produced some memorable works which dealt with the problem of people of the

post war era. Many of the established writers criticized administration of the alien rulers in the past or displayed the psycho-
analysis of the people suffering from the unsettled condition of
divided Korea.

Now coming to the end of the 1960s, in the South writers in
general gradually began to forget the Korean War and intensified their ideological antagonism against communism, while
other authors appealed to the sentiments and ideas of readers
who were no longer interested in analysis of the frustration and
loneliness of individuals in the midst of great historical events or
national anxiety. Thus, a significant and controversial issue
developed in literary circles—the contrast between the renewed
active participation in social affairs and the individual contemplation of the inner spiritual life.

Through these 50 years of modernization of Korean literature there has been also a kind of revival movement of tradition,
with many critics, poets, and writers calling for its restoration.
This spirit of renaissance has been in revolt against the use of
Western technology in the creation of literature. Recently in
some quarters there is a cry for a synthetic compromise between
the traditional features of the Orient and the modern sentiment
of the West.

In short modern Korean literature during the last 50 years
aimed in the beginning at a revolt against the traditional systems
of life which had led the people to accept subjugation to circumstances, and through several movements, indoctrinated by Western
techniques, produced literary works that tried to inspire dreams
of national independence and a hatred for imperialism or totalitarianism. Though sometimes they had art for art's sake or
escapism from reality or revival of traditionalism, all of them
were the thesis, anti-thesis, and synthe-thesis of revolt in
circling dialectics. Literature during recent 50 years in Korea
has been significant in the aspiration of revolt in one way or
another.

*(Delivered at the International P.E.N. Congress,
1971, Dublin)*

PATRONAGE OF MODERN LITERATURE IN KOREA

Under totalitarian regimes state power is used to control literature for establishing its doctrines and as an agent to promote the philosophy and policies of the administration. While on the other hand in free countries such monopolized patronage has not been possible. Intellectuals very often try to eliminate any such controlling power and the commercialism of publishing companies rather tends to induce writers to deal with popular works.

Differing from these two categories mentioned above, in an oppressed country controlled under the yoke of alien's conquest, as, for example, in Modern Korea during the 40 years of Japanese occupation from 1905 until 1945, there was almost no patronage from the ruling class for creative literature or any significant publishing organizations to stimulate it. There were only some self-supporting Korean daily newspapers, such as Dong-A Daily News, Chosun Daily News and others, or magazines, such as Gaebyeog (the Creation), Korean Literary Circle and others, edited by native patriots and conscientious individuals inspired by the motivation of their own self-determination. Indeed, the only true patronage of literature under such circumstances was the genuine motivation of intellectual pursuit of the Korean writers themselves.

After the 2nd World War when Korea was emancipated and the later division of the country into North and South, patronage of literature became different for the two parts. The North tends to be monopolized by the state, while the South has been moulded by a compromise between suggestions of the state, free commercialism of publishing enterprisers, and cultural organizations.

Now in the South either the Ministry of Culture and private organizations often offer rewards for the best literature published. They are inspiring and effective as varied forms of patronage. In addition all daily newspapers and some periodicals established a system of annual prizes—awarded on January 1st of each year—for the best pieces carefully selected among these manuscripts submitted for the contests. Other rewards such as literary awards established in commemoration of deceased writers, such as Dong-In Literature Reward and others, are used to promote the creation of genuine literature.

Recently patronage of literature in Korea has been extended through the cooperation of writers. Several organizations of writers, for example, the Korean Center of International P.E.N. Club, the Korean Writers Association, Korean Women Writers Association and others often take necessary actions through unanimous resolutions to force publishers to raise the amount of copy money and also to defend their copyright within the country against careless publishers—though Korea did not take part in the International Convention of Copyright yet.

Finally we can say that the best patrons of literature are the better circulation of readers who really appreciate the value of literature, but this market is rather limited in the divided country.

(Delivered at the International P.E.N. Congress, 1971, Dublin)

Translation of Literature

TRANSLATING KOREAN LITERATURE
Joint Management for English Versions

Translation has been so far considered by the people as a subsidiary pursuit of literary production, simply because it is, they think, affiliated with the original text of a creative work.

Translation, as we understand it, is to transfer through the transformation of linguistic differences, the literature of one language into another corresponding speech, so that the foreigner may be able to read and appreciate the foreign composition. The work itself is an attached action to the primary harvest.

But nowadays when international communications have been tremendously emphasized, the purpose of translation is multiplied and its area much enlarged. Therefore I would like to establish a new dimension of literature in a categorical sense for various urgent considerations to be made—*Translation Literature*.

Of course, I admit national literature is given the position of a primary source, but we need two criteria for defining its boundary—the language and the nationality. By a national literature we mean a literature produced in the national orthography of a country by native writers of the language.

National Literature
From this point of view a foreign literature, so-called, is also the national literature of a specific country, but it is an alien literature in a relative concept to a nation which does not belong to the area where the language is spoken.

Then, the new terminology I am using here, "Translation Literature" is neither a national literature nor a foreign one, because it does not keep up the above-mentioned two binding criteria, language and nationality.

The language employed in translation is not the original one primarily written. For example, the works of Shakespeare translated into Korean are no more, strictly speaking, English literature, because the language utilized in the translation is not English but Korean. Nor can they be called Korean literature even though written in Korean, because the idea of the works had originally been created by the English author.

The translator can be a Korean, or a Chinese, or an Indian who mastered the Korean language. There is no limitation of nationality and language in translation literature.

Now speaking of translation of Korean literature into English, the similar application of theoretical approach can be made. When a Korean poem *sijo* is translated into English, it is not Korean literature in its true sense, because the Korean language is not maintained, one of the two most important factors with which we usually determine the category of the nationality of a literature. And also the translated verse in English is not English literature at all even if it were transferred into English, because the original nationality of authorship was Korean.

Thus Korean literature transmitted into English is a sort of Bohemian, an international figure or a fosterchild of comparative literature.

Literary Taste

From these conditions Translation Literature requires two careful considerations for its reasonable achievement: selection of works to be translated and technique of translation. The work picked up should meet on one hand the taste of foreign readers while on the other hand it better be a satisfactory object of native evaluation. Some works which we Koreans appreciate very much are often tasteful to foreigners and vice versa.

When I was teaching at the University of London, I prepared two bundles of manuscripts of English translations, one

"Folk Tales From Korea" and the other "Modern Short-Stories From Korea." A British publisher accepted the former at once and immediately printed it, but he would not take the latter.

The reason was very simple. The folk tales were full of different customs and manners which were quite strange and interesting to Westerners, but the modern stories were, as the editor claimed, almost identical with those of western writers in the treatment of material. Thus the former was published on the spot in London and got an international reputation, but the latter had to wait to find a Korean publisher many years later in Seoul.

Thus Westerners paid more attention to the archaic things of Korea. Differing from this the contemporary Korean readers are usually more absorbed in modern literature of Korea which has the up-to-date sentiment of our life, sharing the technique of modern literature of the West. Generally speaking, Korean intellectuals are rather absent-minded in our ancient literature, or those of former days before the restoration of the 1900s. The study or research of old traditional literature is now more or less confined within the circle of scholars of classical literature. How can we fuse these two extreme inclinations differentiating each other?

In the class of my lectures on Korean culture for foreigners, the Westerners or English speaking students are more interested in the appreciation of old literature of Korea than in the modern. But our contemporary writers expect their recent production be better recommended among western readers, because they are proud of their cultural level now highly inspired by their modern intelligence. Thus there is a gap between the literary tastes of two hemispheres. How shall we overcome this parallel of contrasting attitudes?

Honestly speaking, the more urgent necessity of translation from our Korean view is to introduce first modern literature written by our contemporaries because the world should know "Korea Today" and "Koreans Alive" before the things of the past are excavated.

If this is imperative the selection of works for translation into English is advised to be carried out by a joint committee from the two nationalities, that is to say, by Korean experts and western readers together. And their targets should aim at modern literature which has the well-blended idea of Korean flavor plus western technique. This means to supply one for two demands.

For example, we can compare two novels by Yi Gwang-su, the father of modern Korean literature, "Heartlessness" (Mujeong) and the "Death of Yi Chadon." The former had secured one of the highest reputations among Korean readers because of its epoch-making merit for modern enlightenment of our national development as well as the inspiration of individual conscious-ness of new life, but it may not appeal much to Westerners as we expect, because the subject matter and its idea had been prac-tised long ago in the West.

In contrast with this the latter would be, I am sure, en-thusiastically approached by Westerners as well as Asian readers, because this specific fiction has its unique mystery and martyrdom based on historical data and religious piety.

In the selection of works priority should be determined through a sort of joint discussion by native specialists and foreign consultants. Furthermore, if we assume a chance may happen in the future to recommend a candidate for the Nobel Prize of literature, adoption of the above-mentioned cautious policy is quite imperative.

Joint Management

Now turning the focus of our issue to the technique of translation, I also suggest another joint management of translat-ing procedure by two parties, that is, a Korean who mastered English for the purpose and an English-speaking foreigner who has full capacity of reading Korean and a certain amount of writing talent in Korean, too. Thus any translation done by a Korean should be checked by an English-speaking counterpart and vice versa.

But from my own experience, I am rather inclined to advise that a Korean should take the initiative and then the foreigner concerned be seated with the Korean to review the primary translation already accomplished.

It may take time for both of them to polish the translation

literature sitting together identifying simultaneously from two angles, but this type of reciprocal effort is absolutely indispensable for the production of reliable literary craft.

There are two types of translation, literary translation and free translation. The former deals more carefully with the equivalent morphology and syntax in another language while on the other hand the latter is using a free hand in the adjustment of semantic similarity.

But these dual extremes of methodological attitudes should be modified between the two to such an extent that the translation of classics, for example, "Reminiscences of Three Kingdoms" or "The Story of Spring Perfume," are expected to be carried out more by literary translation, but modern fiction may well be done more or less by free translation. In any case a translator's licence should not run over the boundary between exactness and delicacy.

Case of Poetry

Translation of poetry is more complicated. When translating Korean *sijo* into English, symmetrical arrangement of prosody—meter, rhyme, alliteration, and stanza—are to be remembered as much as possible.

But modern poetry can be framed without such strictness of rules and regulations. But even free verse should be provided with a certain amount of consciousness of prosodical scansion though containing irregularities and exceptions.

In Korea, translation of European literature into Korean is much better in quality and abundant in quantity, but translation of Korean literature into English had been practised in the past mostly on an individual basis or rather at-random motivations.

Only recently several group projects have been promulgated by some organizations, such as the International P.E.N. Club, National Committee for Translation of Korean Classics, Asian Writers' Translation Bureau, universities, Ministry of Public Information and Culture, and The Korea Times.

This is a good omen for a better future. The purpose of "translation literature" is to effect lively international exchange of literature through translation and publication of selected works of literature and other related cultural works originating from the nations of Asia, thereby promoting better mutual understanding, cooperation, and lasting friendship among them and further with the American and European people at large.

Finally I hope full financial support be provided by the governmental authority concerned as well as public organizations and individuals.

—1971. 1. 1. Korea Times—

EXCHANGE OF LITERATURE PROMOTED THROUGH TRANSLATION

At the 37th International P.E.N. Congress held at the Chosun Hotel in Seoul on Sunday, June 28th, 1970, the proposal of the Korean Center for the establishment of a Translation Bureau for Asian Literature was seconded by England and endorsed by the United States, India, Japan, Vietnam, Ceylon, China, Australia and France. It was enthusiastically received by other centers and passed unanimously.

During lunch the sixteen Asian countries represented at the congress met and an ad hoc committee of one from each country was formed under the chairmanship of Prof. Zong In-sob (Korea). At the three consecutive meetings of the committee separately held during the congress it passed several resolutions, chose the name of the bureau (the Asian Writers' Translation Bureau), appointed the bureau staff (director: Dr. Zong In-sob), chose the location of its head office (Seoul, Korea), and agreed on publication of a quarterly bulletin (Asian Literature) and an annual anthology of Asian Writers' works translated either in English or in French, etc.

Upon the resolutions aforesaid, the headquarters center was established on July 18th in the office of the P.E.N. Korean Center, and it initiated its activities. Since then the constitution of the bureau has been approved by the member centers, and recently the first issues of the anthology, "Asian Literature," and of "AWTB Newsletter" have been published.

As indicated in Article II of the constitution, the purpose

of this international organization is to effect lively international exchange of literature through translation and publication of selected works of literature and other related cultural works originating from the nations of Asia, thereby promoting better mutual understanding, cooperation, and lasting friendship.

If these two publications of the bureau just brought out meet to a certain extent the original demand of our P.E.N. colleagues and also increase the appetite of the general public throughout the world, we might expect further development of the bureau's activities in full scale.

I would like to point out on this occasion some of the difficulties which I had encountered in the pursuit of this international administration for collection of manuscripts from Asian writers and printing procedures, including the financial background to be secured.

Honestly speaking it took two full years before we started the editing works here in Seoul because of the unavoidable delay of manuscripts. Through several communications with each P.E.N. center in various Asian countries, we found that they had themselves their own complicated problems, such as selection of valuable works, reliable translation of the selected pieces and copy money.

In addition to these, the bureau itself has been keeping up a few covering rules and regulations for the preparation of manuscripts, which were reaffirmed at the annual meeting of Asian representatives when they met in Dublin for the 38th International Congress, in 1972:

(1) Translations into either English or French must be those of Asian literature originally written in the native languages.

(2) Translation already printed and published should not be included.

(3) Manuscripts of translation should be authorized by the respective centers.

Finally regarding the budget of the bureau we have Article IX which says, "The budget of expenditures of the Translation Bureau shall be borne by the member nations, prorated on the basis determined by the working committee at its annual meeting.''

Yet for the primary stages of its administrative actions and the publications concerned, we were rather hesitant to request any amount of their share because of financial situation of member centers and also the uncertain commitment of achievements on our part. So we announced to the member centers that we, the Seoul office, would bear the expenses for printing and publication as well as a certain amount of copy money for the contributors.

At last we secured 17 works from seven Asian countries—China, India, Japan, Korea, Lebanon, the Philippines, and Thailand (15 short stories including five from Korea, and two plays, one modern play from India and one dramatic poetry from Lebanon—all in English except two stories and one play in French). Several lyrics from India and Hawaii had been sent us, but selected poems were excluded from the first issue of the anthology. And also one short story "The Wedding" written by a native writer of New Zealand, named Witi Ihimaera, was submitted, but it was too late for us to include it in this issue. Much earlier than this one article "Folk History in Australia" written by Mr. L.J. Blake had been submitted to us through the Melbourne center, but all these above-mentioned are reserved for a future number being advised by the editing committee here.

Bringing out these two international publications, the anthology, "Asian Literature" and the bulletin "AWTB Newsletter," took more than half a year, including careful proof reading, twice by Korean experts and the third final reading by foreign native scholars.

In concluding I would like to say that this kind of anthology which contains in one volume trustworthy translations of various Asian literature of international level will contribute much to the comparative observations of their national characteristics as well as the appreciation of Oriental literature to revaluate the symphony of the world literature as the counterpart of Occidental works.

Now the Republic of Korea is taking initiative action for this significant undertaking for the international motivation and more positive cooperation from all East Asian Middle East countries will be much appreciated.

—1973. 9. 30 Korea Times—

Asian Writers' Translation Bureau

The 38th International P.E.N. Congress (Dublin), September 13th, 1971.
Asian Writers' Translation Bureau.
Dr. In-Sob Zong, Director of the Asian Writers' Translation Bureau made his greetings and report at the Executive Committee in the morning as follows:

Greetings!

As one of the official delegates from Korea. I am sincerely grateful to you who offered us the opportunity of holding the 37th Congress last year in Seoul. By the warm hearted cooperation of those participants there, we could carry on successfully all the procedures, and particularly the theme of the Congress— Humor in Literature—East and West—made us all happy and pleasant in a witty, humorous atmosphere during the Congress. We just published the complete volume of its proceedings, speeches, and discussions in three equivalent versions reciprocally translated into English, French, and Korean. This will, I am sure, strengthen the immortality of recollection of the Congress in our hearts.

On behalf of the Korean Center I thank you all again, the President, General Secretary and all delegates for your further friendship through this memorable jubilee of the International P.E.N. Club.

Report of Asian Writers' Translation Bureau

By the unanimous resolution passed at the Executive Committee and the Conferences of 17 Asian Centers' delegates we

set up the Headquarters of the Bureau in Seoul with the necessary equipment and staff. As was recommended, we planned
two publications, one, a quarterly named "Asian Literature" in
200 pages in English and French, and the other, an annual Anthology of 500 pages for the works of Asian writers.

As to the quarterly, we asked all Asian Centers to send
their manuscripts as of December 5th, 1970, with the draft of its
constitution attached and we are still waiting for their contributions. The quarterly will be printed as soon as we get enough
manuscripts to become a periodical. A request for financial support was submitted to UNESCO in Paris as of September 25th
1970, through the National Commission in Seoul, but no
response came from it. The Headquarters in Seoul will probably
bear the expences for printing and publication as well as a certain amount of copy money.

And for the publication of the Anthology, a more detailed
scheme will be discussed at a separate meeting of Asian delegates some time during this Congress. There is no financial
problem, because the Seoul office will secure the necessary
amount of funds for this annual publication and we can an-
nounce at this moment that a reasonable amount of copy money
will be paid to those who contribute.

For both I request a more positive effort of all Asian
Centers for their immediate action in the selection of works,
trustworthy translations and administrative responses.

Accordingly the representatives of Asian official delegates,
one from each center, met separately from 5 p.m. as the working committee of this time, and passed the following decisions:

To speed up the publications of its quarterly, "Asian
Literature" and the annual anthology, both of which had
already been planned in the previous year,

1. Any resolutions, policies, or understandings made at the
conferences of representatives should be supported and carried
out by the presidents of their centers.

2. Translations either into English or French must be those
of Asian literatures originally written in the native languages.

3. Works originally written in English or French should
not be reprinted. Accordingly the participations of the two

Australian Centers and New Zealand are not likely to be eligible.

4. Any translation once printed and published should not be included.

5. Manuscripts of translation should be authorized by the respective center.

6. Manuscripts from each center for one periodical of the quarterly should not exceed 2,000 words, those of the anthology not exceeding 3,000 words either in English or in French. A longer piece may be divided between more than one volume (an exception may be made in the case of plays).

7. The quarterly may include book reviews, interviews with or without photographs, recent literary activities or merits, historical surveys, folklore, academic articles, as well as poetry, short stories, novels, plays, criticism, and essays (abbreviated summaries are not recommended).

8. Manuscripts of the quarterly should be sent to the head office (Seoul, Korea) every three months by November, February, May, and August, and those of the Anthology should be sent once every year until June.

Representatives attended:

Turkey	Ulkür Tamer
	(Talat S. Halman)
India	G. S. Khosla
Japan	Ayako Sono
Thailand	Wibha Senanan
Philippines	F. Sionil Jose
Lebanon	C. Aboussouan
Israel	David Lazer
Hawaii	John Young
Korea	In-Sob Zong
	(Kwang-Yong Chun)
	(Yun-Suk Moh)
	(Byung-ro Yun)

Thirty Years of Peace
for World Literature

Immediately after the Second World War a new liberalism prevailed through the world for the creation of intellectual freedom by the cooperative management of world peace by the Allied forces. For example, "The Love of Four Colonels" by the British playwright, Ustinov, visualized on the stage a well-balanced joint maintenance of administration of an occupied town in successive turns of one week each by four colonels from Britain, France, Soviet Russia, and the U.S.A.

Later they were all guided for an excavative sight-seeing tour by the native major of the town to an ancient castle in its suburb where they find the common ideal of a sleeping Beauty, who can be referred to as the symbol of external peace.

This play illustrates the possibility of tentative preservation of world peace. Many writers throughout the world—not only in Europe but also in other hemispheres made the same kind of effort in their literary productions for the common utopia of international tranquility. These experiments have a significant feature of a synthetic thesis of my view of the dialectical process of the world's civilization.

Nevertheless as in the last scene of the above-mentioned theatrical performance, two of the colonels, the American and the French, try to stay forever in the castle of the Sleeping Beauty, each on opposite sides of her bed, while the other two colonels, the British and the Russian, leave the dream of the enchanted castle to come back to the world of reality. Here the playwright seems to have suggested idealism versus realism, or a thesis and its antithesis. Whatever prediction the author may aim at in his writing, the actual literary circles of the world during the latter half of these thirty years after the War were rather divided into two antagonistic arguments in the creation of arts with arbitrary contrasts among ideologically diverse groups or blocks.

These conflicts have been stimulated politically throughout the world during the period of cold war under the pretext of local warfares. These, however, always stopped short of a hot war on an international scale. We must realize indeed that these thirty years of peace owe much to the literature of many writers not only in Europe but also in other regions of the world, including Asia, who have produced their harvests through various genres of art to secure world peace.

Geographical division of hot-spots throughout the world, such as in Korea or Germany, sometimes induced internal or external tumults against the will of those nations concerned, but such unavoidable phenomena of bursting bubbles acted very often as the catharsis for releasing the tension of international indigestions, otherwise the whole world might have been destroyed by nuclear weapons. The peaceful settlement of world issues has to be handled on the basis of coexistence or detente if necessary, the image of which has been deeply rooted in the minds of the people. Thus political features and the influence of literature should be considered on a reciprocal basis.

The role of a neutral country seems to be very heavy in these days. Neutralism so-called should not mean only a vacant zero thesis. it should act as the real peace-maker in its true sense. The world requires genuine peace not in a disguised attire nor in a twisted dogma.

The Asian Writer' Translation Bureau, which had been inaugurated as an organization affiliated to the International P.E.N. Club is doing its best for the promotion of understanding and peace among Asian countries and also extends its services to the world at large as the bridge between Western readers and Asian writers through translations.

We are very glad to meet here in Vienna to talk about the common interest of world peace, through the means of literature.
(Delivered at the International P.E.N. Congress, 1975, Vienna)

"Asian Literature"

Volume I

The proposal for the establishment of an Asian Writers' Translation Bureau was formally introduced at the 36th International P.E.N. Congress held at Menton, France in September 1969. The Congress then approved it in principle, but it was at a meeting of the International Executive Committee of the 37th International P.E.N. Congress held on 28 June 1970 in Seoul, Korea, that the proposal won its final approval. A total of 16 member nations in the Asian and Pacific region participated in the Seoul meeting inaugurating this new organization.

Shortly thereafter, the office of the Bureau was established in Seoul, Korea, and I had the honor of assuming its first directorship. An Advisory Board consisting of 15 persons, all members of the Korean Centre, and an Editorial Committee of four persons were activated next. The Central Committee of the Korean Centre was instrumental in giving birth to these organizations.

The purpose of the Bureau is to effect lively interchange of literature through the publication of selected works of literature and other related cultural works originating from the nations of Asia, thereby promoting better mutual understanding, cooperation and friendship throughout the world.

As one of the major projects to fulfill this purpose, the Bureau has decided to publish an anthology of translated works of literature originating in the region. Letters were sent out to member nations to contribute manuscripts, but as is customary in an undertaking of this nature, communication was often difficult. Thus there has been an inevitable delay in publishing this anthology.

The staff of the Bureau will consider it fortunate if this maiden publication meets the standard of the parent organization and receives the critical attention of our readers abroad.

For this year, a newsletter entitled *Asian Writers' Translation Bureau Newsletter* has been published to replace the quarterly journal, *Asian Literature,* which was originally planned at the time of the Bureau's inauguration. The *Newsletter* is designed to promote the interchange of ideas and information regarding the activity of the Bureau.

The staff of the Bureau welcomes suggestions and advice from the member nations as well as general readers.

April, 1973

Volume II

Upon the resolutions unanimously passed at the 37th International P.E.N. Congress held in Seoul (1970), the Headquarters Centre of the Asian Writers' Translation Bureau was established on July 18th in the office of the Korean P.E.N. Centre.

Henceforth as recommended by the representatives from 17 Asian Centres, two publications were brought out by the Bureau. Namely *Asian Literature* volume I, an anthology which covers 14 short stories and 2 plays from 16 Asian nations, and the first issue of *AWTB Newsletter* attached therewith which aimed at periodical reports from the Head Office, and also the reciprocal communications among the fellow members of the Bureau and the colleagues of the International P.E.N. Club, not to speak of the correspondences with individual contributors.

Now we are presenting the second volume of *Asian Literature* which contains a large amount of literary works from 11 Asian Centres, Australia, Taiwan, Hong Kong, India, Iran, Japan, Jordan, Korea, Lebanon, New Zealand and Turkey, varied in the fields of poetry, short stories, essays, criticisms. And also the second issue of *AWTB Newsletter* attached herewith will give the readers the recent news regarding the activities of those who took part in the pursuit of our projects, including book-reviews on the previous publications.

Particularly we are very grateful to Madame Wadia, the founder of International P.E.N. All-India Centre for her initiative cooperation with us in securing a tremendous amount of manuscripts from India, and also to Professor Halman for his warm-hearted contributions with translation of Turkish poetry.

Finally we would like to draw your attention on the part of those Asian Centres and contributors to our editorial principles already promulgated that the anthology will accept only those unpublished works or not printed yet. And also we request the brief autobiographical data of the authors and translators be submitted together with their manuscripts so that the general readers may appreciate the merits of their works much better.

We sincerely hope that many of those manuscripts not printed in this second volume be included in the third anthology which will emerge in the nearest future. More positive actions for further contributions from Asian P.E.N. Centres to get ready for immediate supply will be much appreciated.

May, 1975

Volume III

Since the establishment of the Asian Writers' Translation Bureau which had been unanimously passed at the 37th International P.E.N. Congress held in Korea (1970) as a separate function directly affiliated to the Headquarters of a world association of writers, "the International P.E.N. Club" itself, the Head Office of the Bureau in Seoul has been engaged in its activities.

The purpose of the Bureau is to effect lively interchange of literature through the publication of selected works originating from the nations of Asia, thereby promoting better mutual understanding, cooperation and friendship between the East and the West throughout the world.

I made greetings at the Executive Committee of the 38th P.E.N. Congress held in Ireland and reported there the

Bureau's activities up to 1972. And the official delegates of Asian P.E.N. Centers met separately during the Congress at Dun Laoghaire to discuss on cooperation of member Centers.

An Anthology of Asian Writers' works, namely *Asian Literature* Volume I (320 pages, 15cm×22cm) was published in June 1973. It contains 14 short stories from six countries, and 2 plays from 2 countries. At the same time attached to it *AWTB Newsletter* Vol. 1 No. 1 (6 pages, 21cm×30cm) was also issued, which contains the History and Constitution of the Bureau, congratulatory messages, reports, letters from members, contributors, etc. Accordingly these two publications were distributed to those concerned as well as to all International P.E.N. Centers throughout the world.

In view of the difficulty of collecting manuscripts from member countries, I visited China (Taiwan) P.E.N. Center in Dec. 1974 to discuss various items for the subsequent publications of the Bureau.

Then the anthology *Asian Literature* Volume II (301 pages 15cm×22cm) was brought out on August 10, 1975, which includes 85 poems by 45 poets from 7 countries, 17 short stories by 17 writers from 8 countries, and 7 essays by 7 writers from 4 countries.

As was in the past the corresponding *AWTB Newsletter* Vol. 2 No. 2 (4 pages 21cm×30cm) was also printed for the Director's report and messages, book-reviews on *Asian Literature* Vol. I, and letters from colleagues. And these two publications were also immediately circulated at home and abroad to those organizations and individuals directly or indirectly concerned.

I made an official report on the activities of the Bureau at the Executive Committee of the 40th International P.E.N. Congress held in Vienna, Austria. And a separate meeting of the Asian Writers' Translation Bureau was held during the Congress, and several topics were discussed for the future projects of the Bureau as well as its achievements so far, including the continuous preparation of the issue of another anthology, *Asian Literature* Vol. III. To chase up the collection of manuscripts I had personal contacts at Mexico City with several scholars on the occasion of my participation in the 30th International Congress of Human Sciences in Asia and North Africa held there in 1976.

It was expected for us to make its debut in 1977. But the heavy financial burden solely imposed on our Head Office here resulted in one year delay even after the completion of editorial works. And also because of the tardy printing procedures the anthology *Asian Literature* Vol. III which we eagerly anticipated has finally emerged now. Instead of issuing another *AWTB Newsletter* to be attached to it this time, we added an Appendix in the anthology.

We owe much to Asan Foundation which patronized the Bureau this time with its financial aid for the publication of this *'Asian Literature,* Volume III'. I, on behalf of all members and colleagues of the Bureau, express my hearty thanks to Mr. Chung Ju Yung, the Chairman of the Board of Directors of the Foundation, who pays much attention to the promotion of academic pursuits of scholars as well as the social welfare services to the nation. Furthermore we hope his additional chairmanship in the activities of the Federation of Korean Industries be twice blessed for the everlasting prosperity of our national economy.

Finally we would like to express our deepest regret over the death of Dr. Lin Yu-tang (Taiwan), Chairman of the Bureau. Instead the former Secretary General of the Bureau, Mrs. Jit K. Sibunruang (Thailand) has been replaced by Mrs. Nancy Chang Ing (Taiwan) since the gathering of Asian delegates at Vienna. And Mr. Se-hun Shyn, a young poet (Korea), is now helping me here in the office as a local secretary.

Feb. 1979

A New Dualistic Interwoven Dialectics for the World's Literature with Korean Contrasts

To deal with the synchronic processes of cultural development of human life both Hegel and Marx established each a monolithic dialectics of three stages—thesis, anti-thesis, and synthesis, the former with Idealism, while the latter with Materialism. But either of the two does not seem to be reasonable, because both of their treatments are against the facts we have experienced so far.

Therefore, as for me, admitting two constituents of a human existence, mind and body, I hereby try to formulate a new dualistic interwoven dialectics of four stages—synthesis, thesis, anti-thesis, and zero-thesis, (or an extended order, thesis, anti-thesis, zero-thesis, and synthesis,) which are systematically arranged with two factors, Spiritualism (hereafter abbreviated with the symbol, S) and Materialism (hereafter signified with the symbol, M). Particularly to trace the chronological order of cultural trends of Korea in comparison with those of the West, I figured out the neuclus of a chart, vertically analyzed and also horizontally emerged therewith— a methodological bird's eye view of their total complex. Now I will illustrate the frame and its contents in the following short-cut interpretation.

Human civilization is divided into cycles, each of which has four periods, starting with a Dawn or Peace or Harmony (Synthesis, S + M, or M + S) and ending by a Chaos or War or Ennui (zero-thesis, hereafter indicated with O), the second and the third period between them being a thesis (S or M) and an anti-thesis (M or S) respectively.

For example, speaking of the physical history of human

週期 Cycles	要目 Items 段階 Stages									
		無限 Infinity	神 God	元素 Elements	混沌 Chaos					

(世界文學의 二元論的 交替 辨證法 및 各 時代의 思潮區分)

A New Dualistic Interwoven Dialectics for the World's Literature with Korean

週期 Cycles	段階 Stages					
歷史以前 Pre-History	1 黎明 Dawn	無限 Infinity				
	2		神 God			
	3			元素 Elements		
	4 混沌 Chaos				混沌 Chaos	
I 週期 Cycle	1 黎明 Dawn			原始時代 Primitive	: 口傳文學 (Oral Literature), 兒童文學 (Literature for Children)	
	2	↓	上代古典 Helle-nism	: 巫俗思想 (Shamanism), 多神教 (Pantheism)		
	3	↓	↓	中世主義 Hebra-ism	: 佛教 (Buddhism), 輪廻思想 (Transmigration)	
	4 混沌 Chaos	↓		暗黑時代 Dark Age	: 佛教 腐敗 (Corruption of Buddhism)	
II 週期 Cycle	1 黎明 Dawn	↓ ↓ ↓	近世古典 Classi-cism	: 儒教 (Confucianism), 形式主義		
	2	↓ ↓	浪漫主義 Romanti-cism	⟶	基督教 (Christianit	
	3	↓ ↓ ↓ ↓	自然主義 Natural-ism	⟶	實學派	
	4 混沌 Chaos	↓	↓	(頹廢思想, 第一次世界大戰) (Decadent, World War I)	世紀末思潮 Fin de Siécle	
III 週期 Cycle	1 黎明 Dawn	↓ ↓ ↓ ↓	↓	新理想主義 Neo-Idealism		
	2	↓ ↓ ↓	↓	新Sa		
	3	↓ ↓ ↓	↓			
	4 混沌 Chaos	↓	↓	(潛在意識, 第 (Subconscious		
IV 週期 Cycle	1 黎明 Dawn	↓ ↓ ↓	↓	↓		
	2	↓ ↓ ↓	↓	↓		
	3	↓ ↓ ↓	↓	↓		
	4 混沌 Chaos	↓	↓	↓		
V 週期 Cycle	1 黎明 Dawn	↓ ↓ ↓	↓	↓		
	2	↓ ↓ ↓	↓	↓		
	3	↓ ↓ ↓	↓	↓		
	4 混沌 Chaos	↓	↓	↓		

Contrasts and Classification of Their Ideological Processes

Ideological Process	命題 Dialectics	M : S	物 : 心	所有慾 Possession	愛情慾 Affection	運命慾 Destination
	綜合命題 Synthesis	(M+S)	(物+心)			
	正命題 Thesis	S	心			
	反命題 Antithesis	M	物			
	零命題 Zerothesis	O	零			
	綜合命題 Synthesis	S+M	心+物	皆有 Everybody owned	母系 Maternal	自然死 Natural Death
	正命題 Thesis	M^1	$物^1$	全有 Monopolizing	美奴 Beauty-slave	神・人對立 Human vs Gods
	反命題 Antithesis	S^1	$心^1$	全無 Nothing	聖母 Holy Mother	全犠牲 Total Sacrifice
	零命題 Zerothesis	O^1	$零^1$			
...mality), 中庸 (Moderation), 兩班思想 (Bureaucracy)	綜合命題 Synthesis	M^1+S^1	$物^1+心^1$	領土所有 Territorial	貴族女性 Ladies	性格運命 Character
...思想 (Resurrection)	正命題 Thesis	S^2	$心^2$	各人所有 Personal Possession	處女禮讚 Virginity	氣質運命 Temperament
...ctical Science Group), 開化思想 (Enlightenment)	反命題 Antithesis	M^2	$物^2$	私有財産 Private Property	婦人 Married Women	環境運命 Environment
...ern Doctrine Guerila, 道教 (Taoism), 清日戰爭 (Chino-Japanese War), 露日戰爭 (Russo-...anese War), 尊日合邦 (Annexation)	零命題 Zerothesis	O^2	$零^2$			
自決主義 (Self-Determination), 民族文學 (National Literature), [自然主義 (Naturalism), ...思想 (Decadent), 浪漫主義 (Romanticism)]	綜合命題 Synthesis	S^2+M^2	$心^2+物^2$	信託管理 Trusteeship	男女同等 Equality	國際運命 International
新傾向派 (New Tendency Group), 카프 (K.A.P.F.)	正命題 Thesis	M^3	$物^3$	階級所有 Class Possession	職業女性 Working Women	集團運命 Collective
日本獨裁 (Japanese Dictatorship), 徵用文學 (Draftee Literature)	反命題 Antithesis	S^3	$心^3$	民族所有 Racial Ownership	家庭女性 House Wives	血統運命 Blood Destiny
不條理時代 Age of Absurdity — 逃避思想 (Escapism), 純粹藝術 (Art for Art's Sake)	零命題 Zerothesis	O^3	$零^3$			
新自由主義 New Liberalism — 韓國解放 (Emancipation of Korea)	綜合命題 Synthesis	M^3+S^3	$物^3+心^3$	U.N. 管理 U.N. Control	内外兼備 Compatible Women	世界運命 World's Destiny
自由民主主義 Free Democracy — 大韓民國 (Republic of Korea)	正命題 Thesis	S^4	$心^4$	救済事業 Welfare Services	女性上位 Superiority of Women	自由의 運命 Destiny of Freedom
共産主義 Communism — 北韓 (North Korea)	反命題 Antithesis	M^4	$物^4$	集團所有 Bloc Possession	勞動英雄 Working Heroine	敎條運命 Destiny of Ideology
(所屬의 喪失, 冷戰, 地域戰) (Alienization, Cold War Local Wars), 不信時代 Age of Distrust, 韓國戰爭 (Korean War), 越南戰爭 (Viet-Nam War)	零命題 Zerothesis	O^4	$零^4$			
共存主義 Co-Existence — 南北會談 (South-North Conference)	綜合命題 Synthesis	S^4+M^4	$心^4+物^4$	共同市場 Common Market	性解放 Free Sex	人類運命 Human Destiny
?	正命題 Thesis	M^5	$物^5$	?	?	?
?	反命題 Antithesis	S^5	$心^5$	?	?	?
?	零命題 Zerothesis	O^5	$零^5$	?	?	?

culture, its first cycle begins with a dawn, that is, the Primitive Life, which can be characterized with a synthesis, S + M, because in this period superstitions (S factor) predominated, and also natural resources (M factor) were equally abundant. This combined conception of Primitive Life is adaptable both in the West and Korea without any difference. The second period shows a thesis M, because the subsidiary member of the preceding synthesis is intensified as Hellenism in the West, and in Korea Shamanism prevailed as a thesis M. Characteristics of both Hellenism and Shamanism are identical with their pantheistic humanism.

Now the third period was prominent with Hebraism in the West, which can be represented with S, as the anti-thesis of Hellenism. The equivalent category in Korea was Buddhism (S), which required total sacrifice on human part, that is to say, the anti-thesis of preceding Shamanism.

Then the Dark Age, a chaos, which is a zero-thesis O, followed in the West just as degenerated corruption of Buddhism induced a chaos in Korea.

Thus the first Cycle as explained above goes with the formula of S + M(synthesis), $\rightarrow M^1$ (thesis)$\rightarrow S^1$ (anti-thesis) $\rightarrow$ O (zero-thesis) (the diacritical figure ^{1} means the first cycle).

Speaking of the Cycle II, the first period (Dawn) initiates the revival of Hellenism, but it was modified by Hebraism. The result was so-called Renaissance, the synthesis of $M^1 + S^1$. The corresponding ideology in Korea was Confucianism which flourished after the degeneration of Buddhism. Main theory of Confucianism was the well-balanced discipline between reason and emotion, which can be formulated with a synthesis $M^1 + S^1$. Then Renaissance, in another word, this Pseudo-Classicism, was followed by Romanticism (S^2)— the diacritical mark ^{2} indicates Cycle II—the intensified factor of the subsidiary member (S^1) of the preceding synthesis ($M^1 + S^1$). In Korea the newly imported Christianity (S^2) inspired Korean people with its romantic idea of resurrection and brotherhood as the resistance against Bureaucracy and Confucian prejudice. Romanticism in the West was followed by Naturalism (M^2) as its anti-thesis, while Practical Science Group (M^2) made a début in

Korea as an enlightenment movement.

The civilization of natural science emphasized by Naturalism finally resulted in the break-out of World War I in the West, a chaos, zero-thesis(O^2). Likewise in Korea the Eastern Doctrine Guerilla caused the Chino-Japanese War and Russo-Japanese War as well, which forced Korea to be annexed to Japan, thereby Korea losing its independent sovereignty, a chaos (zero-thesis O^2).

So far we checked the dialectics of two cycles. Now we found two sets of dualistic structures, which run as $S + M \to M^1 \to S^1 \to O^1$. (or an extended form, $M^1 \to S^1 \to O^1 \to M^1 + S^1$) followed by a reversed form $M^1 + S^1 \to S^2 \to M^2 \to O^2$ (or an extended form, $S^2 \to M^2 \to O^2 \to S^2 + M^2$). These two sets repeat thereafter alternatively, formulas of the remaining cycles being self-explanatory, and furthermore will be ruminated forever as in my Chart, predicting the possible happenings of the future.

In addition to this, to cover the truth of my findings, I would rather apply my interpretation regressively to Prehistory, the metaphysical world, which preceded the physical history already explained. As usual they say that God (S) created elements of the world (M) and then these things collided into Chaos (O). But unless the question "Where is God from?" is solved, still there remains a rub.

I assume God is from Infinity, the dawn (synthesis, a combination of $M + S$), because the actual conception of Infinity consists of two factors, timelessness and spacelessness, in which time-space is the conception of M and -lessnesses being the dimention of S.

Consequently Prehistory has the process of $(M + S) \to S \to M \to O$ (here parentheses mean imaginary assumption,) which precedes the first Cycle of human history already mentioned. Including this imaginary dialectics of metaphysical prehistory, the whole structure of my Chart fulfills the demand of my general equation for the development of human culture.

The chronological order in the Chart is not illustrated by a straight vertical way, but by a slanting steps escalated. The reason shows that each new column is simply an added item to the total of its horizontal heritages of preceding traditions which are inherited by downward arrows.

On the right wing of the Chart three categorical headings, Possession (wealth problem), Affection (love problem), and Destination (death problem) contain in their columns concerned the main current of materials described in the masterpieces created in each period.

In conclusion if this new interwoven dialectics proves the fact and truth of the past and present, we can predict what will happen in the future—the science of futurology. I dare declare an equation does not only exist in natural science, but also it works in the observation of cultural development, including the comparative study of literature between the West and Korea.

The Korean Alphabet

JAN SAFAREWICZ

2. - COMMUNICATION DE M. INSUB JUNG

Romanization of Korean

Professor Insub Jung gave a description, supported by records, of the peculiar articulation of the different series of Korean plosives, and pointed out the various difficulties met with by the phonetician in rendering the Korean sounds by means of the available systems of ·phonetic transcription based on the Latin alphabet. For practical purposes the Korean phonetic writing already adopted by the main authorities of the country ought to be further developed and improved, especially as far as the rendering of foreign sounds is concerned. Still it would be important to have a convenient Romanization of the Korean alphabet for international use. Systems of Romanization of Korean, of Koreanization of foreign sounds and a scheme of an International phonetic transcription of Korean sounds have been worked out by the speaker in his capacity as a member of a committee appointed for that purpose. Typewritten specimens of these systems were presented to the members of the Congress, who were invited to give their opinions on the subject.

Voir la motion du C.I.P.L. approuvée par le Congrès, plus loin, p. 297. (The 4th International Congress of Linguists held in Copenhagen, Denmark, 1936.)

1. THE KOREAN SCRIPT AND THE ROMAN ALPHABET

The Korean script, devised by Korean scholars of the fifteenth century, under the patronage of King Sezong, and reformed and standardized by Korean scholars of the twentieth century, is most admirably suited to the writing of the Korean language. Enthusiasts for its cause, as the author of this article confesses himself to be, would even maintain that it is the best script yet put into practical use anywhere, and there is no suggestion, on our part at any rate, that any system of Romanization should replace the Korean script as the orthography for general use within Korea. However, this script is unfamiliar to most non-Koreans, and, since other peoples are interested in gaining knowledge of Korea, and the Korean wish to make themselves known to other peoples, there must therefore be devised methods of spelling Korean names and words in ways which those other people will be able to read, write, and remember. We are concerned here with the problem of spelling Korean names and words with the letters of the Roman alphabet, not to produce a transliteration of the Korean orthography, but a standardized Romanization for international use.

2. THE STANDARDIZATION OF THE ROMANIZATION OF KOREAN

Some of the letters of western alphabet and many modified forms of them have been given internationally agreed values in the International Phonetic Alphabet (IPA), and one may write down the symbols there adopted, and by specifying that they are being used as the IPA, convey to the reader something very close to the sound which is being recorded, but, since some eighty or more letters, as well as many modifying marks, are used in the IPA, many of the IPA symbols are as unfamiliar to the uninformed reader as is the Korean script, and the IPA is therefore not suitable as a Romanization for the purposes stated. If possible, such a Romanization must use only letters within the usual twenty-six of the Roman alphabet and a minimum of modifying marks. However, the Roman alphabet is traditionally used by peoples speaking many different languages, and all its letters are subject to many different pronunciations, but Romanization must as far as possible meet the convenience of all who traditionally use the Roman alphabet.

The many systems of Romanization which have been adopted by westerners have almost all been designed, for the most part rather carelessly, to be guides to Korean pronunciation for a more or less limited group, such as speakers of English, and these Romanizations which many individual Koreans have adopted, in the absence of any unified system of Romanization, mostly for proper names, have not usually possessed many of the merits which a Standard Romanization must possess. However, although today, in 1953, there still reigns complete confusion in the Romanization of Korean, it was as long ago as 1931 that the Korean Philological Society was requested by various Korean bodies representing writers, educationalists, and others, to unify the methods of spelling foreign words in Korean letters, and Korean words in Roman letters. Over the next ten years, on the initiative of the Korean Phonetic Association, people from all branches of Korean society took part in a most careful investigation of these questions and it is not twelve years since the results were published by the Korean Philological Society on June 25th, 1941, in a small book called "The Unified System of Spelling Foreign Words," with an appendix (pp. 43 to 49) entitled "Rules for the Romanization of Korean Sounds." The system there presented is the Korean Romanization of their language, which though it has not come into universal use in Korea nor been fully understood by westerners yet because of the conditions in Korea so uncongenial to cultural development, was the only unified system of Romanization actually in use. For special purpose, individuals may devise the Romanization which suits those purposes best, but what is about to be because it is the Unified System of Romanization in Korea, and because it will also be shown to have merits of its own which make it far superior to any other Romanization yet proposed.

3. KOREAN LETTERS AND PRONUNCIATION

The Korean script is phonetic, each letter representing ideally one phoneme, and each phoneme being represented ideally by one letter. However, since the pronunciations of the letters in junctions may be modified, there must be some compromise between phonetic exactness and orthographic regularity. We shall now consider the phonetic values of the Korean letters in various positions, and, upon that basis, show the merits of the Unified System of Romanization.

A. The Consonants

i) Stops

a) Letters and sounds of the stops
There are in Korean three groups of stops, bilabial, dental-alveolar, and velar, each of three types, pure, ejective, and aspirated, with pronunciations in various positions which may be stated as follows in IPA terms:

Group:	Bilabial			Dental-alveolar			Velar		
Type:	pure	eject.	asp.	pure	eject.	asp.	pure	eject.	asp.
Letter:	ㅂ	ㅃ	ㅍ	ㄷ	ㄸ	ㅌ	ㄱ	ㄲ	ㅋ
Initial:	b̥	p'	ph	d̥	t'	th	g̊	k'	kh
Medial:	b	p'	ph	d	t'	th	g	k'	kh
Final:	p,		p,	t,		t,	k,	k,	k,

By "initial" is meant following a pause in speech or an unvoiced sound, by "medial," between two voiced sounds, and by "final," preceding a pause in speech or an unvoiced sound. [b̥], [d̥], and [g̊] represent bilabial, dental-alveolar, and velar plosion respectively, without voice, aspiration, or glottalization (The IPA symbols [p], [t], and [k] are avoided, since they are generally understood to be the unvoiced and unaspirated plosives of, for example, French or Chinese, which have been to be liable to be accompanied by weak glottal plosion.) [b], [d], and [g] represent the corresponding voiced stops. ['] (as in [p']) represents glottal plosion simultaneous with the oral plosion. [̦] (as in [p̦]) shows that the oral passage is blocked at the point of articulation indicated by the letter, but the stop is not exploded. [h] (as in [ph]) represents very strong aspiration following the plosion. Where no value is given, the letter is not known to occur in the position. Initial pure stops immediately following unvoiced sounds, and in certain cases immediately following voiced sounds are glottalized. Final stops immediately preceding nasals are nasalized (see §iv below.), and any final stop immediately preceding, or any initial pure stop immediately following a laryngéal fricative (ㅎ —"h"), forms with the laryngeal fricative an aspirated stop. (See § iii, below.)

b) Romanization of the stops
    Romanization must, as will be seen from the above table, distinguish three groups of stops, bilabial, dental-alveolar, and velar, and in initial and medial positions three types, pure, ejective, and aspirated, but in final position only one type of each group. For the pure stops, "b," "d," and "g" will be sufficient for all qualities, since the different qualities within each group are due solely to a difference of position. The ejective stops in initial and medial positions are impossible to spell in Roman letters without modifying marks in such a way that their nature will be immediately obvious to those who traditionally use the Roman alphabet for their own language, since the Korean type of glottalization is not thought of as occurring normally in western languages. "p," "t," and "k" are used in the IPA to represent sounds which are actually often weakly glottalized, but, if they were used in the IPA to represent sounds which are actually often weakly glottalized, but, if they were used in a Romanization, they would not always be given this value, but rather tend to be pronounced as aspirated stops. It is convenient to follow the practice of the Korean script, which uses doubled plosives (ㅃ, ㄸ , and ㄲ) for

the double—oral and glottal—plosion, and write "bb," "dd," and "gg." Furthermore final [p,] and [k,] (Romanized "b" and "g," see below) immediately preceding homographic initial pure stops (Romanized "b" and "g" respectively), and final [t,] (Romanized "d," see below) immediately preceding any initial pure stop (including "d"), may form together with the following pure initial stop an ejective stop (Romanized "bb," "dd," or "gg"). For the aspirated stops in initial and medial positions, "p," "t," and "k" will give a simple, convenient, and unambiguous Romanization. In Korean the primary division of the stops of each group is into unaspirated and aspirated types, just as in most western languages it is into voiced and unvoiced types. The other differences are mainly junction features. In final position, all types of stops may conveniently be represented by the same letters as the pure stops, "b," "d," and "g," in Romanization, since the pronunciation of all types of a group in final position is the same.

Other system of Romanization for the stops which have been used or proposed are inconvenient or misleading. Some have failed to distinguish between the pure and the aspirated stops, using "p," "t," and "k," for instance, for both in initial position, others similarly failed in practice because they use to indicate aspiration some small modifying mark such as an apostrophe, which has been ignored in pronunciation or omitted in print, while yet others have given rise to gross mispronunciations by using "ph," "th," and "kh" for the aspirated stops. These faults have arisen mainly from the initial mistake of using "p," "t," and "k" for the pure stops in initial position because they are unvoiced in that position. However, if one is to make the distinction in Romanization between the phonetically different sounds (unvoiced and voiced) of the pure stops in different positions, one must give two or more Romanizations to each pure stop in a Korean name or word, and thus cause much confusion. For instance, in a table of "Common Geographic Terms" in a recent issue of "Korean Survey" (Jan. 1953), it was found necessary to give four spellings of 북 ("bug" in the Unified System of Romanization), the Korean for "North," namely, "—Puk," presumably for when it follows a pause and precedes a pause or an unvoiced sound, and—"Pung," presumably for when it follows a pause and precedes a nasal sound, "—buk," presumably for when it follows a voiced sound and precedes a pause or an unvoiced sound, and "—bung," presumably for when it follows a voiced sound and precedes a nasal sound, and still the pronunciations which the word would have following an unvoiced sound (when the initial ㅂ would be glottalized) or preceding a vowel (when the final ㄱ would be vocalized) are not specifically indicated. Such variety of spelling is confusing and not necessary.

Nor is it necessary to Romanize differently the different Korean letters used as final stops with the same pronunciation, since such spelling is a matter of Korean orthography. Furthermore, final stops, however they are written in the Korean script, are in some compound words pronounced as pure stops. (For detailed examples of this, see our additional note on the "Table for the Romanization of Korean Sounds," Notes §4, below.)

ii) Affricates

a) Letters and Sounds of the Affricates

The Korean affricates consist of retracted alveolar plosion followed by palatal friction, and are of three types, pure, ejective, and aspirated, with pronunciations in various positions which may be stated as follows:

Type:	pure	ejective	aspirated
Letter:	ㅈ	ㅉ	ㅊ
Initial:	d̥ʒ̊	tʃ'	tʃh
Medial:	dʒ	tʃ'	tʃh
Final:	t̺		t̺

[d̥ʒ̊] represents the affricate without voice, aspiration, or glottalization. (The IPA symbol [tʃ] has been avoided because it has been found that the sound which is generally understood to represent that is liable to be weakly glottalized.) [dʒ] represents corresponding voiced affricate. ['] in [tʃ'] implies besides glottal plosion simultaneous with the oral plosion which is the first element of the affricate, a creaky quality in the palatal friction which is the second element (cf. the ejective fricative, §iii, below). The pure affricate immediately following unvoiced sounds, and, in certain cases, immediately following voiced sounds, is glottalized. All other terms and symbols are the same as those used when describing the stops, §i, above.

b) Romanization of the Affricates

As with the stops, the Unified System of Romanization for the affricates clearly distinguishes in initial and medial positions between the pure and the aspirated, using "z" and "cz" respectively, and for the ejective, doubles the pure affricate, "zz," and in final position uses "d" only, to represent a pronunciation identical with that of the dental-alveolar stop in final position.

It would have been more convenient to discuss the Romanization of the affricates together with that of the stops, but the affricates present a particularly difficult problem of Romanization because hardly any two western languages are agreed upon a spelling of the affricate sounds or on the pronunciation of the various letters which are used to spell the affricate sounds in various languages. However, if it is agreed to use, if possible, only the usual letters of the Roman alphabet, and also not to use, even in combination, for the affricates any of the other nineteen letters which will have to be used for Romanizing other sounds, except for the affricate letters in final position when they actually have the same pronunciation as other letters, there remain only "c," "j," and "z" for Romanization of the affricates, apart from the obviously unsuitable "f," "q," "v," and "x," none of which, as generally understood in western languages, imply either alveolar plosion or palatal friction. "j" has often been used or proposed as Romanization of the Korean affricate by speakers of English, in which language it has a pronunciation very close to the Korean voiced pure affricate [dʒ], but, if Roman letters may be said to have any internationally agreed value at all, that of "j" is rather the IPA [j], as in the German name "Jung" (like the "y" in the English "young"). Therefore "j" has been rejected as a standard Romanization, leaving for the pure affricate only the one other letter which is commonly understood as voiced in western languages, just as the Western "voiced letters" "b," "d," and "g" were selected for the pure stops, namely "z," with its three main pronunciations in western languages of IPA [z], [ʒ], and [ts], all of which are often spelled, when Koreans are spelling foreign words in the Korean script, with affricates, ㅈ having the nearest sound to them. For the aspirated affricate, "c" alone is rejected because it is so commonly pronounced in western languages as IPA [k], [kʰ], or [s]; the combination "ch" which has often been used or proposed is also rejected because of its pronunciations as IPA [x] (as in German "nach"), [ç] (as in German "Munchen"), and [ʃ] (as in French "Cherbourg"); "cz" is adopted as being the only remaining practicable possibility which shows the relationship between the pure and the aspirated affricates, although it is only generally known with this pronunciation in the name "Czecho-slovakia." For the same reasons as with the stops, no attempt is made in Romanization to distinguish between the phonetically different values of the pure affricates initial and medial positions, or the different letters used in the Korean script to write the final dental-alveolar stop.

iii) Fricatives

a) Letters and Sounds of the Fricatives

Korean has two groups of fricatives, retracted alveolar, and glottal, more conveniently here called laryngeal, of which the retracted alveolar is either pure or ejective, with pronunciations in various positions which may be stated as follows:

Group:	Alveolar		Laryngeal
Type:	pure	ejective	
Letter:	ㅅ	ㅅ	ㅎ
Initial:	s	s'	h
Medial:	s	s'	ɦ
Final:	t₁	t₁	(v. below)

[s] represents retracted alveolar friction, without voice or glottalization. ['] in [s'] necessarily has a different implication when used with a fricative from when used with a plosive, here representing a creaky quality in the fricative. The initial pure alveolar fricative immediately following unvoiced sounds, and, in certain cases, immediately following voiced sounds is glottalized. [h] represents voiceless laryngeal friction, and [ɦ] voiced laryngeal friction. ㅎ in final position is pronounced [t₁] before a pause in speech in the one case of the word 히읗 "hiud," the name of the letter ㅎ, [n] before a nasal sound, and as glottalization of a following alveolar fricative; in initial or final position when it immediately follows or precedes a pure stop or affricate, it is pronounced as aspiration of the stop of affricate. In other cases in final position it is not pronounced. (See also the "Table for the Romanization of Korean Sounds," Notes §4, below.) All the other terms and symbols are the same as those used when describing the stops, §i, above. (Note; there is also palatal friction as an element of the affricates, q.v., §ii, above.)

b) Romanization of the Fricatives

The Unified System of Romanization uses "s" for the pure retracted alveolar fricative in initial and medial positions, and, as with the stops and affricates, doubles the same letter for the ejective, "ss," and for both types uses "d" in final position to represent more nearly the actual pronunciation. For the laryngeal fricative "h" is used in initial and medial positions, and in final position "d" is used before a pause in the one case where it is pronounced [t,] quoted above, "n" before a nasal, "ss" for an initial ㅅ preceded by a final ㅎ, and the corresponding aspirated stop or affricate for an initial pure stop or affricate preceded by a final ㅎ. In other cases ㅎ is not Romanized, since it is not pronounced.

These Romanizations have been generally adopted in other systems of Romanization. "sh" has been suggested for the pure retracted alveolar fricative in initial and medial positions, but this is rejected because it would seem to indicate a value too far retracted for the Korean value (except when it is palatalized before the vowel ㅣ [i], and also because, for the sake of simplicity, the Unified System of Romanization uses, wherever possible, only one letter for each pure sound. For ㅎ in medial position, it has been suggested that the "h" be omitted when the voiced laryngeal fricative is not heard as a separate distinct sound between vowels, but this may be taken as a variant of the standard pronunciation where the voiced fricative is heard, which is taken as. the basis of the Unified System's Romanization. For the same reason as with the stops, no attempt is made to distinguish in Romanization between the different letters used in the Korean script to write the final dental-alveolar stop, or between the phonetically different values of the laryngeal fricative in initial and medial positions.

iv) Nasals

There are three groups of nasals in Korean, bilabial, dental-alveolar, and velar.

The bilabial [ㅁ], and the dental-alveolar [ㄴ] are normally voiced in all positions, the IPA [m] and [n] respectively, except that [ㄴ] ("n") in final position is [m] immediately preceding a bilabial consonant and [ŋ] immediately preceding a velar consonant, and is [l] immediately following or preceding a lateral consonant, in all but the slowest rates of utterance and most careful pronunciations.

The Unified System's Romanization of the first two nasals is "n" for the bilabial and "n" for the dental-alveolar, with the palatalization of ㄴ ("n") before the vowel ㅣ [i], being Romanized "ny" (this is dealt with in §B ii, below), and its lateral pronunciation immediately following a lateral consonant being Romanized "l." The only alternative suggestions to these which have been made are the spellings "m," "ng," and "l" for a final ㄴ ("n") in the three junctions given above. The Unified System of Romanization, however, makes it a rule to Romanize syllable finals according to their pronunciations before a pause, and to treat junction forms as a matter of pronunciation and not of Romanization. This rule also applies to the Romanization of the nasalized stops preceding nasal sounds (see §i a, above). The writing of the first syllable of a name or word always in the same way is of great convenience in the understanding of meanings, and in dictionaries and indexes of all kinds.

The velar nasal occurs in final and medial positions only, and is written ㅇ in the Korean script. It is normally voiced, and is the IPA [ŋ], except between two vowels, when the oral passage is not completely blocked and there is passage of air through both the oral and the nasal passages at the same time. There is no single letter of the normal Roman alphabet which is generally understood to have this value, and so the Unified System's Romanizations is "ng," which is generally agreed upon in other systems of Romanization, but, since the letters "n" and "g" are separately used for the Romanization of other sounds, hyphens must occasionally be used to indicate whether these letters occurring together are intended to have their individual or their combined values. Thus, final "ng" followed by a vowel must be distinguished from final "n" followed by initial "g," and final "ng" followed by initial "g" from final "n" followed by initial "gg"; also, for general convenience, final "ng" may be separated from a following initial "gg" by a hyphen. (For examples see the "Table for the Romanization of Korean Sounds," (Notes §2, iii, ff., below.)

The same Korean letter ㅇ in initial position is used to indicate a zero initial, that is to say that the syllable, if initial, begins with a vowel. However, if the syllable with initial ㅇ immediately follows a syllable with a final consonant, that final consonant is pronounced as the initial of the syllable with initial ㅇ.

v) Flapped and Lateral

The Korean letter ㄹ in medial position between two vowels, and in the rare cases where it is used in initial position, is an alveolar flapped, IPA [r]; in final position and in medial position when preceded by ㄴ or ㄹ, it is a voiced lateral, IPA [l]; and in medial position after the nasal sounds IPA [m] and [ŋ] it is a dental-alveolar nasal IPA [n]. The rolled IPA [r] also occurs, especially in phonesthetics, and is written with the letter ㄹ. Though the difference between the various values is due to position and phonetic context only, the values are so distinct that the Unified System of Romanization has adopted "l" for the lateral value (the palatal IPA [y] before ㅣ "i," being shown by "ly," see §B ii, below), "r" for the flapped and rolled values, and "n" for the nasal value, as have almost all systems of Romanization which have been proposed.

vi) Double Syllable Final Consonants

Syllables may have a final consisting of certain pairs of different consonants. Their Romanizations are set out in the "Table for the Romanization of Korean Sounds," below, which makes quite clear, after what has already been said about the individual values of the consonants so used, the pronunciations of those double consonants in various positions, without the need for detailed discussion of them here. It need only be said that to Romanize them by transliteration in every position would produce a Romanized orthography, which would not be suitable for the general purposes of Romanization.

B. Vowels and Semivowels

i) Vowels

The Korean script recognizes nine vowels, that is to say there are nine vowel phonemes in Korean (leaving out of consideration the phenomena of devocalization, nasalization, and glottalization), which must be Romanized with the five letters of the Roman alphabet which are generally used to write vowels in western languages. Some use of modifying marks is therefore unavoidable for the Romanization of the vowels. In the Korean script, some of the vowels are written with combinations of other vowel letters, but since the Korean script is syllabic, it is easier to keep the distinction between the separate and the combined values in the Korean script than it would be if a simple transliteration of the separate elements were used in Romanization. The hyphen or some other such mark would have to be employed so often that it really becomes simpler to decide upon the adoption of a diacritical mark on certain of the vowels from the first. The mark adopted by the Unified System of Romanization is a small semicircle above the vowel, and this is the only diacritical mark used in the Unified System, but it was accepted that, if necessary, for typing an apostrophe may be used after the vowel.

The pronunciation of the letters used to write vowels varies greatly in western languages, and many of the Romanizations of Korean which have been used or proposed have chosen for their vowels letters which are claimed to be pronunciation guides to Korean vowel sounds for speakers of one language only. The Unified System of Romanization rejects such an approach, and seeks to find for the vowel sounds of the Korean language letters which are as far as possible internationally accepted as representing those sounds.

It will be sufficient here to give the values of the Korean vowels in general terms, and not necessary to describe the precise qualities which they may have according to duration, phonetic context, and other factors.

ㅏ, ㅣ, ㅗ, and ㅜ, are respectively the vowels written in the

IPA [a] (slightly retracted), [i] (slightly lowered), [o] (slightly lowered), and [u] (slightly lowered), and so the letters "a," "i," "o" and "u" respectively are adopted for their Romanization.

ᅦ and ᅢ are, in the received pronunciation, [e] (slightly lowered) and [ɛ] (slightly lowered) respectively, though in non-standard pronunciations they are often confused, and the Romanizations "e" and "ē" are satisfactory in every respect.

ᅥ and ─ are the mid and high central vowels [ə] and [ɨ] (or [ẅ]) (slightly lowered) respectively, and are most simply and conveniently Romanized by modifying the mid back vowel "o" for the mid central vowel, to give "ŏ" for ᅥ , and the high back vowel "u" for the high central vowel, to give "ū" for ─.

ᅬ is in received pronunciation [ø] (slightly lowered), which may be described as the lip-rounding of [o] with the tongue position of [e], and it also has the nonstandard pronunciation of [we]. The Unified System's Romanization "oe" is therefore well justified.

Various vowel combinations occur in Korean, amongst them ᅩ "o" may be followed by ᅦ "e," and "ū" may be followed by ᅵ "i," and therefore hyphens must be used to distinguish "o-e" (the Romanization of ᅩ followed by ᅦ) from "oe" (the Romanization of ᅬ), and to distinguish "ū-i" (the Romanization of ─ followed by ᅵ) from "ūi" (the Romanization of the syllable ─ᅵ).

The duration of a Korean vowel may be termed phonetically short, half-long, or long, and it may be convenient in special cases to mark the long duration in Romanization. This is done by doubling the final vowel letter of the syllable when it is necessary.

ii) Semivowels

Six vowels may be preceded by a palatal semivowel, and the semivowel is Romanized in the Unified System "y," thus (giving the Korean letter, the IPA transcription, and the Romanization): ᅣ [ja] "ya," ᅤ [jɛ] "yē," ᅧ [jə] "yŏ," ᅨ [je] "ye," ᅭ [jo] "yo," and ᅲ [ju] "yu." The vowel ᅵ "i" is sometimes palatal, and when it occurs initially or immediately following ㄴ "n" or ㄹ "l," which are in some cases then palatalized, this quality may then be shown by Romanizing "yi," though there is no Korean letter for "yi" as distinct from "i."

The letter "j," which is the IPA symbol for the palatal semivowel, is rejected as a Romanization of it because of the pronunciations very different from a palatal semivowel which it has in, for example, English and French.

Five vowels may be preceded by a labio-velar semivowel. Though this is written in Korean with two letters, ㅗ "o" and ㅜ "u." ㅗ "o" occurs only before ㅏ "a" and ㅐ "ĕ," and ㅜ "u" only before ㅣ 'i,' ㅓ "ŏ," and ㅔ "e"; the pronunciation is always IPA [w], and so the Unified System's Romanization is always "w," thus: ㅘ [wa] "wa," ㅙ [wɛ] "wĕ," ㅟ [wi] "wi," ㅝ [wə] "wŏ," and ㅞ [we] "we." ㅟ "wi" is in certain special cases, such as phonesthetics or in a very rapid rate of utterance, pronounced IPA [y], but this may be taken as a variant of the more generally valid [wi], which is taken as standard for the Romanization.

4. THE SYLLABIC COMBINATIONS OF THE KOREAN LETTERS

The individual Korean letters have already been given in the preceding section, but they may be summed up in the following quotation from 한글 맞춤법 통일안 —"The Unified System of Korean Spelling"—published by the Korean philological Society in Seoul in 1940 (with a Romanization added in brackets after each letter to aid identification):

The number of the Korean letters is twenty-four, and their order is fixed as follows:

ㄱ (g), ㄴ (n), ㄷ (d), ㄹ (r), ㅁ (m), ㅂ (b), ㅅ (s), ㅇ (ng), ㅈ (z), ㅊ (cz), ㅋ (k), ㅌ (t), ㅍ (p), ㅎ (h), ㅏ (a), ㅑ (ya), ㅓ (ŏ), ㅕ (yŏ), ㅗ (o), ㅛ (yo), ㅜ (u), ㅠ (yu), ㅡ (ŭ), ㅣ (i).

Note: sounds which cannot be written with the above letters are written with a combination of two or more letters:

ㄲ (gg), ㄸ (dd), ㅃ (bb), ㅆ (ss), ㅉ (zz), ㅐ (ē), ㅒ (yē),
ㅔ (e), ㅖ (ye), ㅘ (wa), ㅙ (wē), ㅚ (oe), ㅝ (wŏ), ㅞ (wē), ㅟ (wi),
ㅢ (ūi).

The single letters are combined syllables in writing, and word divisions are shown by longer spaces being used at the ends of words than between the syllables which make up a word. Every syllable has at least an initial and a medial letter. The medial letter is always a vowel, including the semivowel if present. The initial letter is always, calligraphically, a consonant —though an initial ㅇ (also used as final "ng") indicates a zero initial—and it is written first in order, with the vowel on the right of it if the main stroke of the vowel letter is vertical (i.e., combining the vowels with the consonant ㄱ (g); 가 (ga), 갸 (gya), 거 (gŏ), 겨 (gyŏ), 기 (gi), 개 (gē), 걔 (gyē), 게 (ge), and 계 (gye)), or beneath it if the main stroke of the vowel letter is horizontal (i.e., 고 (go), 교 (gyo), 구 (gu), 규 (gyu), and 그 (gu)). When a "horizontal vowel" is used before a "vertical vowel" in the same syllable to write the labiovelar semivowel, or in the syllables ㅚ (oe) and ㅢ (ūi), the "horizontal vowel" is written beneath the consonant, and then the "vertical vowel" to the right of that combination (i.e., 과 (gwa), 괘 (gwē), 괴 (goe), 궈 (gwŏ), 궤 (gwe), 귀 (gwi), and 긔 (gūi)). The final consonant, if there is one in the syllable, is written below the combination of initial and medial (e.g., to combine a final ㄱ (g) with some of the examples above, 각 (gag), 국 (gug), and 곽 (gwag)). The pronunciation, and therefore the Romanization of the consonants depends to a certain extend upon their position, whether syllable initial or final, and, if syllable final, whether before a pause, an initial consonant, or an initial vowel, that is a zero initial consonant. The Romanizations in these various positions are set out in the table below. This may be a convenient summary of the Romanization which has been discussed above, perhaps in such great detail that the essential simplicity of the system has been lost to sight.

5. TRANSLATIONS FROM "THE UNIFIED SYSTEM OF SPELLING FOREIGN WORDS IN KOREAN" (KOREAN PHILOLOGICAL SOCIETY, SEOUL, 1941)

A. From the Preface:

Some time ago, after the Korean Philological Society had undertaken the determining of the "Unified System of Korean Spelling," it was carrying on diligent research directed at unifying the diverse and disunited spellings of foreign words, and personal and place names of foreign countries, when, on a request from various quarters, journalists, authors, educationalists, and others, a conference on the spelling of foreign words and related problems was organized and opened by forty-five people under the auspices of the society, on January 6th, 1931. At the conference, there was full discussion and debate, as a result of which all problems in this connection were entrusted completely to the society.

The society, thus charged, first selected a three man committee to be responsible (In-sob Zong, Gug-no Yi, and Hui-sung Yi), and had them prepare drafts on (1) the spelling of foreign words, (2) the spelling of Japanese sounds, (3) the Romanization of Korean sounds, and (4) the international phonetic transcription of Korean sounds. All the members of the society were of course consulted, but, besides theirs, the total knowledge of all quarters of society was collected together. For this purpose, the opinions were consulted and collated, nearer home, of the Korean Phonetic Association, the Japanese Phonetic Association, and researchers in phonetics of various organizations, and, further afield, of the International Phonetic Association, the International Congress of Linguists, the International Congress of Experimental phonetics, the International Congress of Phonology, and phonetic research groups and specialists of various countries. For about eight years researches and investigations were repeatedly made, and, as a result, by the Autumn of 1938, comprehensive basic drafts on the four subjects listed above were drawn up.

After the basic drafts had been made, in order to bring them a practicable perfection, they were first turned over to the editorial board of the society, and for two more years practicable experiments were carried out with them and they were applied in the monthly publications of the society and in publications of all sorts, with sincerity and a meticulous attention. This produced a firm conviction that there were no major mistakes, and, further, when the practical experiments and careful research covering the whole of the four drafts had almost been completed, in order to ensure complete consideration, the opinions of important members of society at large were sought, and the full texts of the four drafts were reproduced and presented to more than three hundred people of all quarters, journalists, authors, educationalists, and others, and criticisms and corrections obtained. Thus, in only ten years from start to finish, the fully determined schemes were made, and by a unanimous decision of all the members of the Society these four schemes are now published by the society.

In the practical use of these schemes, when in the future there are points which will gradually be added to or corrected, it is intended that the guidance and cooperation of respected members of society will be obtained, and efforts made to achieve more and more improvements and enlargements, and it is therefore hoped that the general public will continue, together with the society, to be concerned with these matters.

"The Korean Philological Society, 25th June, 1940."

B. Appendix II

Rules for the Romanization of Korean Sounds

General Principles

When spelling Korean sounds in Roman letters, it is to be the basic rule to write as in the following table for the Romanization of Korean sounds:

TABLE FOR THE ROMANIZATION OF KOREAN SOUNDS

Consonants

	Syllable initial	Syllable final		
		Final sound	Before consonants	Before vowels
ㄱ	가게 g gage (shop)	박 g bag (gourd)	박만 g bagman (with suffix 'man')	박이 g bagi (with suffix 'i')
ㄲ	꿈 gg ggum (dream)	밖 g bag (outside)	밖도 g bagdo (with suffix 'do')	부엌에 k buŏke (with suffix 'e')
ㅋ	칼 k kal (knife)	부엌 g buŏg (kitchen)	부엌도 g buŏgdo (with suffix 'do')	밖에 gg bagge (with suffix 'e')
ㅂ	발 b bal (foot)	입 b ib (mouth)	입과 b ibgwa (with suffix 'gwa')	입을 b ibŭl (with suffix 'ŭl')
ㅃ	뿔 bb bbul (horn)	. . .	. . .	. . .
ㅍ	팔 p pal (arm)	앞 b ab (front)	앞과 b abgwa (with suffix 'gwa')	앞으로 p apŭro (with suffix 'ŭro')
ㄷ	다리 d dari (leg)	곧 d god (namely)	곧다 d godda ('god-' "to be straight" with suffix 'da')	곧아 d goda (with suffix 'a')
ㄸ	땀 dd ddam (sweat)	. . .	. . .	. . .
ㅌ	티 t ti (flaw)	밭 d bad (dry field)	밭만 d badman (with suffix 'man')	밭에 t bate (with suffix 'e')

Syllable initial		Syllable final		
		Final sound	Before consonants	Before vowels
ㅈ	자 z za (Korean foot)	낮 d nad (daytime)	낮과 d nadgwa (with suffix 'gwa')	낮에 z naze (with suffix 'e')
ㅉ	쪽 zz zzog (piece)	. . .	. . .	. . .
ㅊ	차 cz cza (tea)	꽃 d ggod (flower)	꽃도 d ggoddo (with suffix 'do')	꽃이 cz ggoczi (with suffix 'i')
ㅅ	소 s so (cattle)	옷 d od (clothes)	옷과 d odgwa (with suffix 'gwa')	옷이 s osi (with suffix 'i')
ㅆ	쌀 ss ssal (rice)	있 d id (stem of 'to exist')	있고 d idgo (with suffix 'go')	있어 ss issō (with suffix 'ō')
ㄴ	나무 n namu (tree)	손 n son (hand)	손만 n sonman (with suffix 'man')	손을 n sonūl (with suffix 'ūl')
ㅁ	말 m mal (horse)	밤 m bam (night)	밤도 m bamdo (with suffix 'do')	밤에 m bame (with suffix 'e')
ㄹ	오리 r ori (duck)	달 l (v. n. 6) dal (moon)	달도 l daldo (with suffix 'do')	달이 r dari (with suffix 'i')
ㅎ	호미 h homi (hoe)		(v. note 4)	
ㅇ	(v. n. 3)	콩 ng kong (beans)	콩도 ng kongdo (with suffix 'do')	콩이 ng- kong-i (with suffix 'i')
ㄳ	. . .	넋 g nōg (spirit)	넋도 g nōgdo (with suffix 'do')	넋이 gs nōgsi (with suffix 'i')

Syllable initial	Syllable final		
	Final sound	Before consonants	Before vowels
ㅄ ...	값 b gab (price)	값만 b gabman (with suffix 'man')	값이 gs gabsi (with suffix 'i')
ㄵ ...	앉 n an (stem of "to sit")	앉고 u an-ggo (with suffix 'go')	앉아 nz anza (with suffix 'a')
ㄶ ...	끊 n ggŭn (stem of "to cut")	(v. note 4)	끊어 nh ggŭnhŏ (with suffix 'ŏ')
ㄺ ...	흙 g hŭg (earth)	흙도 g hŭgdo (with suffix 'do')	흙이 lg hŭlgi (with suffix 'i')
ㄻ ...	삶 m saam (stem of "to boil")	삶고 m saamggo (with suffix 'go')	삶아 lm salma (with suffix 'a')
ㄼ ...	여덟 l yŏdŏl (eight)	여덟만 l (v. n. 4) yŏdŏlman (with suffix 'man')	여덟에 lb yŏdŏlbe (with suffix 'e')
ㄽ ...	돐 l dol (birthday)	돐도 l dolddo (with suffix 'do')	돐에 lss dolsse (with suffix 'e')
ㄾ ...	핥 l hal (stem of "to lap")	핥고 l halggo (with suffix 'go')	핥아 lt halta (with suffix 'a')
ㄿ ...	읊 b ŭb (stem of "to recite")	읊다 d ŭbda (with suffix 'da')	읊어 lp ŭlpŏ (with suffix 'ŏ')
ㅀ ...	끓 l ggŭl (stem of "to boil")	(v. note 4)	끓어 lh ggŭlhŏ (with suffix 'ŏ')

Vowels

ㅏ	a	아산	Asan (p.n.)	신라	Sinla (p.n.)		
ㅓ	ō	언양	Ōnyang (p.n.)	새터	Setō (p.n.)		
ㅗ	o	오산	Osan (p.n.)	목포	Mogpo (p.n.)		
ㅜ	u	우수영	Usuyōng (p.n.)	무주	Muzu (p.n.)		
ㅡ	ū	은진	Ūnzin (p.n.)	장흥	Zanghūng (p.n.)		
ㅣ	i	인천	Inczōn (p.n.)	장기	Zang-gi (p.n.)		
	yi	승니	sūngnyi (monk)	왕십리	Wangsibnyi (p.n.)		
ㅐ	ē	애인	ēin (lover)	동래	Dongnē (p.n.)		
ㅔ	e	에구	ēgu (an interjection)	휴게	hyugye (rest)		
ㅚ	oe	외금강	Oegūmgang (p.n.)	괴산	Goesan (p.n.)		
ㅟ	wi	위원	Wiwōn (p.n.)	소귀	Sogwi (p.n.)		
ㅢ	ūi	의주	Ūizu (p.n.)	희천	Hūiczōn (p.n.)		
ㅘ	wa	완주	Wanzu (p.n.)	옥과	Oggwa (p.n.)		
ㅝ	wō	원산	Wōnsan (p.n.)	영월	Yōng-wōl (p.n.)		
ㅙ	wē	왜관	Wēgwan (p.n.)	유쾌	yukwē (pleasure)		
ㅞ	we	웬	wen (what sort of?)	금궤	gūmgwe (golden chest)		
ㅑ	ya	양주	Yangzu (p.n.)	춘향	Czunhyang (p.n.)		
ㅕ	yō	연백	Yōnbēg (p.n.)	강경	Gang-gyōng (p.n.)		
ㅛ	yo	용산	Yongsan (p.n.)	벌교	Bōlgyo (p.n.)		
ㅠ	yu	유성	Yusōng (p.n.)	법률	bōbnyul (law)		
ㅒ	yē	애야	yēya (an interjection)	애개	ēgyē (an interjection)		
ㅖ	ye	예산	Yesan (p.n.)	신계	Singye (p.n.)		

P.n. indicates that the word quoted is a proper name.

Notes

§1. Long vowels are not specially indicated, but, should it be unavoidably necessary to do so in certain cases, the final vowel of the syllable is to be written double, e.g.:

밤	baam (chestnut)	별	byōōl (star)
곰	goom (bear)	굴	guul (cave)
들	dūūl (field)	일	iil (work)

*Additional note: Contrast 밤 bam (night), 별 byōl (special), 굴 gul (oyster), and 일 il (one). Vowel length only distinguishes the place name 경성 (京城) Gyōngsōng (= Seoul) from 경성

(鏡城) Gyŏŏngsŏng (a place in Hamgyŏng North Province).

§2. In the following cases a hyphen (-) is put between two syllables:

i) between a syllable final 'o' (ㅗ) and a following syllable initial 'e' (ㅔ) (to distinguish from 'oe'), e.g.: 코에 ko-e (in the nose) (to distinguish from 'koe,' written 쾨).

ii) between a syllable final 'ŭ' (ㅡ) and a following syllable initial 'i' (ㅣ) (to distinguish from ŭi), e.g.: 그이 gŭ-i (that man) (to distinguish from gŭi:, written 긔).

*Additional note: In standard writing, the spelling 긔 is no longer used, and ㅢ is now used as a syllable medial only with the syllable initials ㅇ and ㅎ.

iii) between a syllable final 'ng' ㅇ and a following syllable initial vowel, and also between a syllable final 'n' (ㄴ) and a following syllable initial 'g' (ㄱ) (to distinguish the two), e.g.:

평양 Pyŏng-yang (p.n.) (not 'Pyŏng-gyang')

한강 Han-gang (p.n.) (not 'Hang-ang')

iv) between a syllable final 'ng' (ㅇ) and a following syllable initial, (ㄱ), and also between a syllable final 'n' (ㄴ) and a following syllable initial 'gg' (ㄲ) (to distinguish the two), e.g.:

강경 Gang-gyŏng (p.n.) (not 'Gan-ggyŏng')

산끝 san-ggŭd ("the end of a mountain") (not 'sang-gŭd').

*Additional note: It will also be found to be convenient to separate the three 'g's which come together when a syllable final 'ng' (ㅇ) is followed by a syllable initial 'gg' (ㄲ), e.g.: for 강가 (river-side) 'gang-gga' is easier to read than 'ganggga.'

§3. The consonant ㅇ is written 'ng' as syllable final only, and as syllable initial it is not spelled at all e.g.:

앙 ang (a phonesthetic)

윙 wĕng (a phonesthetic)

§4. When the final of a syllable and the initial of a following syllable meet, and the pronunciations change, the rule is that the final of the first syllable should be written according to the Table, and the initial of the following syllable should be written as it is pronounced, e.g.:

극락 gugnag (paradise)

신라 Sinla (p.n.)

동래   Dongnĕ (p.n.)
삼례   Samnye (p.n.)
물ㅅ약   mullyag (liquid medicine)
겹ㅅ이불 gyōbnyibul (double quilt)
검고   gōmggo (is black, and)
신다   sindda (put on shoes)

*Additional note: The orthographies, romanizations, and phonetic transcriptions of the above words are as follows:

Orthography	Romanization	IPA transcription
gūgrag	gūgnag	[ģ̦ŋnak,]
Sinra	Sinla	[ʃilla]
Dongrĕ	Dongnĕ	[doŋnɛ]
Samrye	Samnye	[samnje]
gōmgo	gōmggo	[ģ̦əmk'o]
sinda	sindda	[ʃiːnt'a]

Since this book was written, the use of the "Inserted ㅅ" has been reformed in the Korean script (V. §5 and additional note, below.) and are now:

물약   muryag   mullyag   [muḷyak,]
겹이불 gyōbibul   gyōbnyibul   [ģ̦jəmnjibul]

It is not necessary that the natural glottalization in Korean of a pure stop, affricate, or alveolar fricative following a final stop should be recorded in Romanization (e.g. 입과 'ibgwa' is IPA [ip, k'wa], but other cases of glottalization are record (as 'sindda,' above).

Note A. ㅎ final is written 'k,' 't,' 'p,' or 'cz' in conjunction with a following ㄱ (g), ㄷ (d), ㅂ (b), or ㅈ (z) respectively, and in other cases it is altered in writing to the consonant which follows after it, but when there is no phonetic need for it, it is completely dropped, e.g.:

i) 좋고   zoko (it is good and)
   좋다   zota (it is good)
   좋지   zoczi (it may be good)
   끊고   ggūnko (cuts and)
   끊다   ggūnta (cuts)
   끊지   ggūnczi (may cut)
ii) 놓네   nonne (puts down)
   놓세   nosse (let us put down)

끊세   ggŭnse (let us cut)
iii) 끊네   ggŭnne (custs)
뚫네   ddulle (bores)
놓치다 noczida (loses)

*Additional note: ㅎ as a final stop before a pause probably occurs only in the name of the letter, ㅎ, 히읗 'hiŭd,' when it is pronounced as a dental-alveolar stop [tᵢ] and so Romanized 'd.'

Note B. ㄷ (d) and ㅌ (t) finals when followed by the suffixes 이 (i) or 히 (hi) are written 'zi' or 'czi,' e.g.:

굳이   guzi (obstinately)
여닫이 yŏdazi (sliding door)
밭이   baczi (a dry field is—)
핥히다 halczida (to be licked roughly)
굳히다 guczida (to stiffen)
묻히다 muczida (to be buried)

Note C. In ㄼ (lb) final, the ㄼ of 밟 (the stem of the verb "to step on") before a consonant, and of 넓적 and 넓죽 (flat) is written 'b' (ㅂ), e.g.:

밟고   babgo 밟다 babda 밟지 babzi
밟다듬이 babdadŭmi 넓적하다 nŏbzŏghada
넓죽하다 nŏbzughada

*Additional note: When a word final stop is pronounced as a medial stop together with a following word initial vowel in the formation of a compound word, the medial value of the stop is that of a pure stop, irrespective of the usual medial value of the letter used to write the final stop. Compare the pronunciations and Romanizations of the following words in isolation, with a suffix, and as the first member of a compound followed by a vowel:

무릎   murŭb - "knee"
무릎에 murŭpe - "to the knee"
무릎아래 murŭbarĕ - "the leg below the knee"
팥   pad - "red beans"
팥에   pate - "to the red beans"
팥알   padal - "a single red bean"
부엌   buŏg - "kitchen"
부엌에 buŏke - "to the kitchen"

부엌안 buōgan - "the inside of the kitchen"
옷   od - "clothes"
옷에   ose - "to the clothes"
옷안   odan - "the inside of the clothes"
젖   zōd - "milk"
젖에   zōze - "to the milk"
젖어미 zōdōmi - "nurse"
꽃   ggod - "flower"
꽃에   ggocze - "to the flower"
꽃아래 ggodarē - "beneath the flower"
값   gab - "price"
값에   gabse - "to the price"
값없다 gabōbda - "to be priceless"
넋   nōg - "spirit"
넋에   nōgse - "to the spirit"
넋없다 nōgōbda - "to be dispirited"

§5. The "Inserted ㅅ " of compound nouns, when occurring before consonants, is written with same letter as that consonant, and when occurring before ㅑ (ya), ㅕ (yō), ㅛ (yo), ㅠ (yu), and ㅣ (i) is written with 'n' e.g.:

i) 문ㅅ간 mun-ggan (door)
   코ㅅ날 konnal (ridge of the nose)
   발ㅅ등 balddūng (top of the foot)
   초ㅅ불 czobbul (candle-light)
   밤ㅅ잠 bamzzam (night-sleep)
   이ㅅ솔 issol (tooth-brush)
ii) 갓ㅅ양 gadnyang (hat-rim)
    담ㅅ요 damnyo (blanket)
    콩ㅅ엿 kongnyōd (bean-candy)
    편ㅅ윷 pyōnnyud (team 'four-sticks')
    흙ㅅ일 hūgnyil (work with soil)

However, when it occurs before 야(ya), 여(yō), 요(yo), 유(yu), and 이(i), if the preceding syllable final is a vowel, it is written, in accordance with the pronunciation, 'nn,' and if the final is ㄹ (l), it is written 'l' e.g.:

i) 동네ㅅ양반 dongnennyangban (gentlemen of the village)
   채ㅅ열   czěnnyōl (whip-lash)
   뒤ㅅ요량   dwinnyoryang (scheme for the future)

뒤ㅅ윷   dwinnyud (the later game of 'four-sticks')
대ㅅ잎   dĕnnyib (bamboo leaves)
ii) 물ㅅ약   mullyag (liquid medicine)
불ㅅ여우   bullyōu (fierce fox)
길ㅅ요강   gillyogang (travelling chamberpot)
놀ㅅ윷   nollyud ('four-sticks' to be played)
들ㅅ일   dūllyil (work in the fields)

*Additional note: The use of the "Inserted ㅅ " has been reformed in Korean writing since this book was published. At present, if the first member of a compound noun ends in a consonant, no "Inserted ㅅ " is used, but the Romanization remains as given above, in accordance with the Notes, §4, above, e.g. 문ㅅ간 [munk'an] is now written 문간 but still Romanized 'mun-ggan'; if the first member of the compound ends in a vowel, the "Inserted ㅅ " is written as a final consonant to it, and the Romanization may therefore follow the Table. e.g. 코ㅅ날 [khonnal] is now written 콧날 and Romanized "kodnal," and 대ㅅ잎 [dɛnnjip] is now written 댓잎 and Romanized 'dĕdnyib.'

§6. When a word with a final "ㄹ" and a word with an initial 아(a), 어(ō), 오(o), 우(u), or 으(ū) form a compound, the ㄹ is written 'r,' e.g.:

울안   uran (with in the fence)
살얼음   sarōrum (thin ice)
물오리   murori (wild duck)
술웃국   surudgug (formented wine)
들음식   dūrūmsig (snack taken to work in the fields)

§7. In special cases reasonable decisions may be taken individually, but we request that they be based always upon the spirit to this scheme.

For Reference

"Though this scheme is chiefly concerned with the spelling of proper names, general speech sounds have been borne in mind as well."

That is the Unified System of the Romanization of Korean. Apart from possessing merits of its own, it has been officially adopted as standard in Korea, and we therefore appeal to westerners to adopt it also.

23rd June, 1953